The Coal Question

*An Inquiry Concerning the Progress of the Nation,
and the Probable Exhaustion of our Coal-Mines*

By William Stanley Jevons

PANTIANOS CLASSICS

Published by Pantianos Classics

ISBN-13: 978-1-78987-646-8

First published in 1865

This reprint is adapted from the Second Edition of 1866

Engraving of William Stanley Jevons

Contents

Additional Information

"The progressive state is in reality the cheerful and the hearty state to all the different orders of the society; the stationary is dull; the declining melancholy."

ADAM SMITH.

Preface

I am desirous of prefixing to the second edition of the following work a few explanations which may tend to prevent misapprehension of its purpose and conclusions.

The expression "exhaustion of our coal mines," states the subject in the briefest form, but is sure to convey erroneous notions to those who do not reflect upon the long series of changes in our industrial condition which must result from the gradual deepening of our coal mines and the increased price of fuel. Many persons perhaps entertain a vague notion that some day our coal seams will be found emptied to the bottom, and swept clean like a coal-cellar. Our fires and furnaces, they think, will then be suddenly extinguished, and cold and darkness will be left to reign over a depopulated country. It is almost needless to say, however, that our mines are literally inexhaustible. We cannot get to the bottom of them; and though we may some day have to pay dear for fuel, it will never be positively wanting.

I have occasionally spoken in the following pages of "the end," of the "instability of our position," and so forth. When considered in connexion with the context, or with expressions and qualifications in other parts of the volume, it will be obvious that I mean not the end or overturn of the nation, but the end of the present progressive condition of the kingdom. If there be a few expressions which go beyond this, I should regard them as speculative only, and should not maintain them as an essential part of the conclusions.

Renewed reflection has convinced me that my main position is only too strong and true. It is simply that we cannot long progress as we are now doing. I give the usual scientific reasons for supposing that coal must confer mighty influence and advantages upon its rich possessor, and I show that we now use much more of this invaluable aid than all other countries put together. But it is impossible we should long maintain so singular a position; not only must we meet some limit within our own country, but we must witness the coal produce of other countries approximating to our own, and ultimately passing it.

At a future time, then, we shall have influences acting against us which are now acting strongly with us. We may even then retain no inconsiderable share of the world's trade, but it is impossible that we should go on expanding as we are now doing. Our motion must be reduced to rest, and it is to this change my attention is directed. How long we may exist in a stationary condition I, for one, should never attempt to conjecture. The question here treated regards the length of time that we may go on rising, and the height of prosperity and wealth to which we may attain. Few will doubt, I think, after examining the subject, that we cannot long rise as we are now doing.

Even when the question is thus narrowed I know there will be no want of opponents. Some rather hasty thinkers will at once cut the ground from under me, and say that they never supposed we should long progress as we are doing, nor do they desire it. I would make two remarks in answer.

Firstly, have they taken time to think what is involved in bringing a great and growing nation to a stand? It is easy to set a boulder rolling on the mountain-side; it is perilous to try to stop it. It is just such an adverse change in the rate of progress of a nation which is galling and perilous. Since we began to develop the general use of coal, about a century ago, we have become accustomed to an almost yearly expansion of trade and employment. Within the last twenty years everything has tended to intensify our prosperity, and the results are seen in the extraordinary facts concerning the prevalence of marriage, which I have explained in pp. 197-200, and to which I should wish to draw special attention. It is not difficult to see, then, that we must either maintain the expansion of our trade and employment, or else witness a sore pressure of population and a great exodus of our people.

The fact is, that many of my opponents simply concede the point I am endeavouring to prove without foreseeing the results, and without, again, giving any reasons in support of their position.

Secondly, I do not know why this nation should not go on rising to a pitch of greatness as inconceivable now as our present position would have been inconceivable a century ago. I believe that our industrial and political genius and energy, used with honesty, are equal to anything. It is only our gross material resources which are limited. Here is a definite cause why we cannot always advance.

Other opponents bring a more subtle objection. They say that the coal we use affords no measure of our industry. At a future time, instead of exporting coal, or crude iron, we may produce elaborate and artistic commodities depending less on the use of coal than the skill and taste of the workman. This change is one which I anticipated. It would constitute a radical change in our industry. We have no peculiar monopoly in art, and skill, and science as we now have in coal. That by art and handicraft manufactures we might maintain a moderate trade is not to be denied, but all notions of manufacturing and maritime supremacy must then be relinquished. Those persons very much mistake the power of coal, and steam, and iron, who think that it is now fully felt and exhibited; it will be almost indefinitely greater in future years than it now is. Science points to this conclusion, and common observation confirms it. These opponents, then, likewise concede what I am trying to show, without feeling how much they concede. They do not seem to know which is the sharp edge of the argument.

A further class of opponents feel the growing power of coal, but repose upon the notion that economy in its use will rescue us. If coal become twice as dear as it is, but our engines are made to produce twice as much result with the same coal, the cost of steam-power will remain as before. These opponents, however, overlook two prime points of the subject. They forget that economy of fuel leads to a great increase of consumption, as shown in the chapter on the subject; and, secondly, they forget that other nations can use improved engines as well as ourselves, so that our comparative position will not be much improved.

It is true that where fuel is cheap it is wasted, and where it is dear it is economised. The finest engines are those in Cornwall, or in steam-vessels plying in distant parts of the ocean. It is credibly stated, too, that a manufacturer often spends no more in fuel where it is dear than where it is cheap. But persons will commit a great oversight here if they overlook the cost of an improved and complicated engine, which both in its first cost, and its maintenance, is higher than that of a simple one. The question is one of capital against current expenditure. It is well known that nothing so presses upon trade as the necessity for a large capital expenditure; it is so much more risked, so much more to pay interest on, and so much more abstracted from the trading capital. The fact is, that a wasteful engine pays better where coals are cheap than a more perfect but costly engine. Bourne, in his "Treatise on the Steam Engine," expressly recommends a simple and wasteful engine where coals are cheap.

The state of the matter is as follows:—Where coal is dear, but there are other reasons for requiring motive power, elaborate engines may be profitably used, and may partly reduce the cost of the power.

But if coal be dear in one place and cheap in another, motive power will necessarily be cheaper where coal is cheap, because there the option of using either simple or perfect engines is enjoyed. It is needless to say that any improvement of the engine which does not make it more costly will readily be adopted, especially by an enterprising and ingenious people like the Americans.

I take it, therefore, that if there be any strong cause exclusive of the possession of coal which will tend to keep manufactures here, economy of fuel and a large employment of capital may neutralise in some degree the increased cost of motive power. But so far as cheap fuel and power is the exciting cause of manufactures, these must pass to where fuel is cheapest, especially when it is in the hands of persons as energetic and ingenious as ourselves.

Finally, I may mention the argument of Mr. Vivian, that the art of coal mining will advance so that coal may be drawn from great depths without any material increase of cost. The very moderate rise of price as yet experienced, apparently supports this view, and for my own part I entertain no doubt that a mine might, if necessary, be driven to the depth of 5,000 feet. The cost at which it must be done, however, is quite another matter. The expenditure on the shaft increases in a far higher ratio than its depth; the influence of this expenditure is more than can be readily estimated, because it is risked in the first instance, and in not a few cases is wholly lost; and not only must the capital itself be repaid, but considerable amounts of compound and simple interest must be met, in order that the undertaking shall be profitable. Were the depth of mines so slight an inconvenience as Mr. Vivian would make it appear, I think we should have more deep mines. It is now forty years since the Monkwearmouth Pit was commenced, and I believe that only one deeper pit has since been undertaken, that at Dukinfield, seventeen years ago. We cannot wonder that there are so few deep pits, when we consider that it required twenty years' labour to complete the Monkwearmouth pit, in consequence of the serious obstacles encountered. The Dukinfield Deep Pit, begun in June, 1849, was more fortunate, and reached the expected coal at a depth of 2,150 feet in March, 1859.

Having now candidly mentioned and discussed the strongest objections brought against the views stated in the following work, I may fairly ask the reader that he will treat these views with candour, not separating any statement from its qualifications and conditions. I have some reason to complain that this has not been done hitherto. A correspondent of the Times and Mining Journal has represented it as a consequence of my suppositions that there would, in 1961, be a population of 576 millions of people in this country, a statement wholly without foundation in the following pages.

One journal, the (London) Examiner, [1] has so far misrepresented me, that the editorial writer, after expressly stating that he has read the book with care, says:—"Professor Jevons shrinks from endorsing the 4,000 feet theory, and stops short at 2,500; but why there precisely, rather than anywhere else, he does not tell us. All we can gather from him on the subject is, that when we get to that depth a complete supply of foreign coals will come in from Pennsylvania and elsewhere." If the above be compared with what I have really said on the subjects in chapter four, and in chapter thirteen, it will be seen that my statements are represented as the direct opposite of what they are. The whole article is full of almost equal misrepresentations.

I have been surprised to find how far the views expressed in some of the following chapters are merely an explicit statement of those long entertained by men of great eminence. The manner in which Mr. Mill mentioned this work in his remarkable speech on the National Debt, [2] was in the highest degree gratifying. I have found indeed, that most of what I said concerning the National Debt was unconsciously derived from Mr. Mill's own works. I have repeated it unchanged in this edition, with the exception of adding references. The fact is that no writer can approach the subject of Political Economy without falling into the deepest obligations to Mr. Mill, and it is as impossible as it is needless always to specify what we owe to a writer of such great eminence, and such wide-spread influence.

Sir John Herschel has most kindly expressed a general concurrence in my views, and has even said that this work contained "a mass of considerations, that as I read them seemed an echo of what I have long thought and felt about our present commercial progress."

As regards the supremacy of coal as a source of heat and power, and the impossibility of finding a substitute, I have again only interpreted the opinions of Professor Tyndall. He has kindly allowed me to extract the following from a recent letter with which he favoured me:—

"I see no prospect of any substitute being found for coal, as a source of motive power. We have, it is true, our winds and streams and tides; and we have the beams of the sun. But these are common to all the world. We cannot make head against a nation which, in addition to those sources of power, possesses the power of coal. We may enjoy a multiple of their physical and intellectual energy, and still be unable to hold our own against a people which possesses abundance of coal; and we should have, in my opinion, no chance whatever in a race with a nation which, in addition to abundant coal, has energy and intelligence approximately equal to our own.

"It is no new thing for me to affirm in my public lectures that the destiny of this nation is not in the hands of its statesmen but in those of its coal-owners; and that while the orators of St. Stephen's are unconscious of the fact, the very lifeblood of this country is flowing away."

And in the following passage Professor Tyndall has lately summed up the sources of power:—

"Wherever two atoms capable of uniting together by their mutual attractions exist separately, they form a store of potential energy. Thus our woods, forests, and coal-fields on the one hand, and our atmospheric oxygen on the other, constitute a vast store of energy of this kind—vast, but far from infinite. We have, besides our coal-fields, bodies in the metallic condition more or less sparsely distributed in the earth's crust. These bodies can be oxydised, and hence are, so far as they go, stores of potential energy. But the attractions of the great mass of the earth's crust are already satisfied, and from them no further energy can possibly be obtained. Ages ago the elementary constituents of our rocks clashed together and produced the motion of heat, which was taken up by the ether and carried away through stellar space. It is lost for ever as far as we are concerned. In those ages the hot conflict of carbon, oxygen, and calcium produced the chalk and limestone hills which are now cold; and from this carbon, oxygen, and calcium no further energy can be derived. And so it is with almost all the other constituents of the earth's crust. They took their present form in obedience to molecular force; they turned their potential energy into dynamic, and gave it to the universe ages before man appeared upon this planet. For him a residue of power is left, vast truly in relation to the life and wants of an individual, but exceedingly minute in comparison with the earth's primitive store." [3]

I learn from Mr. Hunt that his forthcoming report will show the production of coal in the United Kingdom in 1865 to be about ninety-five millions of tons, giving a considerable increase over the great total of 1864.

I would direct the attention of those who think the failure of coal so absurd a notion, and who, perhaps, would add that petroleum can take the place of coal when necessary, to the results of an inquiry lately undertaken by Mr. Hunt concerning an increase of supply of cannel coal. He finds, after a minute personal and local inquiry, that the present yearly production of 1,418,176 tons might be raised to 3,172,000 tons should the gas companies demand it and offer a sufficient price. But it appears to be clear that such a supply could not be maintained for many years. The Wigan cannel is estimated to last twenty years at the longest. Ten years of the assumed production would exhaust the North Wales cannel, and two authorities, Mr. Binney and Mr. J. J. Landale, agree that the Boghead oil-making coal will not last many years.

It is evident, in short, that the sudden demand for the manufacture of petroleum, added to the steady and rising demand of the gas works, will use up the peculiar and finest beds of oil and gas-making coals in a very brief period.

I have to thank Mr. Robert Hunt not only for his kindness in supplying me with a copy of the unpublished report containing these facts, but also for his readiness in furnishing the latest available information from the Mining Record Office. The operations of this most useful institution are still crippled, in spite of Mr. Hunt's constant exertions, by the want of proper power. It was established at the suggestion of the British Association, moved by Mr. Thomas Sopwith, to preserve the plans of abandoned mines in order that the future recovery of coal or minerals now left unworked might be facilitated, and the danger from irruptions of water and foul air from forgotten workings be averted. Colliery owners are, indeed, obliged to possess plans of their workings, and to exhibit them to the Government Inspectors of Mines, but they are not obliged to deposit copies in the Mining Record Office, on the ground of noninterference with vested interests. The deposit of plans then being voluntary, very few are received, and almost all are lost or destroyed soon after the closing of the colliery. Such plans, however, are of national importance, like registers of births, deaths, and marriages, or wills and other records. It is obvious that their destruction should be rendered illegal and penal, and that after the closing of a colliery, when the interference with private interests becomes imaginary, they should be compulsorily deposited in the Mining Record Office. It is more than twenty years since Mr. Sopwith urged these views in his remarkable pamphlet on "The National Importance of preserving Mining Records."[4] Yet our legislation remains as it was in truly English fashion. This subject, I hope, will now receive proper attention from the Royal Commission which is about to be appointed to inquire into the subject of our coal supply.

My great obligations to Mr. Hull will be clearly seen in several parts of the work.

I am inclined to think that a careful consideration of my arguments will show them to be less speculative and more practical than appears at first sight. I have carefully avoided anything like mere romance and speculation. It would be romance to picture the New Zealander moralizing over the ruins of London Bridge, or to imagine the time when England will be a mere name in history. Some day Britain may be known as a second Crete, a sea-born island crowned by ninety cities. Like the Cretans, we are ruled by laws more divine than human; we teach the use of metals, and clear the seas of robbers, and exert a mild governance over the coasts and islands. We too like Crete may form in remote history but a brief and half-forgotten link in the transmission of the arts from the East towards the West—transmission not without improvement.

But the subject of the following chapters, rightly regarded, seems to me to have an immediate and practical importance. It brings us face to face with duties of the most difficult and weighty character—duties which we have too long deferred and ignored. So long as future generations seemed likely for an indefinite period to be more numerous and comparatively richer than ourselves, there was some excuse for trusting to time for the amelioration of our people. But the moment we begin to see a limit to the increase of our wealth and numbers, we must feel a new responsibility. We must begin to allow that we can do to-day what we cannot so well do to-morrow. It is surely in the moment when prosperity is greatest; when the revenue is expanding most rapidly and spontaneously; when employment is abundant for all, and wages rising, and wealth accumulating so that individuals hardly know how to expend it—then it is that an effort can best be made, and perhaps only be made, to raise the character of the people appreciably.

It is a melancholy fact which no Englishman dare deny or attempt to palliate, that the whole structure of our wealth and refined civilization is built upon a basis of ignorance and pauperism and vice, into the particulars of which we hardly care to inquire. We are not entirely responsible for this. It is the consequence of tendencies which have operated for centuries past. But we are now under a fearful responsibility that, in the full fruition of the wealth and power which free trade and the lavish use of our resources are conferring upon us, we should not omit any practicable remedy. If we allow this period to pass without far more extensive and systematic exertions than we are now making, we shall suffer just retribution.

It is not hard to point out what kind of measures are here referred to. The ignorance, improvidence, and brutish drunkenness of our lower working classes must be dispelled by a general system of education, which may effect for a future generation what is hopeless for the present generation. One preparatory and indispensable measure, however, is a far more general restriction on the employment of children in manufacture. At present it may almost be said to be profitable to breed little slaves and put them to labour early, so as to get earnings out of them before they have a will of their own. A worse premium upon improvidence and future wretchedness could not be imagined.

Mr. Baker, the Inspector of Factories in South Staffordshire, has given a deplorable account of the way in which women and children are employed in the brick-yards; and in the South Wales ironworks I have myself seen similar scenes, which would be incredible if described. Dr. Morgan holds that our manufacturing population is becoming degenerate; and it must be so unless, as our manufacturing system grows, corresponding restrictions are placed upon the employment of infant labour.

It will be said that we cannot deprive parents of their children's earnings. If we cannot do it now, we can never do it; and wretched, indeed, must be a kingdom which depends for subsistence upon infant labour. But we can do it to the ultimate advantage of all, and we are bound to do it from regard to the children themselves: and anything which we may lose or spend now in education and loss of labour will be repaid many times over by the increased efficiency of labour in the next generation.

Reflection will show that we ought not to think of interfering with the free use of the material wealth which Providence has placed at our disposal, but that our duties wholly consist in the earnest and wise application of it. We may spend it on the one hand in increased luxury and ostentation and corruption, and we shall be blamed. We may spend it on the other hand in raising the social and moral condition of the people, and in reducing the burdens of future generations. Even if our successors be less happily placed than ourselves they will not then blame us.

To some it might seem that no good can come from contemplating the weakness of our national position. Discouragement and loss of prestige could alone apparently result. But this is a very superficial view, and the truth, I trust, is far otherwise. Even the habitual contemplation of death injures no man of any strength of mind. It rather nerves him to think and act justly while it is yet day. As a nation we have too much put off for the hour what we ought to have done at once. We are now in the full morning of our national prosperity, and are approaching noon. Yet we have hardly begun to pay the moral and the social debts to millions of our countrymen which we must pay before the evening.

[1] *Examiner,* May 19th, 1866.
[2] *House of Commons,* April 17th, 1866.
[3] *Fortnightly Review,* Dec. 31, 1865, p. 143.

Chapter One - Introduction and Outline

Day by day it becomes more evident that the Coal we happily possess in excellent quality and abundance is the mainspring of modern material civilization. As the source of fire, it is the source at once of mechanical motion and of chemical change. Accordingly it is the chief agent in almost every improvement or discovery in the arts which the present age brings forth. It is to us indispensable for domestic purposes, and it has of late years been found to yield a series of organic substances, which puzzle us by their complexity, please us by their beautiful colours, and serve us by their various utility.

And as the source especially of steam and iron, coal is all powerful. This age has been called the Iron Age, and it is true that iron is the material of most great novelties. By its strength, endurance, and wide range of qualities, this metal is fitted to be the fulcrum and lever of great works, while steam is the motive power. But coal alone can command in sufficient abundance either the iron or the steam; and coal, therefore, commands this age—the Age of Coal.

Coal in truth stands not beside but entirely above all other commodities. It is the material energy of the country—the universal aid—the factor in everything we do. With coal almost any feat is possible or easy; without it we are thrown back into the laborious poverty of early times.

With such facts familiarly before us, it can be no matter of surprise that year by year we make larger draughts upon a material of such myriad qualities—of such miraculous powers. But it is at the same time impossible that men of foresight should not turn to compare with some anxiety the masses yearly drawn with the quantities known or supposed to lie within these islands.

Geologists of eminence, acquainted with the contents of our strata, and accustomed, in the study of their great science, to look over long periods of time with judgment and enlightenment, were long ago painfully struck by the essentially limited nature of our main wealth. And though others have been found to reassure the public, roundly asserting that all anticipations of exhaustion are groundless and absurd, and "may be deferred for an indefinite period," yet misgivings have constantly recurred to those really examining the question. Not long since the subject acquired new weight when prominently brought forward by Sir W. Armstrong in his Address to the British Association, at Newcastle, the very birthplace of the coal trade.

This question concerning the duration of our present cheap supplies of coal cannot but excite deep interest and anxiety wherever or whenever it is mentioned: for a little reflection will show that coal is almost the sole necessary basis of our material power, and is that, consequently, which gives efficiency to our moral and intellectual capabilities. England's manufacturing and commercial greatness, at least, is at stake in this question, nor can we be sure that material decay may not involve us in moral and intellectual retrogression. And as there is no part of the civilized world where the life of our true and beneficent Commonwealth can be a matter of indifference, so, above all, to an Englishman who knows the grand and steadfast course his country has pursued to its present point, its future must be a matter of almost personal solicitude and affection.

The thoughtless and selfish, indeed, who fear any interference with the enjoyment of the present, will be apt to stigmatise all reasoning about the future as absurd and chimerical. But the opinions of such are closely guided by their wishes. It is true that at the best we see dimly into the future, but those who acknowledge their duty to posterity will feel impelled to use their foresight upon what facts and guiding principles we do possess. Though many data are at present wanting or doubtful, our conclusions may be rendered so far probable as to lead to further inquiries upon a subject of such overwhelming importance. And we ought not at least to delay dispersing a set of plausible fallacies about the economy of fuel, and the discovery of substitutes for coal, which at present obscure the critical nature of the question, and are eagerly passed about among those who like to believe that we have an indefinite period of prosperity before us.

The writers who have hitherto discussed this question, being chiefly geologists, have of necessity treated it casually, and in a one-sided manner. There are several reasons why it should now receive fuller consideration. In the first place, the accomplishment of a Free Trade policy, the repeal of many laws that tended to restrain our industrial progress, and the very unusual clause in the French Treaty which secures a free export of coals for some years to come, are all events tending to an indefinite increase of the consumption of coal. On the other hand, two most useful systems of Government inquiry have lately furnished us with new and accurate information bearing upon the question; the Geological Survey now gives some degree of certainty to our estimates of the coal existing within our reach, while the returns of mineral statistics inform us very exactly of the amount of coal consumed.

Taking advantage of such information, I venture to try and shape out a first rough approximation to the probable progress of our industry and consumption of coal in a system of free industry. We of course deal only with what is probable. It is the duty of a careful writer not to reject facts or circumstances because they are only probable, but to state everything with its due weight of probability. It will be my foremost desire to discriminate certainty and doubt, knowledge and ignorance—to state those data we want, as well as those we have. But I must also draw attention to principles governing this subject, which have rather the certainty of natural laws than the fickleness of statistical numbers.

It will be apparent that the first seven of the following chapters are mainly devoted to the physical data of this question, and are of an introductory character. The remaining chapters, which treat of the social and commercial aspects of the subject, constitute the more essential part of the present inquiry. It is this part of the subject which seems to me to have been too much overlooked by those who have expressed opinions concerning the duration of our coal supplies.

I have endeavoured to present a pretty complete outline of the available information in union with the arguments which the facts suggest. But such is the extent and complexity of the subject that it is impossible to notice all the bearings of fact upon fact. The chapters, therefore, have rather the character of essays treating of the more important aspects of the question; and I may here suitably devote a few words to pointing out the particular purpose of each chapter, and the bearings of one upon the other.

I commence by citing the opinions of earlier writers, who have more or less shadowed forth my conclusions; and I also quote Mr. Hull's estimate of the coal existing in England, and adopt it as the geological datum of my arguments.

In considering the geological aspects of the question, I endeavour to give some notion of the way in which an estimate of the existing coal is made, and of the degree of certainty attaching to it, deferring to the chapter upon Coal Mining the question of the depth to which we can follow seams of coal. It is shown that in all probability there is no precise physical limit of deep mining, but that the growing difficulties of management and extraction of coal in a very deep mine must greatly enhance its price. It is by this rise of price that gradual exhaustion will be manifested, and its deplorable effects occasioned.

I naturally pass to consider whether there are yet in the cost of coal any present signs of exhaustion; it appears that there has been no recent rise of importance, but that, at the same time, the high price demanded for coals drawn from some of the deepest pits indicates the high price that must in time be demanded for even ordinary coals.

A distinct division of the inquiry, comprising chapters vi. vii. and viii., treats of inventions in regard to the use of coal. It is shown that we owe almost all our arts to continental nations, except those great arts which have been called into use here by the cheapness and excellence of our coal. It is shown that the constant tendency of discovery is to render coal a more and more efficient agent, while there is no probability that when our coal is used up any more powerful substitute will be forthcoming. Nor will the economical use of coal reduce its consumption. On the contrary, economy renders the employment of coal more profitable, and thus the present demand for coal is increased, and the advantage is more strongly thrown upon the side of those who will in the future have the cheapest supplies. As it is in a subsequent chapter on the Export and Import of Coal conclusively shown that we cannot make up for a future want of coal by importation from other countries, it will appear that there is no reasonable prospect of any relief from a future want of the main agent of industry. We must lose that which constitutes our peculiar energy. And considering how greatly our manufactures and navigation depend upon coal, and how vast is our consumption of it compared with that of other nations, it cannot be supposed we shall do without coal more than a fraction of what we do with it.

I then turn to a totally different aspect of the question, leading to some estimate of the duration of our prosperity.

I first explain the natural principle of population, that a nation tends to multiply itself at a constant rate, so as to receive not equal additions in equal times, but additions rapidly growing greater and greater. In the chapter on Population it is incidentally pointed out that the nation, as a whole, has rapidly grown more numerous from the time when the steam-engine and other inventions involving the consumption of coal came into use. Until about 1820 the agricultural and manufacturing populations increased about equally. But the former then became excessive, occasioning great pauperism, while it is only our towns and coal and iron districts which have afforded any scope for a rapid and continuous increase.

The more nearly, too, we approach industry concerned directly with coal, the more rapid and constant is the rate of growth. The progress indeed of almost every part of our population has clearly been checked by emigration, but that this emigration is not due to pressure at home is plain from the greatly increased frequency of marriages in the last ten or fifteen years. And though this emigration temporarily checks our growth in mere numbers, it greatly promotes our welfare, and tends to induce greater future growths of population.

Attention is then drawn to the rapid and constant rate of multiplication displayed by the iron, cotton, shipping, and other great branches of our industry, the progress of which is in general quite unchecked up to the present time. The consumption of coal, there is every reason to suppose, has similarly been multiplying itself at a growing rate. The present rate of increase of our coal consumption is then ascertained, and it is shown that, should the consumption multiply for rather more than a century at the same rate, the average depth of our coal-mines would be 4,000 feet, and the average price of coal much higher than the highest price now paid for the finest kinds of coal.

It is thence simply inferred that we cannot long continue our present rate of progress. The first check to our growing prosperity, however, must render our population excessive. Emigration may relieve it, and by exciting increased trade tend to keep up our progress; but after a time we must either sink down into poverty, adopting wholly new habits, or else witness a constant annual exodus of the youth of the country. It is further pointed out that the ultimate results will be to render labour so abundant in the United States that our iron manufactures will be underbid by the unrivalled iron and coal resources of Pennsylvania; and in a separate chapter it is shown that the crude iron manufacture will, in all probability, be our first loss, while it is impossible to say how much of our manufactures may not follow it.

Suggestions for checking the waste and use of coal are briefly discussed, but the general conviction must force itself upon the mind, that restrictive legislation may mar but cannot mend the natural course of industrial development. Such is a general outline of my arguments and conclusions.

When I commenced studying this question, I had little thought of some of the results, and I might well hesitate at asserting things so little accordant with the unbounded confidence of the present day. But as serious misgivings do already exist, some discussion is necessary to set them at rest, or to confirm them, and perhaps to modify our views. And in entering on such a discussion, an unreserved, and even an overdrawn, statement of the adverse circumstances, is better than weak reticence. If my conclusions are at all true, they cannot too soon be recognised and kept in mind; if mistaken, I shall be among the first to rejoice at a vindication of our country's resources from all misgivings.

For my own part, I am convinced that this question must before long force itself upon our attention with painful urgency. It cannot long be shirked and shelved. It must rise by degrees into the position of a great national and perhaps a party question, antithetical to that of Free Trade. There will be a Conservative Party, desirous, at all cost, to secure the continued and exclusive prosperity of this country as a main bulwark of the general good. On the other hand, there will be the Liberal Party, less cautious, more trustful in abstract principles and the unfettered tendencies of nature.

Bulwer, in one of his Caxtonian Essays, has described, with all his usual felicity of thought and language, the confliction of these two great parties. They have fought many battles upon this soil already, and the result as yet is that wonderful union of stability and change, of the good old and the good new, which makes the English Constitution.

But if it shall seem that this is not to last indefinitely—that some of our latest determinations of policy lead directly to the exhaustion of our main wealth—the letting down of our mainspring—I know not how to express the difficulty of the moral and political questions which will arise. Some will wish to hold to our adopted principles, and leave commerce and the consumption of coal unchecked even to the last; while others, subordinating commerce to purposes of a higher nature, will tend to the prohibition of coal exports, the restriction of trade, and the adoption of every means of sparing the fuel which makes our welfare and supports our influence upon the nations of the world.

This is a question of that almost religious importance which needs the separate study and determination of every intelligent person. And if we find that we must yield before the disposition of material wealth, which is the work of a higher Providence, we need not give way to weak discouragement concerning the future, but should rather learn to take an elevated view of our undoubted duties and opportunities in the present.

Chapter Two - Opinions of Previous Writers

ONE of the earliest writers who conceived it was possible to exhaust our coal mines was John Williams, a mineral surveyor. In his "Natural History of the Mineral Kingdom," first published in 1789, he gave a chapter to the consideration of "The Limited Quantity of Coal of Britain." His remarks are highly intelligent, and prove him to be one of the first to appreciate the value of coal, and to foresee the consequences which must some time result from its failure. This event he rather prematurely apprehended; but in those days, when no statistics had been collected, and a geological map was unthought of, accurate notions were not to be expected. Still, his views on this subject may be read with profit, even at the present day.

Sir John Sinclair, in his great Statistical Account of Scotland, [1] took a most enlightened view of the importance of coal; and, in noticing the Fifeshire coal-field, expressed considerable fears as to a future exhaustion of our mines. He correctly contrasted the fixed extent of a coalfield with the ever-growing nature of the consumption of coal.

In 1812 Robert Bald, another Scotch writer, in his very intelligent "General View of the Coal Trade of Scotland," showed most clearly how surely and rapidly a consumption, growing in a "quick, increasing series," [2] must overcome a fixed store, however large. Even if the Grampian mountains, he said, [3] were composed of coal, we would ultimately bring down their summits, and make them level with the vales.

In later years, the esteemed geologist, Dr. Buckland, most prominently and earnestly brought this subject before the public, both in his evidence before the Parliamentary Committees of 1830 and 1835, and in his celebrated "Bridgewater Treatise." [4] On every suitable occasion he implored the country to allow no waste of an article so invaluable as coal.

Many geologists, and other writers, without fully comprehending the subject, have made so-called estimates of the duration of the Newcastle coal-field. Half a century ago, this field was so much the most important and well known, that it took the whole attention of English writers. The great fields of South Wales and Scotland, in fact, were scarcely opened. But those who did not dream of the whole coal-fields of Great Britain being capable of exhaustion, were early struck by the progressive failure of the celebrated Newcastle seams. Those concerned in the coal trade know for how many years each colliery is considered good; and perhaps, like George Stephenson in early youth, have had their homes more than once moved and broken up by the working out of a colliery. [5] It is not possible for such men to shut their eyes altogether to the facts.

I give, on the following page, a tabular summary of the chief estimates of the duration of the Newcastle field.

Author of Estimate.	Date of Estimate.	Supposed Area of Coal Measures unworked. Square Miles.	Estimated Amount of Coal. Millions of Tons.	Assumed Annual Consumption of Coal. Tons.	Duration of Supply. Years.
Mac Nab [1] . .	1792	300	—	—	360
Bailey [2] . . .	1801	—	—	1,866,200	200
Thomson [3] . .	1814	—	5,575	3,700,000	1000
Bakewell [4] . .	—	—	—	—	350
Hugh Taylor [5]	1830	732	6,046	3,500,000	1727
Buckland [6] .	1830	—	—	—	400
Greenwell [7] .	1846	—	—	10,000,000	331
T. Y. Hall [8] .	1854	750	5,122	14,000,000	365
E. Hull [9] . .	1864	685	7,226	16,001,125	450

[1] Treatise on the Coal Trade, quoted in Appendix to J. Williams' History of the Mineral Kingdom: Edinburgh, 1810, vol. ii. p. 267.
[2] Edinburgh Review, vol. cxi. p. 84, note. This estimate, however, seems to refer to Durham only, and to a later year than 1801. See John Bailey, "General View of the Agriculture of the County of Durham," 1810, p. 28.
[3] Annals of Philosophy, December, 1814.
[4] Introduction to Geology, p. 192.
[5] Report on Coal Trade, 1830, p. 77. Edinburgh Review, vol. li. p. 190. M'Culloch's Dictionary, art. Coal.
[6] Report on Coal Trade, 1830.
[7] T. Y. Hall. Transactions of the North of England Institute of Mining Engineers, 1854. Fordyce, History of Coal, Coke, and Coal-Fields: Newcastle, 1860, p. 32.
[8] T. Y. Hall. Transactions of the North of England Institute of Mining. Engineers, 1854. Fordyce, History of Coal, Coke, and Coal-Fields: Newcastle, 1860, p. 32.
[9] The Coal-Fields of Great Britain, by Edward Hull, B.A. 2d Ed. p. 161. (Stanford.)

Suffice it to remark, concerning these estimates, that the amounts of coal supposed to exist in the Newcastle field are much more accordant than the conclusions as to the probable duration of the supply. The reason of course is that the annual consumption is a rapidly-growing quantity, and it is a most shortsighted proceeding to argue as if it were constant. These so-called estimates of duration are no such thing, but only compendious statements how many times the coal existing in the earth exceeds the quantity then annually drawn.

The apparent accordance of these writers often arises, too, from the compensation of errors. Some of them assumed, most wrongly, that the known seams extended continuously over the whole area of the field; they did not allow for the less extension of the higher seams, a point we shall have to consider; and then again, even Dr. Buckland, in accordance with the prevalent opinion of those times, did not suppose that any coal existed under the magnesian limestone strata at the southern angle of the Newcastle field. In Mr. Hull's estimate, however, allowance is made for hidden coal likely to exist. He takes 460 square miles as the area of the open coal measures, and 225 square miles as the available area covered by newer geological formations.

Some writers, without going into numerical detail, have explained very clearly the bearings of this question. John Holland, for instance, the author of an excellent anonymous work on coal, has made very sound remarks upon the probable duration of our coal. "While," he says, [6] "it is manifestly inconclusive to estimate according to present demand the consumption of coals for centuries to come; and still more so to assign any specific condition of society to such a remote period; we are warranted, in the first place, in assuming that the demand for this species of fuel will not diminish, but increase, with every imaginable condition of the progress of society; and, secondly, we have before us the undoubted fact, that our mines are not inexhaustible. In addition to this, there is the most direct evidence to show how far some of the most valuable beds in the northern coalfields have been worked out already; at the same time, that tolerably satisfactory calculations have been made as to the quantity remaining unwrought."

Mr. T. Sopwith, in 1844, in an essay on "The National Importance of Preserving Mining Records" (p. 50), made the following very excellent remarks:—"The opinion that our stores of coal are all but inexhaustible rests wholly on assumed data, and not upon any accurate and detailed statistical accounts such as alone could warrant a confident opinion. This question will, ere long, become a subject of serious concern, unless some measures are taken to found our calculations on a solid basis. It is an easy matter to assume that a considerable thickness of available coal extends over hundreds of square miles; but the different opinions formed by men of the highest respectability and talent, strongly prove how meagre and unsatisfactory are the only data on which these estimates are founded. It is not, however, the mere quantity of coal that is to be considered. Especial regard must be had to its quality, depth, thickness, extent, and position. Many of the inferior seams can only be worked in conjunction with those which, by their superior quality, repay the expense of working them at depths varying from 300 to 600 yards; and it may readily be conceived, that inferior coal only could not be profitably raised from pits equal in depth to three or four times the height of St. Paul's Cathedral, unless the price of such inferior coal was raised to more than the present price of the best coal. It is the additional expense and consequent additional difficulty of competing with other countries, that is the vital question to be considered. It is not the exhaustion of mines, but the period at which they can be profitably worked, that merits earnest and immediate attention."

Among statistical writers the late Mr. M'Culloch characterised the notions of the exhaustibility of our coal mines as utterly futile, both in the article on Coal, in his "Dictionary of Commerce," and in his "Account of the British Empire." [7] For his views, however, the reader may be referred to works so well known and accessible.

Mr. Waterston, in his "Cyclopædia of Commerce," [8] treated the question with more caution, but erroneously supposed that modes of economising coal would compensate the evil of the increasing cost.

The progress of the Geological Survey, and the establishment of a Mining Record Office, [9] have placed this question upon a new footing: and when, in 1860, public attention was drawn to the subject by the warm debates on the French Treaty, Mr. Edward Hull, of the Geological Survey, was induced to prepare a concise description of our coal-fields with an estimate of their total contents. The latest views of the same geologist have been given in an excellent paper on the coal-fields, forming the first article of the Journal of Science for January 1864.

Referring the reader for all geological details to Mr. Hull's very useful works, and leaving over for discussion some points of his calculations, I will now state his general results. The following table gives Mr. Hull's estimate of the probable contents of each of our chief coal-fields: [10] —

Coal-field.	Area of open Coal Measures. Square Miles.	Area covered by newer formations. Square Miles.	Total Coal to depth of 4,000 feet. Millions of Tons.
Anglesea	9	—	*
Bristol & Somerset	45	105	2,488
Coalbrookdale . .	28	—	28
Cumberland . .	25	—	97
Denbighshire . .	47	20	902
Derby and York .	760	400	16,800
Newcastle . . .	460	225	7,270
Flintshire . . .	35	(?)	20
Forest of Dean. .	34	—	561
Forest of Wyre. .	—	—	*
Lancashire . . .	217	25	4,510
Leicestershire . .	15	30	450
North Stafford . .	75	20	2,237
South Stafford . .	93	—	973
Shrewsbury . . .	—	—	*
South Wales . .	906	—	16,000
Warwickshire . .	30	107	2,184
Scotland	1,720	—	25,323
Totals	4,499	932	79,843

[*] Inconsiderable amounts.

In his later publication, [11] Mr. Hull gives his estimate in the following form:—

Coal Group.	Area in Square Miles.	Coal Contents. Millions of Tons.	Produce in 1861. Tons.	Number of Collieries, 1861.
Scotch	1,920	25,300	11,081,000	424
Newcastle . . .	1,845	24,000	34,635,884	848
Lancashire, Staffordshire, &c. .	535	7,594	25,643,000	1,158
South Wales . .	1,094	26,560	13,201,796	516
Cumberland . .	25	90	1,255,644	28
Totals . . .	5,419	83,544	85,817,324	2,974

It will be seen that his estimate, in 1864, of the total contents of our coal-fields, exceeds by only an inconsiderable quantity his estimates in 1860 and 1861. I shall accept this quantity of 83,544,000,000 tons of available coal as a convenient basis for discussion, subject to whatever may be said later on, as to some of Mr. Hull's assumptions. As Mr. Hull possesses the most intimate practical acquaintance with the Lancashire and some of the Midland coal-fields, acquired in carrying out the Geological Survey, and has at his command all the published results of the survey, the experience of his coadjutors, and the writings of previous geologists, his estimate must certainly be accepted for the present.

But whether this estimate be accurate or not, it will appear that the exact quantity of coal existing is a less important point in this question than the rate at which our consumption increases, and the natural laws which govern that consumption. The question is mainly one of statistical science, and it is only as such that I venture to have anything to do with it.

Mr. Hull, indeed, has not confined himself to the geological side of the question, and his remarks upon the statistical bearings of his estimate must not be passed over, though they are far from having the same weight as his geological statements. Throughout his work, he compares the contents of each coal-field with the present annual quantity of coal drawn from it, and his remarks on the condition of the several fields are interesting and significant. The present generation, he thinks, may see the end of the Flintshire coalfield, which was largely worked in the days of shallow pits, and contains little more than twenty millions of tons for future supply. [12] The Coalbrookdale coal-field, where the present mode of iron manufacture was first established, is even further advanced towards exhaustion, and can hardly last more than

23

twenty years. The South Staffordshire field has passed the meridian of its career, and is on the verge of old age. "Its extraordinary richness has been the principal cause of its early decline, and the treasures easily acquired have been often recklessly squandered." [13]

It is true that the great South Wales and Scotch coal basins contain some thousands of times their present annual yield of coal. But it is obvious they will have, in future years, to compensate the falling off in all the smaller and older fields, as well as to bear their own increased local demand. Coal will be got where it can most cheaply and easily be got, and the exhaustion of one field will only throw a new demand upon fresher fields. This is a process already extensively going on.

"The supply of coal in the South Staffordshire district," says Mr. William Mathews, [14] "has seriously fallen off of late years, and has become quite inadequate to meet the demand occasioned by the development of its other manufacturing resources. We are, therefore, obliged to lean somewhat on the aids which the produce of the northern coal-fields opens up to us; and if, by any chance, the resources we now enjoy, from that and other districts in England, should be withheld, we should feel the inconvenience of being deprived of such resources very sensibly indeed."

The same process is taking place, by aid of railways, in many shallow coal districts, and it may proceed until the whole country is mainly dependent on one or two of the greatest coal basins. We ought, therefore, to compare the total supply within the kingdom with the total probable demand, paying little or no regard to local circumstances.

Mr. Hull has made such a comparison. He compared the 79,843 millions of tons of his first estimate [15] with the 72 million tons of coal consumed in 1859, and deduced that, at the same rate of consumption, the supply would last 1100 years.

"Yet we have no right," he very truly remarked, "to assume that such will be the actual duration; for the history of coal mining during the last half century has been one of rapid advance." Our consumption, in short, had about doubled itself since 1840; and, supposing it to continue doubling every twenty years, our "total available supply would be exhausted before the lapse of the year 2034." [16]

"If we had reason," he continues, [17] "to expect that the increase of future years was to progress in the same ratio, we might well tremble for the result; for that would be nothing less than the utter exhaustion of our coal-fields, with its concomitant influence upon our population, our commerce, and national prosperity, in the short period of 172 years!"

No sooner has Mr. Hull reached this truly alarming result than he recoils from it. "But are we," he says, "really to expect so rapid a drain in future years? I think not." Economy will reduce our consumption; the burning waste-heaps of coal will be stopped; America will relieve us from the world-wide demand for our coal, and will eventually furnish even this country with as much as we want. Such are some of the fallacious notions with which Mr. Hull, in common with many others, seeks to avoid an unwelcome conclusion. More lately, he has said: [18] "Notwithstanding these facts, however, it would be rash to assume that the experience of the past is to be a criterion of the future. We neither wish for, nor expect, an increase during the remainder of the second half of this century, at all proportionate to that of the earlier half; and this view is borne out by some of the later returns. Some of our coal-fields, as has been shown, have passed their meridian, and, having expended their strength, are verging to decay. Others have attained their maximum, or nearly so; this, indeed, is the case with the majority. The younger coal-fields will have much of their strength absorbed in compensating for the falling off of the older; so that, in a few years, the whole of our coal-producing districts will reach a stage of activity beyond which they cannot advance, but around which they may oscillate. Entertaining these views, I am inclined to place the possible maximum of production at 100 millions of tons a year; and yet it has been shown that, even with this enormous 'output,' there is enough coal to last for eight centuries."

The reader will easily see, in the course of our inquiry, how mistaken is Mr. Hull, in supposing our production of coal to be limited to 100 millions. It has already exceeded 92 millions without counting the waste of slack coal, and is yet advancing by great strides. And the public seems unaware that a sudden check to the expansion of our supply would be the very manifestation of exhaustion we dread. It would at once bring on us the rising price, the transference of industry, and the general reverse of prosperity, which we may hope not to witness in our days. And the eight centuries of stationary existence he promises us would be little set off against a nearer prospect so critical and alarming.

Facts, however, prove the hastiness of these views. The number of collieries is rapidly increasing up to the very last accounts (1864); and new collieries being mostly larger works than the old ones laid in, we may conclude that coal owners are confident of pushing the production for many years to come.

The remarks of Sir W. Armstrong on this subject, in his Address to the British Association at Newcastle, in 1863, are so excellent that I quote them at length:—"The phase of the earth's existence, suitable for the extensive formation of coal, appears to have passed away for ever; but the quantity of that invaluable mineral which has been stored up throughout the globe for our benefit is sufficient (if used discreetly) to serve the purposes of the human race for many thousands of years. In fact, the entire quantity of coal may be considered as practically inexhaustible.

"Turning, however, to our own particular country, and contemplating the rate at which we are expending those seams of coal which yield the best quality of fuel and can be worked at the least expense, we shall find much cause for anxiety. The greatness of England much depends upon the superiority of her coal, in cheapness and quality, over that of other nations; but we have already drawn, from our choicest mines, a far larger quantity of coal than has been raised in all other parts of the world put together; and the time is not remote when we shall have to encounter the disadvantages of increased cost of working and diminished value of produce.

"Estimates have been made at various periods of the time which would be required to produce complete exhaustion of all the accessible coal in the British Islands. The estimates are certainly discordant; but the discrepancies arise, not from any important disagreement as to the available quantity of coal, but from the enormous difference in the rate of consumption at the various dates when the estimates were made, and also from the different views which have been entertained as to the probable increase of consumption in future years. The quantity of coal yearly worked from British mines has been almost trebled during the last twenty years, and has probably increased tenfold since the commencement of the present century; but as this increase has taken place pending the introduction of steam navigation and railway transit, and under exceptional conditions of manufacturing development, it would be too much to assume that it will continue to advance with equal rapidity.

"The statistics collected by Mr. Hunt, of the Mining Record Office, show that, at the end of 1861, the quantity of coal raised in the United Kingdom had reached the enormous total of 86 millions of tons, and that the average annual increase in the eight preceding years amounted to 2¾ millions of tons.

"Let us inquire, then, what will be the duration of our coal-fields if this more moderate rate of increase be maintained. By combining the known thickness of the various workable seams of coal, and computing the area of the surface under which they lie, it is easy to arrive at an estimate of the total quantity comprised in our coal-bearing strata. Assuming 4,000 feet as the greatest depth at which it will ever be possible to carry on mining operations, and rejecting all seams of less than two feet in thickness, the entire quantity of available coal existing in these islands has been calculated to amount to about 80,000 millions of tons, which, at the present rate of comsumption, would be exhausted in 930 years; but with a continued yearly increase of 2¾ millions of tons would only last 212 years.

"It is clear that, long before complete exhaustion takes place, England will have ceased to be a coal-producing country on an extensive scale. Other nations, and especially the United States of America, which possess coal-fields thirty-seven times more extensive than ours, will then be working more accessible beds at a smaller cost, and will be able to displace the English coal from every market. The question is, not how long our coal will endure before absolute exhaustion is effected, but how long will those particular coal-seams last which yield coal of a quality and at a price to enable this country to maintain her present supremacy in manufacturing industry. So far as this particular district is concerned, it is generally admitted that 200 years will be sufficient to exhaust the principal seams, even at the present rate of working.

If the production should continue to increase as it is now doing, the duration of those seams will not reach half that period. How the case may stand in other coal mining districts, I have not the means of ascertaining; but, as the best and most accessible coal will always be worked in preference to any other, I fear the same rapid exhaustion of our most valuable seams is everywhere taking place."

With almost every part of this statement I can concur, except the calculation by a fixed annual increase of consumption, which I shall show to be contrary to the principles of the subject, and not to reach the whole truth.

Dr. Percy, the eminent metallurgist of the School of Mines, is one whose opinions will bear great weight on this subject; and in several passages of his new treatises on Metallurgy, he has expressed his misgivings. Our coal, he says, "is not only being consumed at a prodigious rate at home, but is being largely exported; and the question as to the probable duration of our coalfields has, of late, been discussed with reasonable anxiety. In 1862 we raised 84,000,000 tons of coal, and the demand continually increases. Hitherto, owing to the abundance of our mineral fuel, we have been, and we still are, comparatively regardless of economy in its consumption. The time has now arrived when necessity will compel us to act differently, both in our manufactories and in our households."

I conclude this chapter with the following passage from the work of two eminent geologists, who wrote, however, when the question was not so urgent as at present:—

"The manufacturing industry of this island, colossal as is the fabric which it has raised, rests principally on no other base than our fortunate position with regard to the rocks of this series. Should our coal-mines ever be exhausted it would melt away at once, and it need not be said that the effect produced on private and domestic comfort would be equally fatal with the diminution of public wealth; we should lose many of the advantages of our high civilization, and much of our cultivated grounds must be again shaded with forests to afford fuel to a remnant of our present population. That there is a progressive tendency to approach this limit is certain; but ages may yet pass before it is felt very sensibly, and, when it does approach, the increasing difficulty and expense of working the mines of coal will operate, by successive and gradual checks against its consumption, through a long period, so that the transition may not be very violent: our manufacturers would first feel the shock; the excess of population supported by them would cease to be called into existence, as the demand for their labour ceased; the cultivation of poor lands would become less profitable, and their conversion into forests more so." [19]

[1] Vol. xii. p. 547.
[2] P. 94.
[3] P. 97.

[4] See also his Address to the Geological Society, Feb. 19th, 1841, p. 41.

[5] Smiles' Engineers, vol. iii. pp. 18, 22.

[6] A History and Description of Fossil Fuel: 1835, chap. xxiv, p. 454.

[7] Fourth Edition, vol. i. p. 600.

[8] 1846, p. 163.

[9] As suggested by Mr. Sopwith at the British Association in 1838.

[10] Coal-Fields of Great Britain, 2d Ed. p. 187.

[11] Journal of Science, No. I. p. 33.

[12] Journal of Science, No. I. p. 29.

[13] Journal of Science, No. I. p. 30.

[14] Trans. of the North of England Institute of Mining Engineers, vol. x. p. 74. (1862.)

[15] Coal-Fields of Great Britain, 2d Ed. p. 236.

[16] The calculation is not strictly correct.

[17] P. 237.

[18] Journal of Science, No. I. p. 35.

[19] Conybeare and Phillips, Outlines of Geology, pp. 324, 325.

Chapter Three - Geological Aspects of the Question

I cannot pretend to do more, as regards the geological aspects of this question, than to give some brief account of the way in which geologists argue concerning it. At the most I must only try to point out what is clear and easy, and what is yet involved in doubt.

In the first place, when we know the extent and thickness of a coal seam, we easily calculate its contents by weight. Coal varies in specific gravity, from about 1.25 to 1.33, or is from one and a quarter to one and a third times as heavy as an equal bulk of water. A cubic yard of solid coal therefore weighs from 2,103 lbs. to 2,243 lbs. And since 2,240 lbs. make one ton, it is quite exact enough to say that a cubic yard is a ton in weight.

Supposing a seam, then, to be exactly a yard thick, an acre of it will contain 4,840 tons of coal, and a square mile 3,097,600 tons. We may say in round numbers that a coal seam gives a million tons of coal per foot thick per square mile.

Our task is now reduced to that of defining the area and thickness of the coal seams of any district. The manner, however, in which the seams have been formed and disposed in the crust of the earth gives rise to several difficulties.

1. The seams are of very different thickness and quality, some workable and others unworkable; we are not certain how many we may count upon.

2. The area of the seams in a district is not uniform, some having been much more denuded or swept away by aqueous agency than others.

3. Coal seams are more or less broken up by faults and hitches, and a greater or less quantity of coal must be sacrificed to the necessities of mining.

4. Coal seams on one side often sink to unexplored depths, and we are uncertain how far we can follow them. There are reasons, too, for supposing that coal measures may exist where they have never yet been reached.

The first question, of the thickness of workable seams, will be more fitly discussed in the next chapter. The fact is sufficient here, that, under the present prices of coal, seams of less than eighteen or twenty-four inches do not repay the cost of working.

We have next to consider the superficial extent of coal seams. It is obvious that so far as seams lie one above the other co-extensively, we may lump them together in our estimate. Thus, in the Newcastle field, there are ten seams of more than two feet thickness, and in workable condition. Of these the High main and Low main coal seams are each six feet thick, and the intermediate Bensham seam is nearly three feet. Adding in the seven other less valuable seams, we have a total thickness of coal of thirty-six feet. As the area of the field, according to Mr. Hull, is 460 square miles, we might be inclined to reckon the total contents according to the rule at 460 × 36 millions of tons, or 16,560 millions. But we should here commit a considerable error, because the seams are not co-extensive. The quantity assumed by Mr. Hull, "corrected for denudation," is only 8,548 millions of tons.

The origin of the difference is very easily explained, though overlooked by many early and some late estimators. It arises from the very large portions of the upper seams that have been swept away or denuded during geological ages. The coal measures consist of many alternated beds of sand, mud, coal, and ironstone, deposited during a long interval of time in estuaries, great swamps, fresh-water lakes, deltas, or flat shores, which gradually sank as the beds were added. As first deposited, the strata must have been nearly level, but they are seldom so now. They lie at every angle from the horizontal to the vertical. Nowhere have we such good opportunities as in our coal mines of observing the upraisals, the downfalls, the dislocations, contortions, and denudations which rocks have suffered. The Scotch coal-fields must, at one time, have formed a nearly continuous and level sheet, but are now broken up into many separate irregular basins, and the seams are sometimes, as in the Mid-Lothian mines, turned up quite vertically on their edge. In the French fields the beds are sometimes folded in and out in a highly complicated and troublesome manner.

In general the coal measures have only been tilted up on one side in sloping plains, or bent into gentle curves and basin-like depressions. These movements could not take place without destroying the continuity of the strata; for though rocks seem to us solid and immovable, they are in comparison with volcanic forces but as thin and incoherent crusts. Accordingly, the beds are transversed in every direction by cracks, fissures, faults, where the whole mass of strata many thousand feet thick has been cloven through, one side comparatively to the other being thrown up. The great ninety fathom dyke, for instance, which crosses the Newcastle field, in a somewhat curved line to the north of the River Tyne, has caused the downthrow of the strata on the north side to the depth of 540 feet, and has had curious influences upon the progress of the English coal trade. On the whole, the Newcastle field is one of the least disturbed, and presents few great difficulties to the miner.

The Lancashire field is more troubled. The new map of the Geological Survey, prepared by Mr. Hull, a complete copy of which may be seen in the Museum of Practical Geology, represents it as scored and broken by a number of cracks, small and great, interlacing in a very complex manner. In short, a sheet of coal measures, to use Dr. Buckland's expression, is like a sheet of ice broken into numerous irregular pieces, but soldered together again without any bit being wholly lost.

Now, when all these disturbances took place, the surface of the ground must have been affected as well as the underground strata. We might expect to find on the south side of the ninety fathom dyke at Newcastle, a perpendicular rocky cliff of corresponding height. But no such thing is known on any of the coal-fields. The surface of our English coal-fields is either quite flat, or only swelling in one direction into round topped hills, showing no conformity to the underground disturbances. We cannot mistake the reason. While earthquakes and intrusions of lava were breaking up the strata, winds and rains and streams, or perhaps the tides of a shallow estuary, were wearing away all prominences, and carrying off great masses of rock. It has been shown, for instance, by Professor Ramsay, that the whole body of the coal measures between the South Wales field and that of the Forest of Dean, has been swept away; and the missing portion, far larger than mountains in mass, is conjecturally restored in the plates to one of the earlier memoirs of the Geological Survey.

During this process the upper beds of course would be soonest carried off. And when the beds are thrown up on one side into an inclined plane, we find the seams of coal more and more cut away as they are nearer the surface. Thus the coal measures, as they usually appear to us, successively crop up to the surface, like the layers of a piece of wood that has been planed off obliquely to its grain.

Thus it happens that the High main seam of coal at Newcastle is quite near the surface, and of comparatively limited extent; while the lower seams crop up to the surface at successively greater distances from the centre of the field, and the lowest crow coals not included in the true measures appear far away.

It is obvious, therefore, that in estimating the contents of a coal-field as we find it, we ought to lay down on a map the line of out-crop of each seam, that line at which it is cut by the surface of the ground. Then we should measure separately the area of each seam, and multiply each area by the thickness of the seam. On many of the maps of the Geological Survey the out-crop of the seams is beautifully shown in series of devious curves, sharply dislocated here and there by the faults. But I am not aware that any person has yet estimated the seams separately. The subject has hardly required so much nicety as yet, and Mr. Hull arrives at a corresponding result by what he calls a "correction for denudation," or an allowance for the large part of the upper beds worn away in the Newcastle field. How he estimates this "correction," almost amounting to half, I do not know.

But the amount of coal ascertained by multiplying the area into the thickness of a seam must not be taken as the amount available. Some part of a seam is always broken up, burnt, or spoiled by the faults and dykes which traverse it. Another considerable part is always lost in mining. Up to the end of last century it was not usual to extract more than four-tenths of the coal in a seam, when working at a greater depth than 100 fathoms; the rest was left in the form of thick pillars to keep the roof from falling in. The free use of timber to support the roof, and the introduction of long-wall, and panel working, has allowed the extraction of nearly all the coal in favourable positions. Still, in unfavourable circumstances, the highest mining skill will probably be unable to get the whole coal; and besides this it is always necessary to leave thick barriers of coal around the limits of the property in order to shut out the water, or the foul air of neighbouring works. A clause to this effect is always introduced into a mining lease, and if not observed, the mine may easily become unworkable. If to these barriers and the wasted pillars of coal, we add the small coal burnt at the pit mouth, or consumed in the ventilating furnaces and engines, we cannot estimate the coal available for commerce at more than two-thirds of that which the continuous seams would contain. Accordingly, Mr. Hull allows one-third for waste.

The contents of a coal-field may then be estimated with some certainty, provided that the boundaries of the seams on every side be known. This is the case in a perfect coal basin like that of the Forest of Dean. In the case of fields abutting on the sea, like those of Newcastle and Whitehaven, we have only the uncertainty concerning the distance to which coal can be worked under the sea. From one to three miles is the greatest distance we can conceive possible, except under a rise of price, which would constitute the scarcity of coal to be apprehended.

It is only when coal seams sink down beyond our knowledge on one side, as in the Yorkshire field, that we are in thorough uncertainty as to the quantity of available coal. The question here becomes a two-fold one. Firstly, *how far may the coal measures be supposed to dip and extend under more modern formations?* Secondly, *how far can we follow them with profit, considering the growing costs and difficulty of deep mining?*

Leaving the second question for discussion in the next chapter, there is but little that can be said concerning the first.

If the science of geology had no other claims upon our attention, it would repay all the labour spent upon it, many times over, by showing where coal may reasonably be looked for. By fixing the geological date of each rock, it points out in what interval the coal measures must appear, if they appear at all. One-third of the whole kingdom, it is said, is excluded from the search by being formed of rocks older than the coal-bearing age. On the other hand, there are large areas of country under which coal may reasonably be expected to occur, although there are no signs of it at the surface: and geology may enable us even to fathom the thickness of overlying rocks and tell with some certainty the depth at which coal will probably occur, if at all. [1]

Mr. Hull includes in his estimate 932 square miles of such country. Of these 225 square miles occur at the south-east corner of the Durham field, where the coal measures dip under the Magnesian Limestone and the New Red Sandstone. Another 400 square miles occur similarly on the eastward dip of the great Yorkshire and Derbyshire field. Wirral and other parts of the Cheshire New Red Sandstone are probably underlain by bands or sheets of coal measures, connecting the Flintshire and Denbighshire fields with the great Lancashire field. The North and South Stafford, Warwick, Coalbrookdale, and Forest of Wyre fields are more or less completely connected. On the other sides the fields are definitely terminated by the appearance of the carboniferous or mountain limestone, that great basement rock which in nearly every part of the kingdom bears the coal measures.

As these sunken coal-fields are continuous with those now worked, there can be little or no doubt as to their existence. But while they can hardly contain better seams than those already known, the seams may very possibly thin out if followed far. And in many cases the overlying Permian and New Red Sandstone rocks may contain so much water and swell to such a thickness as to be quite impenetrable.

A band of coal seams connecting the Durham and Yorkshire fields is of a more conjectural character. In the country between these two fields the Magnesian Limestone, which is above the coal, lies directly upon the millstone grit and carboniferous limestone below the coal. As there is no sign of coal measures at the junction, coal cannot now exist at the point. If it ever existed in the interval, it must have been swept away before the era of the Permian or Magnesian Limestone.

Noticing, then, the rectangular direction in which the northerly edge of the Yorkshire coal, and the southerly edge of the Durham coal run under Permian beds, it seems to be wholly a matter of uncertainty how far the denudation, or absence of the coal measures, may extend.

Another possible position of coal measures is beneath the cretaceous and Wealden beds of Wilts, Berks, Surrey, and Kent. In 1855, Mr. Godwin-Austen published a remarkable argument, showing that a range of rocks, an underground ridge of mountains, as it were, probably stretched from the Mendip Hills to the Ardennes in Belgium; and "we have strong à priori reasons for supposing that the course of a band of coal measures coincides with, and may some day be reached, along the line of the valley of the Thames, whilst some of the deeper-seated coal, as well as certain overlying and limited basins, may occur along and beneath some of the longitudinal folds of the Wealden denudation." His deductions were partially verified immediately after publication by the actual discovery of old rocks in the boring of wells at Kentish Town and Harwich. But Mr. Whitaker, to whose able memoir [2] and kind aid I am indebted, remarks on the uncertainty of such deductions concerning coal. "It must not be supposed that because there is almost a certainty of there being a ridge of old rocks at some depth below the surface along part of the valley of the Thames, and a likelihood of some of those old rocks belonging to the *coal measures,* therefore coal will be found at a workable depth in parts of the London District; for the alternations of sandstone, shale, &c., that so generally contain workable beds of coal, and are therefore known as the 'coal measures,' are sometimes almost without that mineral."

In short, all that is shown is a *bare possibility of finding coal.* But as it is uncertain whether the coal measures are there at all—whether, if there, they contain good coal—and if so, whether they are within workable depth and circumstances, it must still be held very unlikely that coal will ever be got in this tract.

And on the principle that "a bird in the hand is worth two in the bush," we should avoid putting too much reliance on possible coal-fields. Their existence is doubtful—they cannot well contain better coal than that we now enjoy, and may contain much worse, and they are very probably at depths, and in conditions, where they are commercially out of the question, as regards competition with foreign coals. There is plenty of coal known to exist out of our reach without resorting to coal that may or may not exist, but is in any case perhaps out of reach.

Here I may notice the differences of opinion that have arisen concerning the amount of accessible coal in the Great South Wales coal tract. For a long time it was considered an inexhaustible store, to which we might have final recourse some centuries hence.

Mr. H. H. Vivian, a great land and coal owner of that district, Member of Parliament for Glamorganshire, yet insists upon its being regarded in this light. During the discussions on the French Treaty of Commerce in 1860, some opposition having been raised to the 11th clause, on the ground that free exportation of coals must accelerate the exhaustion of our mines, Mr. Vivian roundly asserted that the South Wales field alone would serve the whole consumption of England for 500 years, and it would sustain its own present consumption for 5,000 years. "It was perfectly absurd," he said, "to talk of the exhaustion of coal in this country."

Now, when Mr. Hull came to estimate the amount of available coal in this field, he found it to be only 2,000 times its present yield, or two-fifths as much as Mr. Vivian's estimate.

Having the accuracy of his statement then called in question, Mr. Vivian published a small pamphlet containing, in addition to a reprint of his speech, and of a lecture on coal, a brief critique on Mr. Hull's calculations. "Mr. Hull," he says, "takes the total thickness of strata at 10,000 feet, containing 84 feet of valuable coal; he then deducts for denudation 48,000 millions of tons; he next deducts one half the remainder, or 24,000 millions of tons, for those seams which lie below 4,000 feet; he further deducts one third for waste, and the quantity already extracted, leaving a balance of 16,000 millions of tons out of his original quantity, which he does not state, but which I calculate from his data at 78,000 millions of tons, as the quantity likely to be available for man's use, equal to the present rate of the consumption of South Wales for 2,000 years, my estimate having been 5,000 years." Mr. Vivian then objects to the first of these deductions, that it is wholly arbitrary, and beyond the power of any person, however intimate his local knowledge, to estimate. The second deduction he considers opposed to fact.

But when Mr. Vivian defends and explains his own estimate, what has he to urge? "I took the thickness of coal," he says, "after the most careful consideration, at 60 feet. I had mainly in view the 'Great Lower Veins,' varying from 50 feet on the northern to 100 feet on the southern upcrop, and upwards of 70 feet on the central upheave. I looked at the area over which now, and ages hence, those beds might probably be won. I considered the comparatively limited area under which they would lie too deep, but where the 'Upper Vein,' to some extent, supplied their place, and I concluded that I might fairly take 60 feet as an average workable thickness over the entire area. I then took the produce at 40 per cent. less than the actual contents, that is to say, I calculated the cubic yard at 1,500 tons instead of 1,613 tons, or 6.66 per cent. (less), and I allowed one-third, equal to 33.33 per cent. for waste, faults, quantity already worked, &c., together 40 per cent.; and upon these data I arrived at the conclusion that South Wales could supply all England for 500 years, and her own consumption for 5,000; to that I adhere in spite of the calculations which Mr. Hull has adduced."

Now this sort of argument may be very satisfactory to Mr. Vivian's own mind, and, in a Parliamentary debate, a confident assertion by a man of local knowledge and influence has a good deal of weight, and rightly so. But will Mr. Vivian's views bear a moment's criticism? Would Mr. Vivian accept such an estimate from a witness before him on a Parliamentary Committee? Would he be satisfied with taking the thickness of coal, "after the most careful consideration, at 60 feet?" Why, what are the facts? Geologists of the highest standing—Sir T. De La Beche and Sir W. E. Logan, after a long geological survey, most admirably conducted, proved that the coal measures of South Wales are 10,000 or 12,000 feet thick, and contain altogether 84 feet of coal in seams of workable thickness, the most of which lie near the base. Mr. Vivian assumes, apparently, by nothing more than conjecture, that 60 out of the 84 feet on an average may be taken as available over the whole area!

Mr. Hull may have deducted too much for denudation, and possibly too much for depth; but Mr. Hull's is an estimate—Mr. Vivian's is no more than a guess. And, of course, when Mr. Vivian asserts that South Wales can supply all England for 500 years, he means at the present rate of consumption, which is quite beside the question. The question is, *how long will South Wales supply us at the present price with the present growing demand?*

[1] E. Hull, British Association, 1854, Report, p. 87.
[2] The Geology of Parts of Middlesex, Hertfordshire, &c. by William Whitaker, B.A. F.G.S. 1864, p. 107. (Geological Survey.)

Chapter Four - Of the Cost of Coal Mining

The difficulty and cost of winning and working coal-mines form an aspect of the question that obviously contains the solution of the whole.

In a free industrial system, such as we are developing and assisting to spread, everything is a question of cost. We have heard of moral and physical impossibilities, but we ought to be aware that there are also *commercial impossibilities*. We must ask, in undertaking a work, not whether it can be done, or is physically possible, but whether it will pay to do it—whether it is commercially possible. The works of the two Brunels were, in a mechanical point of view, at least as successful and wonderful as those of the Stephensons; but, commercially speaking, they were disastrous failures, which no one would have undertaken had the consequences been seen. Commerce and industry cannot be carried on but by gain—by a return exceeding the outlay.

Now, in coal-mining, we must discriminate the physical and commercial possibility. The second presupposes the first, but does not follow from it. The question is a twofold one:—Firstly, is it physically possible to drive our coal-mines to the depth of 4,000, 5,000, or 6,000 feet? and, secondly, is it commercially possible when in other parts of the world coal is yet being worked in the light of day? The very existence of Britain, as a great nation, is bound up in these questions.

Now I apprehend that there is not the least danger of our reaching any fixed limit of deep mining, where physical impossibility begins. In mines already 2,000 or 2,500 feet deep, there is no special difficulty felt in going deeper. But we must consider the matter a little, because the Quarterly Review has confidently asserted that 2,500 feet is the limit, [1] and Mr. Hull, after an express inquiry into the matter, thinks that 4,000 may be taken as the limit. [2] It has often been suggested that the increase of temperature of the earth's crust as we descend into it will prove an insuperable obstacle, and Mr. Hull and others have been inclined to hold, that beyond a depth of 4,000 or 5,000 feet the temperature will entirely prevent further sinking.

The increase of temperature varies in different mines from one degree in 35 to one degree in 88 feet. The increase in the deep Monkwearmouth Pit was one degree for 60 feet; but the observations of Mr. Astley in the sinking of the Dukinfield Deep Pit showed an average increase of one degree in 83 feet, nearly the lowest rate known. If with Mr. Hull we take one degree in 70 feet as a safe average rate of increase, we easily form the following table, starting from the depth of 50 feet from the surface, at which depth in this country an uniform temperature of about 50° Fahr. is found to exist.

Depth in feet.	Increase of temperature of rock.	Actual temperature of rock.
50	0°	50°
1,000	14°	64°
2,000	28°	78°
3,000	42°	92°
4,000	56°	106°
5,000	71°	121°

The air in mines, independently of the rock, is also warmer than at the surface, owing to its greater density; for just as in ascending a mountain the barometer falls and the air grows rare and cold, so in descending a mine the barometer rises and the air grows warmer. The barometer, roughly speaking, varies about an inch for every 1,000 feet of elevation, and the temperature about one degree for every 300 feet. On these data, the following table is roughly calculated:—

Depth in feet.	Height of Barometer.	Increase of temperature of air.	Actual temperature of air.
0	30·0	0°	50°
1,000	31·0	3°	53°
2,000	32·0	7°	57°
3,000	33·0	10°	60°
4,000	34·0	13°	63°
5,000	35·0	17°	67°

If air, then, of the temperature of 50° at the surface descend 5,000 feet, it will acquire the temperature of 67°. The rocks at that depth will have the temperature of 121°, and will therefore warm the air as it circulates through the mine up to their own temperature. But Mr. Hull has fallen into a very evident mistake in adding together the increments of temperature of the air and rocks. He makes the temperature, for instance, at a depth of 4,000 feet, to be 120°·08 as follows:—

Invariable temperature of surface...	50°·5
Increase due to depth...	56°·42
Increase due to density of air...	13°·16
Resulting temperature (sum)...	120°·08

On the contrary, even at 5,000 feet deep, the temperature will not exceed 121°, the temperature of the rock, and at 4,000 feet it will not exceed 106°. It may be reduced, too, by plentiful ventilation, or by letting out in the mine air compressed and cooled at the surface, as is done in the new coal-cutting machines. Now, as men can work at temperatures exceeding 100°, we are not likely to encounter the physical limit of sinking on this account.

But the cost of sinking and working deep pits is quite another matter. The growing temperature will enervate, if it does not stop the labourers. Thus it is stated [3] that in one Cornish mine men work in an atmosphere varying from 110° to 120° Fahr. But then they work only for twenty minutes at a time, with nearly naked bodies, and cold water frequently thrown over them. They sometimes lose eight or ten pounds in weight during a day's work. Much increased ventilation will be a matter of expense and difficulty; the hardening of the coal and rocks will render hewing more costly; creeps and subsidences of the strata will be unavoidable, and will crush a large portion of the coal or render it inaccessible; while explosions, fires, floods, and the hundred unforeseen accidents and disappointments to which mining is always subject, will lie as a burden on the whole enterprise, a risk which no assurance company will venture upon. In addition to these special difficulties, the whole capital and current expenditure of the mine naturally grows in a higher proportion than the depth. The sinking of the shaft becomes a long and costly matter; both the capital thus sunk has to be redeemed and interest upon it paid. The engine powers for raising water, coals, miners, &c., increase, and, beyond all, the careful ventilation and management of the mine render a large staff of mechanics, viewers, and attendants indispensable.

Much may be done by working larger areas from the same shaft; by forming consolidated companies for economical drainage; by perfecting machinery, and organizing labour to contend with the growing cost. But increased areas and distances of working, though comparatively diminishing the capital expense of the shafts and works above ground, will increase the current expenses of drainage, ventilation, and general maintenance.

A full analysis of the detailed accounts of a number of collieries of various depths would throw great light on this question, and might go far to solve the question of England's future career. But private commercial accounts are shrouded in such impenetrable closeness, that no individual inquirers can hope to gain the use of them. Even the several Parliamentary Committees, in their prolonged inquiries into the coal trade some thirty years ago, were continually frustrated by Mr. Buddle and other mining engineers, who declined to communicate information known to them professionally and confidential-ly. The investigation of such a subject might perhaps be best undertaken by a Committee of the British Association, or some other learned Society.

An account of the South Hetton Colliery establishment, a recent and well-arranged mine, throws light on this subject. It is published in a little work of the *Traveller's Library*, [4] remarkable for the amount of information it con-tains on the subject of coal.

Of 529 men employed in or about the colliery, 140 only are hewers of coal, representing the productive power of the establishment. We may divide the staff as follows:—

Hewers of coal...	140
Putters, screeners, &c...	227
Employed in administration and maintenance of mine...	123
Boys, variously employed...	39

The "putters," "screeners," and others, to the number of 227, are occupied in pushing the coal along the tramways from the hewer to the shaft; in rais-ing it to the surface; screening it, and removing the stones, and, finally, load-ing it into the railway waggon or ship's hold. They represent, as it were, the trading part of the community, while the administration represents the gov-ernment; consisting of a manager, viewers, engineers, clerks, and a surgeon; with a great number of joiners, sawyers, enginewrights, smiths, masons, carters, waggon-wrights, and common labourers, as well as ventilators, shift-ers, foremen, and others of responsible duties underground; all occupied in keeping the mine, the ventilation, machinery, engines, and the works gener-ally, in repair.

Now, if coal were quarried at the surface, and wheeled straight away, each hewer would scarcely require more than one subsidiary labourer. In a deep mine we find that nearly three subsidiary labourers are required, so that four only accomplish what two would do at the surface, to say nothing of the tim-ber and other materials consumed, and the great capital sunk in the shaft, engines, and works of the deep mine.

As mines become deeper and more extended, the system of management necessary to facilitate the working and diminish the risk of accidents, must become more and more complicated. The work is not of a nature to be made self-acting, and capable of execution by machinery. Even in the West Ardsley Colliery, belonging to the patentees of the coal-cutting machine, who natural-ly carry out its use to the utmost possible extent, this machine is found [5] to diminish the staff only *ten per cent.* The labour saved is only that of twenty-seven hewers, while other branches of the staff must be rather increased than diminished. So different, too, are the conditions of coal-mining, that in many collieries the use of coal-cutting machines is perhaps impracticable.

The deeper a mine the more fiery it in general becomes. Carburetted gas, distilled from the coal in the course of geological ages, lies pent up in the fissures at these profound depths, and is ever liable to blow off and endanger the lives of hundreds of persons. It was supposed that George Stephenson and Sir H. Davy had discovered a true safety lamp. But, in truth, this very ingenious invention is like the compass that Sir Thomas More describes in his Utopia as given to a distant people. It gave them such confidence in navigation that they were "farther from care than danger."

No lamp has been made, or, perhaps, can be made, that will prevent accidents when a feeder of gas is tapped, or a careless miner opens his lamp, or a drop of water cracks a heated glass, or a boy stumbles and breaks his lamp. The miner's lamp, in fact, is never a safety lamp, except when carefully used in a perfectly ventilated mine. Long experience shows that perfect ventilation is the only sure safeguard against explosion. But it is no easy matter to ventilate near a hundred miles of levels, inclines, stalls, and goaves in a fiery mine.

The amount of drainage required in deepening our mines is another point of the greatest importance. The coal-measures themselves, containing many beds of clay and shale, are dry enough in general, except where interrupted by faults which allow the water to penetrate. Thus, the lower parts of deep mines will in general be dry enough, but the passage through the overlying Permian and New Red Sandstone beds may often be extremely costly, or almost impossible.

"In all the sinkings through the Magnesian Limestone, feeders of water, more or less considerable, are met with at a certain distance from the surface, derived not so much by percolation through the mass of the rock—for this can obtain to a small extent only—but collected in and coming off the numerous gullets and fissures which everywhere intersect and divide the mass of strata. If the shaft be not drained by pumping or otherwise, the water from these feeders rises to a point which remains, save in exceptional cases, constant.... Immediately underlying the limestone is a bed of sandstone of very variable thickness, which, when exposed to the action of the atmosphere, disintegrates rapidly, and has hence acquired its local name of 'friable yellow sandstone.' It is in sinking through this bed of rapidly decomposing sandstone that such great engineering difficulties have been encountered, owing to the enormous quantity of water which in some cases is met with, more especially if the bed be thick and much below the level of saturation."

"A very full account of the sinking of the Murton Winning is given by Mr. Potter. [6] ...Nearly 10,000 gallons of water per minute were pumped out of this bed by engines exceeding in the aggregate 1,500 horse-power. The circumstances which favour the remarkable accumulation of water in the limestone, and the rapidity with which it is drained off into pits sunk through it, are due to several causes, some of which are peculiar to this formation, and perhaps to this district. They are:—

"1. The arrangement of the beds of stratification.

"2. The contour of the country.

"3. The permeability of this formation to water." [7]

In the sinking of Pemberton's Pit at Monkwearmouth, a stratum of free-stone sand at the base of the Magnesian Limestone poured 3,000 gallons of water per minute into the sinking. And when this flood of water had been overcome by an engine of 180 or 200 horse-power, and had been "tubbed back," a new "feeder" was met at the depth of 1,000 feet, requiring fresh pumps, and an additional outlay of money. [8] The shaft was commenced in May, 1826; it was continued for eight and a half years before the first workable coal was reached; and it was only in April, 1846, twenty years afterwards, that the enterprise was proved successful by the winning of the "Hutton Seam." The South Hetton and Great Hetton pits were also very costly, difficult winnings, on account of the quicksands and irruptions of water. And the winning of a pit at Haswell, in the county of Durham, through the Magnesian Limestone and the underlying sand, was found impracticable for a like reason, in spite of engines capable of raising 26,700 tons of water per diem. [9]

In the continuous working of pits, even where "tubbing" is used to keep the water out of the shaft as much as possible, the quantity of water is not unusually seven or eight times as great as that of the coal raised. At the Friar's Goose Colliery, near Gateshead, 6,000 tons of water are raised from the mine every day, about twenty times as much as the weight of the coal extracted. In some, such as Percy Main and Wylam collieries, it reaches thirty times the weight of the coal.

Now, when it becomes necessary to sink, not only through the Magnesian Limestone, but through the New Red Sandstone, in order to reach new supplies of coal, may not the water be found overpowering? Mr. Hull, in a valuable paper "On the New Red Sandstone and Permian Formations, as Sources of Water-supply for Towns," [10] has noticed the extremely porous and absorbent nature of the New Red Sandstone. "Rain rapidly sinks into it, leaving a dry soil," and "under and around all the towns built on this formation (or on the Permian) there lie natural reservoirs of pure water." Now, when we come to sink two or three thousand feet through such formations, may not the water prove an insuperable obstacle?

A question of secondary importance concerns the limit of thinness of workable coal seams. This is, of course, a question of the cost of mining. It is found that, at the present price of coal, it is not profitable to work seams of less than 18 or 24 inches thickness. The reason is obvious. In working a four-foot seam little rock has to be mined, since the spaces from which the coal has been removed furnish the levels and communications of the mine. In working a two-foot seam, however, large quantities of rock have to be removed in addition to the coal, and while the cost is hardly less than in a four-foot seam, the produce of coal is only one half. A one-foot seam, again, would be worked at a very great cost, and would furnish less than one fourth of the produce of a four-foot seam. Either the larger seam must yield extraordinary profits, or else the thinner seam cannot be worked.

In estimates of existing coal, 24 or 18 inches is taken as the limit of workable seams; how will this limit be affected by probable changes in the conditions of coal-mining? A considerable advance in the price of coal will, of course, enable thinner seams to be worked with profit. Thus, to some extent, the rise of prices will be slackened. The higher the price rises, the more thoroughly will the coal-measures be worked, and the more coal becomes workable. As, however, the high price of coal constitutes the evil of exhaustion, the dreaded results are only somewhat mitigated, not prevented. And it would be wholly erroneous to suppose that when once the thicker seams of a coal district have been worked out, we can readily, at a future time, work out the thinner seams, when the increased price of coal warrants it. For it must be observed, that a very large part of the cost of mining consists in the cost of draining, ventilation, and maintenance of the shaft, and works at the bank, which we may call the general mining expenses. Now, when these expenses are undertaken for the purpose of working a thick and valuable seam, it is often possible to work thin seams of 18 or 24 inches without any considerable increase in the general expenses. In short, the thick seam pays the general expenses of the mine as well as its own cost of hewing, while it is sufficient if the thin seam leaves a small profit on the expenses of hewing only. But the price of coal must rise in a very extreme degree, that an unworked thin seam should, at a future time, pay the general costs of drainage, ventilation, and maintenance, as well as the cost of hewing.

The same is true of immense masses of coal left underground during the former working of mines, as small or crushed coal, as pillars and barriers, or as outlying portions rendered difficult to mine by faults, or other mining troubles. If such portions of coal could not pay for removal when the mine was in full working efficiency, they cannot pay the whole costs of restoring and maintaining the mine in a workable condition, not at least until the price of coal has risen manifold.

All then that we can hope from thin seams, or abandoned coal, *is a retardation of the rise of price after a considerable rise has already taken place.* This will hardly prevent the evils apprehended from exhaustion.

Nor will the use of the coal-cutting machine much affect this question. By reducing the cost of hewing and the waste of coal in the "kirving," or cut made by the hewer, it will, undoubtedly, to some extent, allow thinner seams to be worked. At the same time, it will not affect the cost of removing large masses of profitless rock, which is essential in working thin seams, nor the general cost of the maintenance of the mine. If seams of 18 inches are now occasionally workable, the coal-cutting machine may reduce the limit a few inches; but it is evident that seams of less than 12 inches could never be worked while the price of coal remained at all tolerable.

Coal-mining is a fair fight with difficulties, and just as the balance inclines between the difficulties and the powers we possess to overcome them, will the cost of coal and the prospects of this country oscillate. What we can do to cheapen extraction, indeed, is chiefly effected by turning the powers of coal against itself, by multiplying steam power to pump and wind, and cut and draw the coal. But then the greater part of the work within the colliery is of a kind that cannot be executed by machinery, just as the building of houses, or the digging of holes, never has been, and scarcely can be, done by machinery.

But be the difficulties what they may, we would have ingenuity and energy enough to overcome them, were the question one of a simple absolute amount of difficulty. But in reality we must consider our mines not by themselves, but in comparison with those of other countries. Our main branches of iron industry grew up at places like Wednesbury, in South Staffordshire, "where there being but little earth lying over the measure of coal, the workmen rid off the earth and dig the coal under their feet, and carry it out in wheelbarrows, there being no need for windlass, rope, or corf." [11]

Our industry will certainly last and grow until our mines are commonly sunk 2,000 or 3,000, or even 4,000 feet deep. But when this time comes, the States of North America will still be working coal in the light of day, quarrying it in the banks of the Ohio, and running it down into boats alongside. The question is, *how soon will our mines approach the limit of commercial possibility, and fail to secure us any longer that manufacturing supremacy on which we are learning to be wholly dependent?*

[1] Vol. CX. p. 329.
[2] Coal-fields, &c. 2d Ed. p. 219.
[3] Report of Commission on Health of Mines, 1865.
[4] Our Coal and our Coal-pits. London: 1853.
[5] Prof. H. D. Rogers, in Good Words, April, 1864, p. 338.
[6] Trans of the North of England Institute of Mining Engineers, Vol. V.
[7] Brit. Assoc. Report, 1863, pp. 726, 727.
[8] Our Coal and our Coal Pits, p. 113.
[9] Ibid. p. 115.
[10] Manchester Memoirs, 3d series, 1861-2. Vol. II. pp. 256, 257.
[11] Dr. Plot's Natural History of Staffordshire, quoted in the "History of Wednesbury," p. 101.

Chapter Five - Of the Price of Coal

"Cheapness and goodness," said Yarranton, "is, and always will be, the great master and comptroller of trade," and the reader will see that the whole question of the exhaustion of our mines is a question of the cost of coal. All commerce, in short, is a matter of price. "Will it pay to do this at this price?" or, "Will it pay better to do this here at this price or there at that price?" Such are the leading questions which govern every commercial undertaking in a free system of industry.

The exhaustion of our mines will be marked pari passu by a rising cost or value of coal; and when the price has risen to a certain amount comparatively to the price in other countries, our main branches of trade will be doomed. It will be well, therefore, to inquire whether there has been any recent serious rise in the price of coal such as would be the sign of incipient exhaustion. Had a considerable recent rise occurred, as I have heard asserted, it might be argued that no such evil results have followed as alarmists prophesy, and then the optimist would conclude that, perhaps, after all, "dear coal" is not the fatal thing some suppose; this country may surmount that evil, it will be said, as it has surmounted worse evils.

From what reliable accounts I have been able to meet with, it is certain that there has been no such recent rise of price as could at all operate as a check upon our industry. Yet it is certain that coal has been cheaper in the past than it can again be, and that in the Great Northern market the growth of demand during the last century has been accompanied by a considerable but indefinite rise of price.

Where coal, indeed, used formerly to be had almost for the asking, it now bears a fair price. In the palmy day of the Staffordshire "Thick Coal" the price of the best large coal was 6s. per ton of 21 cwts., and 120 lbs. to the cwt., or 5s. 4d. per ton of 2,240 lbs. Coal was a drug about Birmingham, "so much so, as to cause the coalowners to give great extra weight.... There are many other veins at present not thought worth getting, or from one to three yards thick; inferior coals are sold at 3s. per ton, and from that upwards, in proportion to their quality; the small coals, for working engines, are sold from 1s. to 1s. 6d. per ton; the supply produced for the manufactures of the country would always be sufficient, in my opinion, without increasing the present price, as there are many new collieries now opening." [1]

The anticipations of the Ironmaster who gave this opinion before the Committee of 1800 have not proved true. The price of best coal in Staffordshire is now nine shillings or more per ton, and many writers concur in stating that the magnificent "Thick Coal" of South Staffordshire has been either used or wasted away. The wonderful "black country" already leans for its supplies of coal and ore upon neighbouring parts; [2] it seems to be already overshadowed by the approaching decline of prosperity. "He that liveth longest, let him fetch fire furthest," was a proverb quoted by Dudley, [3] two and a half centuries ago, with reference to the lamentable waste of the Thick Coal, and now the force of the proverb is becoming apparent.

The late strike of Staffordshire miners was occasioned by the high price of coal. The activity of the iron trade for the last year or two had led to several advances in the price of coal and rate of wages; but though the price of iron remained pretty high, it was found the trade could not bear the cost of coal. To prevent injury to the staple industry of the district, the coal proprietors, somewhat arbitrarily, determined to reduce the price of coal by cutting down the wages of the miners, and in this they have been at least temporarily successful. But it is feared that the interruption of business occasioned by the strike may have already contributed to forward that migration of the iron trade to the newer coal-fields which must soon take place.

It is almost impossible to get such general and uniform statements of the price of coal as would warrant us in drawing comparisons over long periods of time. The variations in the quality, size, and distance of supply constantly affect the price, independently of duties and other obstacles. Almost all the quotations of prices refer to the London market, and are useless, because the prices there are not only affected by freights, but have been burdened, more or less, by duties and charges of a most complicated character.

The only series of prices I have been able to make out gives the average price of the best large coal as put free on board at Newcastle, and the other shipping places of the North. The first two prices (1771 and 1794) are derived from the Report of the Select Committee of the House of Commons on the Coal Trade in 1830 (p. 7). The prices of 1801—1851, are from a table of yearly prices published by Mr. Porter, in his "Progress of the Nation" (p. 277), and are the average shipping prices as returned to the Coal Exchange in London under Act of Parliament. The last price (1860) is an average computed for the General Committee of the Coal Trade of Newcastle, and communicated to the Mining Record Office. [4]

Average Shipping Price of Newcastle Coal.

Year.	s.	d.
1771...	5	4 per ton.
1794...	7	6 per ton.
1801...	10	4 per ton.
1811...	13	0 per ton.
1821...	12	8 per ton.
1831...	12	4 per ton.
1841...	10	6 per ton.
1850...	9	6 per ton.
1860...	9	0 per ton.

This is probably as good and comparable a series of prices as could be got; yet it is very difficult to draw inferences from it beyond the contradiction of any recent considerable rise. The great rise of price up to 1811 was more or less due to the depreciation of gold and paper currency, or to the other causes, whatever they may have been, of the great general rise of prices. The subsequent fall is, of course, partly due to the restoration of our currency, and to the other debatable causes of a general fall of prices. [5]

There are, however, at least two other circumstances not to be lost sight of in comparing early and late prices of coal.

Firstly, there is the *limitation of the vend,* an arrangement which used to exist among the coal proprietors of the North, to limit the amount sold by any colliery, in order that each colliery might have a share of the trade proportional to its capabilities. This combination maintained itself at intervals for about two centuries, and was much complained of because it was supposed to raise the price of coal. It may have had some effect, especially upon those better kinds of coal of which the price is quoted.

Secondly, there is the practice of screening coals, whereby a considerable portion of the coal raised at the beginning of the century used to be separated out and burnt as waste, the whole cost of raising the coal being paid in the price of the large coal sold. Though coals are still generally screened, the "seconds," "nuts," and even the "dead small," or "slack," are usually sold for manufacturing purposes at prices proportional to the size of the coal. The total price thus returned is increased by more than is represented in the price of the large coal.

Both the limitation of the vend and the practice of screening would thus tend to raise the earlier quotations of price of large coal, as compared with late quotations, and thus disguise the real rise of price due to the growing demand and the depth of the mines.

I take it, therefore, to be pretty certain that the cost of the best quality of Newcastle coal has been considerably more than doubled within a century by the growing depth of the collieries. It is not to be said that trade is much affected by the price of the very best coals, which are chiefly valued for household purposes. But from the price of such coal we learn what we should have to pay were all coals drawn from the depths of 1,000 or 2,000 feet or more. The mines of South Wales, Scotland, and Yorkshire are yet shallow, and the coal cheap enough. The cost of the coal, especially, which supports the great and rising iron trade in South Wales and Scotland, is only four or five shillings per ton.

The following are some returns of the price of coal published by Mr. Hunt in the Mineral Statistics for 1860:—

	Description of Coal	Price per Ton	
		s.	*d.*
Newcastle...	House Coal...	9	0
	Steam...	8	0
	Gas, Coking, and Manufacturing	5	6
Derbyshire...	Best Coal...	9	0
	Common...	6	6
	Cost of Getting...5*s.* to	5	6
North Staffordshire...	Best...	9	2

	Description of Coal	Price per Ton	
		s.	*d.*
	Common...	6	0
	Cost of Getting...2*s.* 6*d.* to	4	6
Lancashire...	Best Coal...	6	3
	Lately...	5	6
South Wales and Monmouth-shire...	Large Coal...	6	6
	Small...	4	6
Scotland...	Average...	4	0
	Cost of Getting...	2	8

The average cost of getting coal throughout the country was stated to be 4s. 10d. per ton, not including profits, rent, and other charges.

In the very various prices of coal from the several collieries of the Newcastle district, we have evidence of the rise of price due to the depth of mines. Shipping prices of coal are given in full detail in the Report of the Committee of 1838 (p. 240); and taking the coals classed as Newcastle Wallsend only, we find the price varying from 6s. 6d. to 11s. 6d., the nuts and small coal ranging down to 3s. 9d. It is obvious that *the difference of five shillings per ton in Wallsend coal must either be absorbed by the expenses of deep mining, or else it must make the fortune of the proprietors or workers of the mines.* That in some cases prodigious profits are made, as in the case of the original Wallsend mine, is well known. But this cannot usually be the case, otherwise the wide areas of land yet known to contain untouched seams of coal of the finest qualities, would at once be broken up by speculators, who are never wanting. *That deep mines are so deliberately opened is a sufficient proof that the highest prices obtained are, taking all mining risks and charges into account, only an average equivalent for the capital invested.* These deep pits can only be undertaken at present in search of coal of the finest household quality. The Monkwearmouth Pit was sunk to win the Hutton seam, which yields coal of the highest possible character. The Dukinfield Deep Pit was undertaken to follow the celebrated Lancashire "Black Mine," a four feet seam of the finest coal, selling for 10s. per ton at the pit's mouth, the small coal returning 5s. 6d. per ton.

The high prices, which are necessary in order to tempt speculators to undertake deep mining, afford a rough but sure indication of the effect of depth upon the cost of coal. When the general depth of coal workings has increased to 2,000 feet, little or no coal will be sold for less than 10s. per ton, and the choice large coal will have risen to a much higher price. Our iron and general manufacturing industries will have to contend with a nearly double cost of fuel. And when with the growth of our trade and the course of time our mines inevitably reach a depth of 3,000 or 4,000 feet, the increasing cost of fuel will be an incalculable obstacle to our further progress.

[1] Evidence of Alex. Raby. First Report on Coal Trade, 1800, pp. 76, 77.
[2] See Chap. XV.
[3] Metallum Martis, p. 8.
[4] Mineral Statistics for 1860, p. xxiii.
[5] The comparison in the First Edition of the change of price of coal with the average change of price of commodities was erroneous, owing to a numerical oversight. The fall of prices between 1794 and 1860 was in the ratio of 100 to 81. See Journal of the Statistical Society, June 1865, p. 294.

Chapter Six - Of British Invention

The history of discovery and invention, like history in general, can never be the matter of an exact science. The extension of the sciences and arts is the last thing that can be subjected to rigorous laws. But in a long course of progress, like that which marks the rise of civilization in England, we may observe tendencies, not free from exception, of an instructive kind, and bearing powerfully upon the general subject of our inquiry.

The usefulness of Britain greatly depends upon the arts she has contributed for the use of mankind, and her own pre-eminence in the use of those arts. But an Englishman who goes with the current of insular opinion, is too apt to assume that Britain is great in everything. There is no discrimination in popular opinion. As Shakespeare is the acknowledged poet of modern times, so Francis Bacon is supposed to be the philosopher who brought about the revival of knowledge and the arts. Now, though we have poets and philosophers, works and discoveries, which in their own way are unrivalled, we should remember that other nations have their triumphs in their way unrivalled. And if we at present possess a certain leading and world-wide influence, it is not due to any general intellectual superiority, but to the union of certain happy mental qualities with our peculiar material resources.

We may observe, in the first place, that almost all the arts we practised in England, until within the last century, were of continental origin. England, until lately, was young and inferior in the arts.

Secondly, we may observe that almost all the arts and inventions we have of late contributed, spring from our command of coal.

Such generalizations are very subject to exception. Roger Bacon is an illustrious exception, and it seems likely that there were other Englishmen in his days of lofty talents. Still, they drew their education and information from the Continent, and they lived in such a time and place that their works were unappreciated, and left no mark in the creation of the arts. Francis Bacon has usurped much of the fame due to Roger Bacon. No one the least acquainted with the history of science in Europe, can suppose that Francis Bacon gave rise to the sciences and arts which were rising and flourishing in Italy, and France, and Germany, before his time. Great as was Bacon in many ways, we cannot regard him as more than an expounder of the scientific tendency of his age. And after the severe and partially true exposure of his claims by Baron Liebig, [1] it is to be hoped that we shall give up some of our absurd national fallacies concerning him.

How much of the arts we owe to continental nations, may be learnt from a simple enumeration of our principal debts. It is in Mr. Smiles' volumes that the history of the arts in Britain has been brought to our notice. These volumes seem to me a most valuable contribution to our general history, and the facts adduced by him clearly establish that until about the middle of last century we were wholly behindhand in all that relates to skilled industry, and were justly treated by the great advanced nations of the Continent—by Italy, Spain, France, and Holland —as poor, uncultivated, but proud islanders. "England," he says, "was then regarded principally as a magazine for the supply of raw materials, which were carried away in foreign ships, and partly returned to us in manufactures, worked up by foreign artisans. We grew wool for Flanders, as America grows cotton for England now. Even the little manufactured at home was sent to the Low Countries to be dyed." [2]

Generalizations on this subject, I have said, are open to exceptions. It is not true that England made no contributions to the arts down to the time of the steam-engine, and the coal-blast furnace; but I know of only one exception, the knitting-frame of William Lee, a truly singular invention of the year 1589. It is favourably mentioned by Sturtevant in his curious treatise on Metallurgy of the year 1612. Its solitary character is shown by the fact that an Act prohibiting the export of stocking-frames was passed as early as 1696, but that no other Act of the same kind was thought needful until 1750. It was not till 1774 that a third Act of the kind made a beginning of our general system of prohibiting the export of machinery, contrived to protect our rising success in the cotton, linen, and other manufactures. In this mistaken and illiberal system we persevered until August, 1843.

Mining is an art in which we are now at least eminent. But a century ago, as most Englishmen will be surprised to learn, our engines and contrivances in common use were only those familiar to the Germans 100 or 200 years before.

The horse-gin, the double reversing water-wheel, the chain-pump, ventilating contrivances, such as bellows, fans, lamps, furnaces, together with the underground wheeled carriage, were introduced from Germany, probably by the German miners brought over in considerable numbers during the reigns of Elizabeth and the Stuarts. These inventions, in fact, were described in the work of Agricola published in 1556, and this writer was acquainted with such valuable contrivances as the fly-wheel, and the crank and beam. [3] Hooson, an early writer on coal-mining, expressly says, "We do not know of anything material or useful that has been found out for the better, than what has been left us by our forefathers; but rather much impaired by neglect and idleness." [4]

Gunpowder is an almost indispensable agent in mining, and was used by the Germans as early as 1613. Its use in blasting was introduced into this country in 1665, and, according to Robert Bald, [5] the ancient method of drilling and wedging rocks open by the stook and feathers, without powder, was still used in Scotland at the beginning of last century.

Metallurgy is a kindred art that we now carry out on a vast scale; but, with the exception of the processes depending on the superior abundance and excellence of our coal, both the theory and practice of metallurgy are mainly due to the Germans. Dr. Percy, in the preface to his important work on Metallurgy, has drawn attention to the fact that we have scarcely any literature on the subject, and must draw our information from the two leading works of Agricola in 1556, or Karsten in 1831, or from the large collection of monographs, periodical publications, and complete treatises on Metallurgy, with which the German language abounds. Even the Swedes, Scheele and Berzelius, have made greater contributions to the art than individual Englishmen can boast of.

Many of the arts of working iron were drawn from the Continent. It will be shown in the chapter on the Iron Trade, that the first efforts towards the erection of our great iron manufacture were made by German metallurgists. It was Godfrey Box, of Liège, who erected at Dartford, in 1590, the first iron mill for slitting bars; and from the slitting-mill was no doubt derived the notion of the rolling-mill as used by Cort. Yarranton went to Saxony to learn the process of tinning iron plates, as carried on there with great profit, and he was allowed to engage workmen and inspect all the steps of the manufacture. The making of clasp-knives was introduced into Sheffield in 1650, by Flemish workmen, such knives having been previously known as *joctelegs*, [6] from Jacques de Liège, a celebrated foreign cutler. [7] The casting of iron cannon was a French invention, introduced into Sussex in 1543, by Peter Baude, a Frenchman, brought over by Ralph Hogge, the Sussex ironmaster, who also employed a Flemish gunsmith, Peter Van Collet, to make his explosive shells. [8]

Engineering was taught us by continental nations until we developed our own new modes of engineering with iron. The Dutch, having redeemed their own country from the sea, were masters of the art of embankment, drainage, and inland navigation. The history of the works carried out by them in our fens, of the skill, capital, and labour they expended here, and the precarious profits they carried back, is to be found in Mr. Smiles' volumes. [9] We are reminded of the part which we play in the railways, canals, and public works of the United States and our Colonies. Even as late as 1748, we owed to Labelye, the Swiss architect, the reconstruction of the south level of the Fens, and the building of Westminster Bridge. [10] When a tidal engine was required to pump water from the Thames for the supply of London, Peter Morice, a Dutchman, was employed to erect it. [11]

Scotland was even more backward than England. When in 1708 windmills were wanted to try and drain certain Scotch coal-mines, John Young, the millwright of Montrose, was found to be the only man in the country who could erect windmills. He had "been sent at the expense of that town to Holland, in order to inspect the machinery of that country," and "it was suggested that, if this millwright could not be procured, application should be made to the *Mechanical Priest in Lancashire* for his advice." [12]

In maritime enterprise we were always daring, but only of late have we been eminently expert or successful. "At a time," says Mr. Smiles, [13] "when Spain, Holland, France, Genoa, and Venice were great maritime powers, England was almost without a fleet, the little trade which it carried on with other countries being conducted principally by foreigners. Our best ships were also built abroad by the Venetians or the Danes, but they were mostly of small tonnage, little bigger than modern herring boats."

The herring fishery was regarded both by Holland and England as the "chiefest trade and gold-mine," and "the way to winne wealth." It was thought to be a pure creation of riches, and to nourish at the same time a race of hardy seamen that are the pride and safety of the kingdom. But it raised unutterable feelings in English writers of a century or two ago, to observe that the Dutch fished our own seas. Holland, "not exceeded in quantity by Norfolk and Suffolk, hath gotten the sea," bitterly says the author of The Trades' Increase. And when we got herrings, we had to learn from the Flemings how to cure them.

The Dutch, as is well known, were our predecessors in trade. A writer of the year 1615 thus speaks, "Without love or anger, but with admiration of our neighbours, the now Sea Herrs, the nation that get health out of their own sicknesse, whose troubles begot their liberty, brought forth their wealth, and brought up their strength, that have, out of our leavings, gotten themselves a living, out of our wants make their own supply of trade and shipping there; they coming in long after us, equal us in those parts in all respects of privilege and port; that have devanced us so farre in shipping that the Hollanders have more than one hundred saile of shippes that use those ports, continually going and returning, and the chiefest matters they doe lade outward be English commodities, as Tinne, Lead, and Bailes, of such like stuffe, as are made at Norwich." [14]

Campbell was aware of their commercial superiority. "By keeping their customs low," he says, "they have their warehouses always full of goods and manufactures of every kind....Rough and raw materials they cleanse and sort; gross and bulky commodities they import in one kind of vessels, divide and export them in others. A low interest keeps the bulk of their cash in trade; working cheap, and selling at a small profit, secures them in continual employment." [15] The Dutch, in short, understood the principles and practice of commerce, and had a free and far-spreading trade when we were yet sunk in poverty and the fallacies of the mercantile and restrictive systems. And it was the Venetians, Jewish, and other foreign merchants of Lombard Street, who laid the foundations of our vast trading and monetary system.

While we were so much inferior to continental nations in the fundamental operations of trade and industry, it is almost needless to observe, that in the more luxurious arts of life we were wholly indebted to them. "Our first cloth-workers, silk-weavers, and lace-workers were French and Flemish refugees. The brothers Elers, Dutchmen, began the pottery manufacture; Spillman, a German, erected the first paper-mill at Dartford; and Boomen, a Dutchman, brought the first coach into England." [16] The name of the fabric, Brown Holland, shows whence we derived it. The arts, indeed, of weaving and whitening linen attained high perfection in Flanders and Harlem especially, while the common processes of dyeing were wholly the work of foreigners, chiefly Germans. [17]

France was then, as now, supreme in many little branches of manufacture, such as those of glass, hats, paper, linen, sail-cloth, sword-blades, scissors, and many steel "toys." The "running" of such light articles fortunately could not be prevented. We also drew from them "wine, brandy, linen, fine lace, fine cambricks, and cambrick lawns, to a prodigious value; brocades, velvets, and many other rich silk manufactures, which are either run in upon us, or come by way of Holland." [18]

Generally the advanced arts and knowledge of continental nations seem to have been communicated to us without jealousy or reserve. Yarranton, for instance, in his tours of observation in Holland, enjoyed every facility. Sometimes we resorted to deceit; as when Foley, according to one account, gained the art of splitting iron from the Swedes, and Sir Thomas Lombe the use of the water-frame in the silk manufacture. Such achievements, when in our favour, are treated as romantic and courageous adventures; but when foreigners now come prying into our factories, forges, and chemical works, we are apt to treat them as rogues.

Even the steam-engine cannot be claimed as a purely indigenous invention. But before we consider this point, or go on to enumerate the undoubted contributions we have made, it is necessary to discriminate the conditions of invention.

There seem to be three essential conditions, too often confused or overlooked:—First, a distinct PURPOSE, arising from an urgent need of some new means of accomplishing a given end. Secondly, a new PRINCIPLE, or mode, by which it is to be accomplished. Thirdly, the material, power, and skill for embodying this principle in a successful machine,—in short, the CONSTRUCTION.

For instance, as a maritime nation, we felt during last century the most urgent need of some certain method of determining the longitude of a ship at sea: here was a strong *purpose*. Astronomy pointed out several different *principles* on which it might be done, the most convenient one involving the use of a good time-keeper. It was Harrison, of Liverpool, who, under the stimulus of a large Government reward, invented the ship's chronometer, and supplied the material *construction* of the method commonly employed.

Now, as regards the history of the steam-engine, there is no doubt that an urgent need was felt at the beginning of the seventeenth century for a more powerful means of draining our mines. Sir George Selby, in Parliament, said, as early as 1610, that "the coal-mines of Newcastle could not hold out the term of their lease of twenty-one years." [19] This was on account of the cost or impossibility of draining them to any depth. The terms in which the engine was described, and the way in which it was actually used for nearly two centuries, show that the raising of water out of our mines was the all important object aimed at—the first condition—the purpose.

The cheap coal, drawn from the self-same mines, was to prove the material power or third condition of the great invention; but, in the meantime, we needed a new natural principle of action. Now candour obliges us to allow that we owe this principle to science and to France. It is true that the English writer Hugh Platte had, in 1594, shown how the steam of boiling water might be made to issue in a powerful jet, sufficient to blow a fire. [20] But he probably owed this notion to some of the works of practical science and ingenuity which abounded at that time on the Continent. No doubt Arago was right in insisting [21] that Solomon de Caus, a French engineer employed by King Charles, first spread abroad in England scientific notions of raising water by the expansive force of steam. His work, "Les Raisons des Forces Mouvantes," was first published in the year 1615, several years before the era of Bacon's Organum. A print in this work showed a metallic globe, containing water heated by a fire. A long, upright, open pipe passed air-tight through the top of the globe, and terminated in the water near the bottom of the globe. The water, urged by the expansive force of the steam within the globe, is represented as issuing forcibly from the top of the pipe.

A second edition of the work appeared in 1624; and in 1644 was published, *at London,* by Isaac de Caus, a partial reprint, distinctly entitled, *"Nouvelle Invention de lever l'Eau."* [22]

Now, considering that the earliest patents which apparently refer to a steam-engine are of the years 1627 and 1631; [23] that the Marquis of Worcester's "water-commanding engine" and his almost prophetic statements were of the year 1663; that Sir S. Morland's proposals were made in 1683; and Thomas Savery's success in 1698,—it is hard to deny that we owe the engine, as regards the second or scientific condition, to a French work.

The Marquis of Worcester's engine was the first we know to have been really constructed. Its purpose is clearly stated in the "Exact and True Definition," by "an ancient Servant of his Lordship."

"There being, indeed, no place but either wanteth water, or is overburdened therewith, (and) by this engine either defect is remediable." Its principle, there is little doubt, was that enunciated by De Caus, from whom it was in all probability derived. For, as Mr. Dircks admits, [24] the Marquis "evidently availed himself of every suggestion that either reading, accident, experience, or travel, threw into his way." With the construction of Worcester's Engine we are not acquainted, but it seems to have been in part due to his assistant Caspar Kaltoff, a Dutchman and an "unparalleled workman both for trust and skill."

It is in Thomas Savery's description of his engine that we can most clearly discriminate the conditions of the great invention. The purpose was clearly to raise water and drain mines, as indicated by the title of his excellent little publication, "The Miner's Friend," but most explicitly stated within. "I do not doubt," he says, [25] "that, in a few years, it will be a means of making our mining trade, which is no small part of the wealth of this kingdom, double if not treble to what it now is." He continues, [26] —"The coals used in this engine are of as little value as the coals commonly burned on the mouths of the coal-pits are;" and "the charge of them is not to be mentioned, when we consider the vast quantity of water raised, by the inconsiderable value of the coals used, and burned in so small a furnace." Here we have the most distinct statement that the purpose of the engine was to use the waste and valueless slack coals to overcome the great obstacle to the progress of our mines. The position which Savery contemplated for his engine was clearly the mouth of a coal-pit.

As to the principle of the invention, it was that of De Caus, with the additional principle of the vacuum, which may have been the discovery of Savery himself.

It is, however, in the construction of the machine that Savery's highest credit seems to lie. "I have met," he says, [27] "with great difficulties and expense to instruct handicraft artificers to forme my engine, according to my design." And whoever examines the picture of his engine, either in the original work or copies, will be struck by the very compact and work-manlike form of the machine, which would be a creditable piece of mechanism even at the present day. There is no doubt that by this time the use of cheap and excellent coal at Wolverhampton, Birmingham, and Sheffield, had enabled our artisans to acquire remarkable skill in the working of metals; [28] and it is to this facility of construction, joined to the principle published by De Caus, but especially to the strong purpose and incitement offered by the condition of our coal-mines, that I should attribute the complete invention of the steam-engine.

Savery's engine was extremely wasteful of heat, because the steam came in actual contact with the cold water to be moved. It was so uneconomical, that, in spite of the cheapness of coals, it could not come into use. Denis Papin, a French refugee, and an engineer of the highest mechanical talents, supplied and published, before the Royal Society, in 1699, the new principle required to perfect the engine, that of a piston intervening between the steam and water. But the Frenchman was deficient in constructive power; and it was reserved for Newcomen to accomplish the atmospheric engine, which proved capable of draining our mines and reviving our industry.

The subsequent steps in the improvement of the engine consisted chiefly in methods of using the steam more economically. They will be considered in the following chapter.

The atmospheric engine, perfected in some mechanical details by Smeaton, was employed throughout the century, not only to drain the coal and Cornish mines, but, in the absence of the crank, or the sun and planet wheels of Watt, to raise water *to turn water-wheels* where a natural supply of water was deficient, an employment anticipated by Ramsey, Worcester, Morland, and Savery.

The engine, from an early period of its history, turned the tide of the arts. As Briavoinne remarks, [29] it was indispensable that other nations should follow England in adopting this newly found power; and, between 1722 and 1733, the first engine was sent from England to Belgium, and set to work by the aid of English mechanics. [30]

Its effect upon the English mines was extraordinary. "The steam-engine produced a new era in the mining and commercial interests of Britain, and, as it were in an instant, put every coal-field, which was considered as lost, within the grasp of its owners. Collieries were opened in every district, and such has been the astonishing effect produced by this machine, that great coal was shipping free on board in the River Forth, in the year 1785, at 4s. 10d. per ton; that is, after a period of seventy years, coals had only advanced 2d. per ton, while the price of labour and all materials was doubled." [31]

Of hardly less importance than the steam-engine are the new modes of conveyance, gradually introduced or discovered here, during the last two hundred and fifty years. Common roads, worth, calling such, only began to be made in the middle of last century, when the enterprise of the country was roused by the new influence of steam and iron. Between 1760 and 1774, no fewer than 452 Acts for making or repairing highways passed through Parliament; [32] and it is necessary to read Mr. Smiles' volume to form a notion of the previous wretched state of our communications. Common roads, however, have little further connexion with our subject.

Canals might also seem utterly disconnected from the use of coal. Certainly, both in principle and construction, they have nothing to do with it. Holland, France, Sweden, and Russia had created and developed, on a large scale, the art of making canals long before we had a single canal. Holland enjoyed a magnificent system of artificial water communication. France had connected the Loire and Seine, the Loire and Saône and the Atlantic Ocean with the Mediterranean; Peter the Great had constructed a canal from the Don to the Volga.

But until coal supplied the purpose there was not spirit enough in this country to undertake so formidable a work as a canal. In spite of Yarranton's demonstration of the advantages of inland navigation, the first true canal Act was that passed in 1755 for making the Sankey Brook Cut, to enable the coal of St. Helen's to reach the Mersey. This small work drew the Duke of Bridgewater's attention to the profit to be derived from a more economical mode of conveying coal to Manchester. In getting an Act passed to cut the celebrated canal from his mines at Worsley to Salford, he bound himself not to charge more freight on coal than 2s. 6d., the previous cost of carriage having been 9s. or 10s. The opening of the canal at once reduced the price of coal in Manchester, from 7d. per cwt. (120 lbs.) to 3½d.; [33] and it is impossible to say how much such a reduction may not have contributed to the growth of industry in this great centre. And, while one branch carried fuel, the other branch of this grand work was carried from Manchester to the Mersey, in order that raw materials might be brought into conjunction with the fuel, and the finished products conveyed back. The Duke of Bridgewater's view of the innate power of England was clearly shown in his saying that "a navigation should always have coals at the heels of it." [34]

Railroads, however, are perhaps our great, and it would seem, our purely indigenous invention. The principle involved is little more than that of a wheel upon a hard road, but it is surprising how entirely the development of the principle has been connected with our coal trade. The first known use of the rail is due to Beaumont, in the year 1630. This gentleman went to Newcastle at a period of our history when enterprise and ingenuity seemed the rule. But his merits and his reward are summed up in a quaint passage:— "One Master Beaumont, a gentleman of great ingenuity and rare parts, adventured into the mines of Northumberland with his 30,000l. and brought with him many rare engines, not then known in that shire, and waggons with one horse, to carry down coals from the pits to the river; but within a few years he consumed all his money, and rode home upon his light horse."

The early rails were simple bars of wood, laid parallel upon wooden sleepers, or embedded in the ordinary track to diminish friction. They were gradually introduced into the other coal districts of Wales, Cumberland, and Scotland—at Whitehaven as early as 1738. It was soon found that a slip of iron, nailed upon the wooden rail, was economical in preventing wear; and when the abundance of iron had been increased by the coal-blast furnace, rails made entirely of iron were substituted. Such iron rails were first used by Reynolds at the Coalbrookdale works, the birthplace of the smelting furnace, to facilitate the conveyance of coal and ore. In 1776, again, a cast-iron tramway, or plate-way, was introduced into the underground workings of the Duke of Norfolk's colliery, at Sheffield, by John Curr, whose writings prove his perception of the importance of the improvement. [35] It was in 1789 that William Jessop made a railway at Loughborough, with cast-iron edge rails, and a flange transferred to the waggon wheel. Finally, in 1820, nearly two hundred years after the employment of wooden rails, wrought-iron rails, invented by Mr. Birkenshaw, were rolled at the Bedlington iron-works, on the river Blyth, near Newcastle. [36]

But the railway was incomplete without steam power. Every one knows the history of the locomotive—that it was brought into successful use by *George Stephenson, the colliery engineman, for the purpose of leading coals from the pit to the shipping place;* that, after long exertions, it was proved more economical than horse-power, and that when the growing goods traffic between the coal-driven factories of Manchester and the port at Liverpool had altogether exceeded the powers of the canal, a railway was undertaken which led to our present system.

Throughout the history, then, of this great and indigenous invention, we constantly find the *purpose* and *construction* alike dependent on the working of coal. The conveyance of great weights of coal was the purpose; the energy that is in coal, and the cheap iron it yields, supplied the constructive means of accomplishing that purpose. Not unnaturally, then, was Newcastle the cradle of the railway system.

Although, in later years, railways have been extended through purely agricultural countries, such as Russia or some of the States of North America, yet we may observe, in many places, and especially in England, that the rapid extension of railways is mainly due to the traffic and wealth occasioned by the use of coal in manufactures. It was long ago observed by a writer on the coal trade, that "the numerous canals, and conveyances from the distant parts of the kingdom, and to local stations, owe their existence to the wealth acquired by the use of coal." [37] Now, if a series of railway-maps of Great Britain, for the last twenty or thirty years, be closely examined, it will be apparent, not only that the railway system was developed on the coal-fields, but that it yet converges upon them, just as the arteries and veins of the animal body converge upon the heart and lungs. The densely crowded lines of railway around Newcastle, Manchester, and Wolverhampton, form the heart of the railway system. There are, indeed, several great aortal lines, which connect the coal-fields with each other or with the metropolis, the head of the body; or the metropolis with the Continent; but, in every other direction, it will be observed that the railway system becomes sluggish in proportion to its distance from a coal-field, the traffic subdividing and dwindling away like the arterial streams of the animal body. The least successful railways are the Great Western, the Great Eastern, and other lines of railway which run into the most purely agricultural parts of the kingdom. Wise and far-seeing, then, were the favourite notions of George Stephenson:—"The strength of Britain," he used to say, "lies in her iron and coal-beds; and the locomotive is destined, above all other agencies, to bring it forth. The Lord Chancellor now sits upon a bag of wool, but wool has long ceased to be emblematical of the staple commodity of England. He ought to sit upon a bag of coals." [38]

As regards bridges, the command of iron has given us advantages of construction never before enjoyed. Italian and French engineers were altogether our superiors in bridge-building until near the end of last century; but they failed, as in an instance at Lyons, in 1755, in iron bridges, "chiefly because of the inability of the early founders to cast large masses of iron, and also because the metal was then more expensive than either stone or timber." [39] The first iron bridge was erected at Coalbrookdale, by Messrs. Reynolds and Darby, in 1777; and we know what has since been accomplished, in the construction of iron bridges, when the extension of roads and railways presented an adequate purpose.

Iron presents the necessary material condition of several things, which would not be supposed to be dependent on it. The supply of water depends on the use of iron pipes. When Sir H. Middleton had brought the New River to London, he found the distribution of the water a matter of the greatest difficulty—the old wooden pipes wasting one-fourth of the supply, and being subject to rapid decay. [40] Coal-gas, again, itself an important product of coal, could not be used in its present abundance and economy, without the use of iron distributing-pipes. [41]

A more important use of iron is in the development of mechanical engineering in general. Our inventions for spinning and weaving by machinery are not, in their origin, dependent on coal. The early mills were turned by water, and involved but little iron work. The development and perfection of our factory system, however, could never have been carried far without abundance of iron. "The inventions of Arkwright, Crompton, and others," says Mr. Fairbairn, [42] "could not have been executed but for iron; and it is fortunate for the industrial resources of the country, that the manufacture of iron has kept pace with our industrial progress. I am not able to state the amount of consumption of iron in machine-making alone, but taking that for cotton machinery in only one of our largest firms, that of Messrs. Platt and Co. of Oldham, I should average it at 400 or 500 tons per week; and in that of my late brother, Sir Peter Fairbairn, of Leeds, in flax and other machines, at 250 to 300 tons per week."

In some of the old water-mills, yet working in remote country places, we may see ponderous wooden shafts, spindles, and wheels, which seem hardly adapted now-a-days to receive motion, much less to communicate it. Brindley was brought up as a millwright, in the use of wood, and long clung to it- even making wooden-hooped cylinders for engines, which were naturally apt to break down. But having at last discarded brick, stone, and wood, he constructed in 1763 at Coalbrookdale, an engine that was a "complete and noble piece of iron-work." [43] Smeaton carried forward the substitution of iron for wood; but it was Rennie who established its general use, in his celebrated Albion Mills, the whole of his wheels and shafts being made of cast-iron. We find, then, in cast-iron, a material condition which allowed a general advance in the construction of our machines.

A second substitution, however, has taken place, of wrought-iron for cast-iron. It is Mr. Fairbairn who chiefly introduced the use of light wrought-iron shafting for heavy, slow cast-iron work, and thus effected a general economy and advance in the employment of machine power, almost comparable with that of Brindley, Smeaton, and Rennie. [44]

It only remains to be added, that the use of steel, could Mr. Bessemer produce it sufficiently cheap, would occasion a third, and as far as we can see, a final substitution of steel for nearly every other material; so that our machines would be carried to an apparent maximum of efficiency, economy, and elegance, as regards the material of our works.

The shaping and moulding of iron, on the large scale, demanded a wholly new set of arrangements. A purpose having arisen for new inventions, the ancient principles of the lathe, the hammer, and the plane were developed by workmen such as Bramah, Maudslay, Clements, Roberts, Whitworth, Nasmyth, and Wilson. Thus there gradually grew up a system of machine-tool labour, the substitution of iron hands for human hands, without which the execution of engines and machines, in their present perfection and size, would be impossible.

"When I first entered this city," said Mr. Fairbairn, in his address to the British Association at Manchester, in 1861, "the whole of the machinery was executed by hand. There were neither planing, slotting, nor shaping machines; and, with the exception of very imperfect lathes, and a few drills, the preparatory operations of construction were effected entirely by the hands of the workmen. Now everything is done by machine tools with a degree of accuracy which the unaided hand could never accomplish."

Any one who reflects upon what has been brought to pass by the use of abundant iron will agree with the remark of Locke, that "he who first made known the uses of iron may be truly styled the Father of Arts, and the Author of Plenty." Such has been our work in recent times.

It would be absurd to try to follow out in detail the mechanical contrivances of the present age. Reflection will show that they are mainly but the completions of a system of machine labour, in which steam is the motive power, and iron the fulcrum and the lever. The principles of science involved are in no way our own property, being quite as successfully studied on the Continent as here. But from the cheapness of coal and iron we have a peculiar advantage in developing their use; and therefore all the details of machine construction are pushed forward in one great system, of which no part can advance far without the rest.

The Britannia Bridge, our truest national monument, "was the result of a vast combination of skill and industry. But for the perfection of our tools, and the ability of our mechanics to use them to the greatest advantage; but for the matured powers of the steam-engine; but for the improvements in the iron manufacture, which enabled blooms to be puddled of sizes before deemed impracticable, and plates and bars of immense size to be rolled and forged; but for these the Britannia Bridge would have been designed in vain. Thus it was not the product of the genius of the railway engineer alone, but of the collective mechanical genius of the English nation;" [45] and Mr. Robert Stephenson himself said, "The locomotive is not the invention of one man, but of a nation of mechanical engineers." [46]

There is no better example of what our united inventions can accomplish than the iron or steel screw steam-vessel, the product of coal from truck to keel,—hull, engines, masts, rigging, anchors.

Of this product of our industry, Mr. Porter remarked, that "it was one in which our mineral riches and our great mechanical skill will secure to us a virtual monopoly." And any one who considers the present progress of iron ship-building in this country must see that half a century hence our chief ocean conveyances will be wholly by steam. Sailing vessels will not be entirely discarded, but will occupy a subordinate rank, similar to that of canal boats and coasting vessels. Our world-wide communications will be improved in a degree now perhaps unthought of; but we cannot forget that a steam-vessel is endowed with a constant and voracious appetite for coal, that must fearfully accelerate the drain upon our mines.

There yet remains a whole class of inventions, of a chemical rather than a mechanical nature, where a substance has to be altered in its intimate constitution, instead of its outward form. In these inventions iron is in a very minor degree useful; and accordingly, it can hardly be asserted that in the chemical and experimental sciences and arts we are more than barely equal to the French or Germans. Photography, for instance, presents an instance of equal progress in several different nations.

Many remarkable instances have occurred of the commercial replacement of one chemical substance by another. The progress of commerce often depends on such replacements, as when the palm and cocoa oils are used instead of tallow and linseed oils; silk instead of wool, cotton instead of flax, Spanish grass instead of rags, wheat instead of rye or buckwheat, turnips instead of hay.

So far as such substances are beyond the constructive arts, and of purely organic origin, they are beyond our present subject. But many of the more important substitutions are due to coal. Most chemical processes depend on the use of heat; and our cheap fuel has enabled us to raise many great branches of chemical manufacture. Our Cheshire salt mines, with the aid of cheap coal, give us a supremacy in the salt trade, reversing the import trade which used to be carried on, when salt was made by the natural evaporation of sea-water on the coasts of France, Spain, and the Mediterranean. Cheap salt, again, with abundance of fuel, was made to yield carbonate of soda, which replaced, with a great reduction of price, the soda formerly got from kelp or barilla, the ashes of sea-weed. This cheap supply of alkali is all-important in our soap and glass trades, and in a great variety of minor chemical manufactures. Potash, on the contrary, still continues to be obtained from the ashes of wood, and is accordingly imported at a high price from

Canada or Russia. If ever it be extracted from its natural source in felspar, it must be done by an abundant use of fuel.

When the Government of the Two Sicilies placed an exorbitant tax on sulphur, Italy having as it was thought a monopoly of native sulphur, our manufacturers soon had resort to the distillation of iron pyrites, or sulphide of iron; and it has been remarked by Liebig that sulphur could have been extracted, if necessary, from gypsum, or sulphate of lime. [47] Cheap fuel would still be the all-important condition.

Perhaps the most wonderful mode of employing coal is in the ice-machine, two kinds of which, of French and English invention respectively, were at work in the Exhibition of 1862. By such machines, *we may make fire, in the hottest climate, produce the cold of the Polar Regions!*

With fuel and fire, then, almost anything is easy. By its aid in the smelting furnace or the engine we have effected, for a century past, those successive substitutions of a better for a worse, a cheaper for a dearer, a new for an old process, which advance our material civilization. But when this fuel, our material energy, fails us, whence will come the power to do equal or greater things in the future? A man cannot expect that because he has done much when in stout health and bodily vigour, he will do still more when his strength has departed. Yet such is the position of our national body, unless either the source of our strength be carefully spared, or something can be found better than coal to replace it, and carry on the substitution of the better for the worse. Whether the consumption of coal can be kept down in our free system of industry, or whether in the process of discovery we can expect to find some substitute for coal, must next be considered. The dispassionate conclusion will be far from satisfactory.

[1] Macmillan's Magazine, June, July, 1863.

[2] Smiles' Engineers, vol. i. Pref. p. v.

[3] Taylor's Archæology of the Coal Trade, p. 186, in Memoirs of the British Archæological Association, 1858.

[4] Hooson's Miner's Dictionary, 1747, quoted by Taylor, p. 187.

[5] Scotch Coal Trade, p. 12.

[6] See Burns "On the late Captain Grose's Peregrinations." "A faulding jocteleg." In some parts of Yorkshire a large clasp-knife is still known as a "jack-a-leg's knife."

[7] Smiles' Industrial Biography, p. 68.

[8] Smiles' Industrial Biography, p. 33.

[9] Lives of the Engineers, vol. i. pp. 39, 40.

[10] Ibid. p. 66.

[11] Ibid. Pref. p. vi.

[12] Bald, Scotch Coal Trade, p. 7.

[13] Lives of the Engineers, vol. i. p. 276.

[14] The Trades' Increase, p. 7.

[15] Campbell's Survey, vol. i. p. 15.

[16] Smiles' Engineers, vol. i. Pref. p. vi.

[17] Barlow's Cyclopædia, p. 521.

[18] Joshua Gee, The Trade and Navigation of Great Britain considered. 1738, 4th ed. p. 18.

[19] Taylor's Archæology of the Coal Trade, p. 186.

[20] Jewell House of Art and Nature, No. 21. London.

[21] Life of Watt, 1839, p. 46.

[22] Mr. Dircks in his new Life of the Marquis of Worcester strangely overlooks this work of Isaac de Caus.

[23] Rymer's Fœdera, vol. xviii. p. 992; or, Calendars of the State Paper Office, Domestic Series.

[24] H. Dircks, Life of Worcester, p. 354.

[25] Page 6.

[26] Pages 35, 36

[27] Miner's Friend. Prefatory Address to the Royal Society.

[28] See Dr. Plot's account of the artisans of Wolverhampton, Walsall, and the Neighbourhood, Natural History of Staffordshire, p. 376. Also Smiles' Lives of Boulton and Watt, p. 163.

[29] Briavoinne, De l'Industrie en Belgique, Bruxelles, 1839, p. 201.

[30] Toilliez 'Mémoire sur l'Introduction des Machines à Vapeur dans le Hainaut." Quoted by Briavoinne, p. 226.

[31] Bald on the Scotch Coal Trade, p. 24.

[32] Smiles' Lives of the Engineers, vol. i. p. 206.

[33] Smiles' Lives of the Engineers, vol. i. pp. 344-361.

[34] Ibid. vol. i. p. 401

[35] Coal Viewer's and Engine Builder's Practical Companion, 1797.

[36] Report of British Association, 1863, p. 760.

[37] C. Beaumont, Treatise on the Coal Trade, 1789, p. 2.

[38] Smiles' Engineers, vol. iii. p. 357.

[39] Smiles' Engineers, vol. ii. p. 355.

[40] Ibid. vol. i. p. 126.

[41] Hearn's Plutology, 1864, p. 193.

[42] Two Lectures on Iron and its Applications. Newcastle, 1864, p. 15.

[43] Smiles' Engineers, vol. i. pp. 332, 333.

[44] Fairbairn on Mills and Millwork.

[45] Smiles' Engineers, vol. iii. p. 440.

[46] Ibid. p. 8.

[47] Liebig's Letters on Chemistry, pp. 152, 153.

Chapter Seven - Of the Economy of Fuel

It is very commonly urged, that the failing supply of coal will be met by new modes of using it efficiently and economically. The amount of useful work got out of coal may be made to increase manifold, while the amount of coal consumed is stationary or diminishing. We have thus, it is supposed, the means of completely neutralizing the evils of scarce and costly fuel. [1] It is shown, in fact, by the mechanical theory of heat, that the work done by coal, in a good engine of the present day, does not exceed about one-sixth part of what the coal is capable of doing. In furnaces, too, the portion of heat actually used is a small and often infinitesimal fraction of the heat wasted; and in the domestic use of coal, in open grates, at least four-fifths of the heat escapes up the chimney unheeded.

I speak not here of the *domestic consumption of coal*. This is undoubtedly capable of being cut down without other harm than curtailing our home comforts, and somewhat altering our confirmed national habits. The coal thus saved would be, for the most part, laid up for the use of posterity. But even if our population could be induced to abstain from the enjoyment of a good fire, the saving effected would not extend over more than about one-third of the total consumption of coal; the domestic consumption being, on an average, about one ton per annum, per head of the population. Of the other two-thirds, nearly one-third is used in our iron manufactures; and the remainder in our factories, furnaces, and machine shops generally.

But the economy of coal in manufactures is a different matter. *It is wholly a confusion of ideas to suppose that the economical use of fuel is equivalent to a diminished consumption. The very contrary is the truth.*

As a rule, new modes of economy will lead to an increase of consumption according to a principle recognised in many parallel instances. The economy of labour effected by the introduction of new machinery throws labourers out of employment for the moment. But such is the increased demand for the cheapened products, that eventually the sphere of employment is greatly widened. Often the very labourers whose labour is saved find their more efficient labour more demanded than before. Seamstresses, for instance, have perhaps in no case been injured, but have often gained wages before unthought of, by the use of the sewing-machine, for which we are so much indebted to American inventors.

So it is a familiar rule of finance that the reduction of taxes and tolls leads to increased gross and sometimes even nett revenues; and it is a maxim of trade, that a low rate of profits, with the multiplied business it begets, is more profitable than a small business at a high rate of profit.

Now the same principles apply, with even greater force and distinctness, to the use of such a general agent as coal. It is the very economy of its use which leads to its extensive consumption. It has been so in the past, and it will be so in the future. Nor is it difficult to see how this paradox arises.

The number of tons of coal used in any branch of industry is the product of the number of separate works, and the average number of tons consumed in each. Now, if the quantity of coal used in a blast-furnace, for instance, be diminished in comparison with the yield, the profits of the trade will increase, new capital will be attracted, the price of pig-iron will fall, but the demand for it increase; and eventually the greater number of furnaces will more than make up for the diminished consumption of each. And if such is not always the result within a single branch, it must be remembered that the progress of any branch of manufacture excites a new activity in most other branches, and leads indirectly, if not directly, to increased inroads upon our seams of coal.

It needs but little reflection to see that the whole of our present vast industrial system, and its consequent consumption of coal, has chiefly arisen from successive measures of economy.

Civilization, says Baron Liebig, *is the economy of power,* and our power is coal. It is the very economy of the use of coal that makes our industry what it is; and the more we render it efficient and economical, the more will our industry thrive, and our works of civilization grow.

The engine is the motive power of this country, and its history is a history of successive steps of economy. Savery recommended his engine for its cheap drawing of water and small charge of coals. But as he allowed the steam to act straight upon the water, without the intervention of a piston, the loss of heat was tremendous. Practically, the cost of working kept it from coming into use; *it consumed no coal, because its rate of consumption was too high.* [2] Newcomen made the first step towards the future use of the engine, by interposing a piston, rod, beam, and pump, between the steam and water. It was asserted that mines formerly drowned out and abandoned might sometimes, *when coal was very cheap,* be profitably drained by his rude atmospheric engine. But when Brindley went to Wolverhampton, to inspect one of these engines, he formed the opinion "that, unless the consumption of coal could be reduced, the extended use of this steam-engine was not practicable, by reason of its dearness, as compared with the power of horses, wind, or air." [3]

Smeaton, the most philosophical of engineers, after a careful study of the atmospheric engine, succeeded in nearly doubling its efficiency. The engine had long been hanging on the verge of commercial possibility; he brought it into successful use, and made it both possible and profitable. But in this branch of his art he willingly gave place to that even greater man, who, after long continued scientific and practical labours, made the steam-engine the agent of civilization. I need hardly say that Watt's two chief inventions of the condenser and the expansive mode of working are simply two modes of economising heat. The double cylinder of Woolf, the method of surface-condensing, of super-heating, &c. are other inventions, directed to economy of coal. To save the loss of heat in the boiler, and the loss of power by friction, are two other points of economy, to which numberless inventions are directed. And with the exception of contrivances, such as the crank, the governor, and the minor mechanism of an engine, necessary for regulating, transmitting, or modifying its power, it may be said that *the whole history of the steam-engine is one of economy.*

"The economy of fuel is the secret of the economy of the steam-engine; it is the fountain of its power, and the adopted measure of its effects. Whatever, therefore, conduces to increase the efficiency of coal, and to diminish the cost of its use, directly tends to augment the value of the steam-engine, and to enlarge the field of its operations." [4]

The result of these efforts at economy is clearly exhibited in a table of the duty done by engines at different periods. This work or duty is expressed by the number of pounds of water raised one foot high by the expenditure of a bushel (84 lbs.) of coal. [5]

	Duty in lbs
1769. Average of old atmospheric engines...	5,590,000
1772. Smeaton's atmospheric engine...	9,450,000
1776. Watt's improved engine...	21,600,000
1779-1788. Watt's engine working expansively...	26,600,000
1820. Engine improved by Cornish engineers...	28,000,000
1830. Average duty of Cornish engines...	43,350,000
1859. Average duty of Cornish engines (per 112 lbs.?)...	54,000,000
1859. Extreme duty of best engine (per 112 lbs.?)...	80,000,000

In less than one hundred years, then, the efficiency of the engine has been increased at least ten-fold; and it need hardly be said that it is the cheapness of the power it affords that allows us to draw rivers from our mines, to drive our coal-pits in spite of floods and quicksands, to drain our towns and lowlands, and to supply with water our highest places; and, finally, to put in motion the great system of our machine labour, which may be said, as far as any comparison is possible, to enable us to do as much as all the other inhabitants of the world with their unaided labours.

Future improvements of the engine can only have the same result, of extending the use of such a powerful agent. It is usual with a certain class of writers to depreciate science in regard to the steam-engine, and to treat this as a pure creation of practical sagacity. But just as the origin of the engine may be traced to a scientific work, so it is now theory and experiment in their highest and latest developments, which give us a sure notion how great will be the future improvement of the engine, and through what means it is to be aimed at.

"A well constructed and properly working ordinary double-acting steam-engine," of the present time, consumes about 4.00 lbs. of bituminous coal per horse-power per hour. "A double-acting steam-engine, improved to the utmost probable extent, would use 2.50 lbs. of the same coal;" while a theoretically perfect engine, working between such limits of temperature as are usual in steam-engines, "would require only 1.86 lbs." [6]

But theory further points out, what practice has partially confirmed, that the work done by an engine for a certain expenditure of fuel is proportional to the difference of the temperatures at which steam enters and leaves the engine. From this principle arises the economy of using high-pressure and super-heated steam; for we have, as it were, all the old force of the low-pressure and less-heated steam, with a great addition from the initial high pressure and the increased store of useful heat in the steam. The economy already effected in this manner is wonderful. The very engines which had burned 12 or 14 lbs. of coal per hour, when worked with steam at 4, 6, or 8 lbs. pressure, have been found to burn only 3½ or 4 lbs. of coal when supplied with stronger boilers, and worked at steam-pressures from 30 to 70 lbs. per square inch. [7]

Such simple changes as the shortening of the steam supply, the addition of a second cylinder, the felting of the boiler and steam-vessels, the enlarging of the boiler, the raising of the pressure, or the acceleration of the speed of travelling of an engine, are the simple means by which the self-same engine has often been made to give a manifold result.

It is true that, as we go on improving, the margin of improvement becomes narrower, and its attainment more difficult and costly. The improvement of the boiler mainly depends upon the amount of capital expenditure against current expenditure. For the efficiency of a boiler grows with the surface of water we can expose to absorb the heat of the fire; but the more we extend this surface, the less additional economy will an equal extension effect.

So the accomplishment of a new steam-engine, with much increased limits of temperature and economy, will probably require a wholly new set of mechanical expedients, because heated steam destroys the lubricating oil which is an essential part of all machinery, and is even said to attack the iron itself. Many of the difficulties inherent in the steam-engine are, however, absent in the *air-engine,* which presents a wide prospect of economy, as seen in the following numbers:—

	Actual consumption of Coal per horse-power, per hour.	Consumption of theoretically perfect engine.
Sterling's air-engine...	2.20lb.	0.73lb.
Ericsson's engine of 1852...	2.80	0.82

"Sterling's engine," it is said, "as finally improved, was compact in its dimensions, easily worked, not liable to get out of order, and consumed less oil, and required fewer repairs, than any steam-engine; still, the advantages shown by that engine over steam-engines were not so great as to induce practical men to overcome their natural repugnance to exchange a long-tried method for a new one." [8]

Still, the fact is established, that an engine has worked at about one-half the expenditure of an ordinary good engine of the present day. [9] The ultimate improvement of the air-engine will probably reduce the consumption to less than one-third of the present consumption. The gradual progress of mechanical workmanship, and long continued efforts incited by the extraordinary profits of success, can alone lead to such an advance. The inventor who can bring a new and economical air-engine into use will reap a fortune to be counted by millions, and will gain the rank of a second Watt.

But such an improvement of the engine, when effected, will only accelerate anew the consumption of coal. Every branch of manufacture will receive a fresh impulse—hand labour will be still further replaced by mechanical labour, and greatly extended works will be undertaken by aid of the cheap air-power, which were not commercially possible by the use of the costly steam-power. At least three great employments of the steam-engine are now in their germ, or scarcely beyond it, which would grow beyond conception by a great improvement of the engine. The pumping of liquid sewage out of our great towns, and its distribution over the country, is one mode which would return a clear profit of many millions a year. The steam-plough is a second instance. Its efficiency is beyond question, and the soil is said to be quickened by its irresistible tillage, as a fire is quickened by the poker. But it yet hangs upon the verge of commercial possibility, as did Stephenson's locomotive-engine, when he had got it to draw, but scarcely cheaper than horses. Taking the first and current costs into account, it is yet doubtful whether the steam-plough works as cheaply as the old horse-plough; but James Watt, to the surprise of his contemporaries, asserted that steam-ploughing was possible; [10] and Mr. Fairbairn, at the British Association in 1861, confessed his belief that many of those present would live to see the steam-plough in operation over the length and breadth of the land. Now, an improvement in the engine, reducing the cost of fuel, will turn the balance in favour of coal-power, and its common use in agriculture will be a certainty.

But it is in steam navigation that the improvement of the engine will have most marked effects. Any extensive saving of fuel, saving its stowage-room as well as its cost, will still more completely turn the balance in favour of steam, and sailing-vessels will soon sink into a subordinate rank.

What is true of economy in the engine is true of several other important, and many less important instances of economy. The extraordinary increase of the iron trade is a trite example. "This rapid and great increase, shown in the last few years, has been, in some part, caused by the economy introduced through the use of the hot blast in smelting, a process which has materially lowered the cost of iron, and, therefore, has led to its employment for many purposes in which its use was previously unknown." [11] In fact, as shown in a subsequent chapter, [12] *the reduction of the consumption of coal, per ton of iron, to less than one-third of its former amount, has been followed, in Scotland, by a ten-fold total consumption*, not to speak of the indirect effect of cheap iron in accelerating other coal-consuming branches of industry.

Siemens' regenerative furnace is a very good example of economy, now coming into use. It is somewhat on the principle of the hot blast. The current is passed alternately in opposite directions through two brick chambers, between which lies the furnace. Much of the waste heat, on its way to the chimney, is absorbed by the bricks, and again given out, when the current is reversed, to the cool air on its way to the furnace. Much less fuel is required, in such a furnace, to maintain a given temperature, than if cold air were allowed to flow directly into the fire. The general application of such regenerative chambers to furnaces would require the investment of a large amount of capital; and *the question in such improvements, as in the case of the boiler, lies between a large initial investment and large current expenses*.

The utilization of spare heat from a puddling or reheating furnace, by passing it through a steam-boiler; the saving of the waste gases of a blast-furnace, to heat the blast, or work the engines; the employment of spare heat in salt pans; the use of small gas flames, or gas furnaces, where large coal fires were before used: such are a few of the very many modes in which coal may be greatly saved. In fact, there is hardly a single use of fuel in which a little care, ingenuity, or expenditure of capital may not make a considerable saving.

But no one must suppose that coal thus saved is spared—it is only saved from one use to be employed in others, and the profits gained soon lead to extended employment in many new forms. The several branches of industry are closely interdependent, and the progress of any one leads to the progress of nearly all.

And if economy in the past has been the main source of our progress and growing consumption of coal, the same effect will follow from the same cause in the future. Economy multiplies the value and efficiency of our chief material; it indefinitely increases our wealth and means of subsistence, and leads to an extension of our population, works, and commerce, which is gratifying in the present, but must lead to an earlier end. Economical inventions are what I should look forward to as likely to continue our rate of increasing consumption. Could we keep them to ourselves, indeed, they would enable us, for a time, to neutralize the evils of dearness when coal begins to get scarce, to keep up our accustomed efficiency, and push down our coal-shafts as before. But the end would only thus be hastened—the exhaustion of our seams more rapidly carried out.

Let us remember that we are dependent on the *comparative cheapness of fuel and motive power*. Now comparative cheapness of fuel cannot be procured or retained by inventions and modes of economy which are as open to our commercial competitors as to ourselves, which have in many cases been introduced by them, and are more readily adopted by versatile foreigners than by English manufacturers bound by custom and routine. Even our superior capital will not avail us against dear fuel, because nothing more readily flows abroad in search of profitable employment than capital. And if we are to uphold a worldwide freedom of intercourse, let us not deceive ourselves as to its natural results upon the material basis of our prosperity.

[1] See for instance the remarks of Waterston in his Cyclopædia of Commerce, 1846, pp. 163, 164.

[2] Farey, Treatise on the Steam-Engine, p. 117.

[3] Smiles' Engineers, vol. i. pp. 329, 330.

[4] C. W. Williams, The Combustion of Coal, 1841, p. 9.

[5] Taylor's Records of Mining, p. 152, &c. Much confusion has been introduced into these accounts by the change of measure from bushels to cwts. In March 1866 the average duty of 27 Cornish engines was only 51.7 millions per 112 lbs. and the highest duty 64.6 millions. The performance of an engine easily falls back.

[6] W. J. M, Rankine on the Air-Engine. Report of the British Association, 1854, p. 159.

[7] James Nasmyth, in Tooke's History of Prices, vol. vi. p. 533.

[8] W. J. M. Rankine, British Association, 1854, p. 159.

[9] A new air-engine is said to be successfully working, but it burns nearly 4 lbs. of coal per horse-power per hour.

Mining Journal—Supplement, 12th May, 1866.
[10] *Gentleman's Magazine,* 1819, part 2, p. 632.

[11] Porter's Progress, 1851, p. 575.
[12] Chap. xv.

Chapter Eight - Of Supposed Substitutes for Coal

A notion is very prevalent that in the continuous progress of science some substitute for coal will be found—some source of motive power as much surpassing steam as steam surpasses animal labour.

The popular scientific writer Dr. Lardner, in the following passage of his Treatise on the Steam Engine, contributed to spread such notions—in him, as a scientific man, inexcusable. [1] "The enormous consumption of coals, produced by the application of the steam-engine, in the arts and manufactures, as well as railways and navigation, has, of late years, excited the fears of many as to the possibility of the exhaustion of our coal-mines. Such apprehensions are, however, groundless. If the present consumption of coal be estimated at sixteen millions of tons annually, it is demonstrable that the coal-fields of this country would not be exhausted for many centuries.

"But, in speculations like these, the probable, if not certain, progress of improvement and discovery ought not to be overlooked; and we may safely pronounce that, long before such a period of time shall have rolled away, other and more powerful mechanical agents will supersede the use of coal. Philosophy already directs her finger at sources of inexhaustible power in the phenomena of electricity and magnetism. The alternate decomposition and recomposition of water, by magnetism and electricity, has too close an analogy to the alternate processes of vaporization and condensation not to occur at once to every mind; the development of the gases from solid matter, by the operation of the chemical affinities, and their subsequent condensation into the liquid form, has already been essayed as a source of power. In a word, the general state of physical science at the present moment; the vigour, activity, and sagacity with which researches in it are prosecuted in every civilized country; the increasing consideration in which scientific men are held, and the personal honours and rewards which begin to be conferred upon them: all justify the expectation that we are on the eve of mechanical discoveries still greater than any which have yet appeared; and that the steam-engine itself, with the gigantic powers conferred upon it by the immortal Watt, will dwindle into insignificance, in comparison with the energies of nature which are still to be revealed; and that the day will come when that machine, which is now extending the blessings of civilization to the most remote skirts of the globe, will cease to have existence, except in the page of history."

Such high-sounding phrases would mislead no scientific man at the present day; but there is a large class of persons whose vague notions of the powers of nature lay them open to the adoption of paradoxical suggestions. The fallacious notions afloat on the subject of electricity especially are unconquerable. Electricity, in short, is to the present age what the perpetual motion was to an age not far removed. People are so astonished at the subtle manifestations of electric power, that they think the more miraculous effects they anticipate from it the more profound the appreciation of its nature they show. But then they generally take that one step too much which the contrivers of the perpetual motion took—they treat electricity not only as a marvellous mode of distributing power, they treat it as a source of self-creating power.

The great advances which have been achieved in the mechanical theory of nature, during the last twenty or thirty years, have greatly cleared up our notions of force. It has been rendered apparent that the universe, from a material point of view, is one great manifestation of a *constant whole of force.* The motion of falling bodies, the motions of magnetic or electric attractions, the unseen agitation of heat, the vibration of light, the molecular changes of chemical action, and even the mysterious life-motions of plants and animals, all are but the several modes of greater or lesser motion, and their cause one general *living force.*

These views lead us at once to look upon all machines and processes of manufacture as but the more or less efficient modes of transmuting and using force. If we have force in any one of its forms, as heat, light, chemical change, or mechanical motion, we can turn it, or may fairly hope to turn it, into any other of its forms. But to think of getting force except from some natural source, is as absurd as to think of making iron or gold out of vacant space.

We must look abroad then to compare the known sources of force. Some distinct sources are of inconsiderable importance, such as the fall of meteoric stones, the fall of rocks, or the heat derivable from sulphur, and other native combustible substances. The internal heat of the earth, again, presents an immense store of force, but being powerfully manifested only in the hot-spring or the volcano, it is not available to us.

The tides arising from the attractions of the sun, earth, and moon, present another source of power, which is, and often has been, used in one way or another, and shall be considered.

The remaining natural sources of force are the complicated light, heat, chemical and magnetic influences of the sun's rays. The light, or chemical action, is the origin of organic fuel, in all its forms of wood, peat, bitumen, coal, &c.; while the heat occasions the motions of the winds and falling waters. The electricity of the air and the thunder-storm, and the electric currents of the earth, are probably secondary effects of the other influences. *Among these several manifestations of force, our choice must, in all reasonable probability, be made.*

Now it will be easily seen that nature is to us almost unbounded, but that economy consists in discovering and picking out those almost infinitesimal portions which best serve our purpose. We disregard the abundant vegetation, and live upon the small grain of corn; we burn down the largest tree, that we may use its ashes; or we wash away ten thousand parts of rock, and sand, and gravel, that we may extract the particle of gold. Millions, too, live, and work, and die, in the accustomed grooves for the one Lee, or Savery, or Crompton, or Watt, who uses his minute personal contribution of labour to the best effect.

So material nature presents to us the aspect of one continuous waste of force and matter beyond our control. The power we employ in the greatest engine is but an infinitesimal portion withdrawn from the immeasurable expense of natural forces. [2] But *civilization,* as Liebig said, *is the economy of power,* and consists in withdrawing and using our small fraction of force in a happy mode and moment.

The rude forces of nature are too great for us, as well as too slight. It is often all we can do to escape injury from them, instead of making them obey us. And while the sun annually showers down upon us about a thousand times as much heat-power as is contained in all the coal we raise annually; yet that thousandth part, being under perfect control, is a sufficient basis of all our economy and progress.

The first great requisite of motive power is, that *it shall be wholly at our command, to be exerted when and where and in what degree we desire.* The wind, for instance, as a direct motive power, is wholly inapplicable to a system of machine labour, for during a calm season the whole business of the country would be thrown out of gear. Before the era of steam-engines; windmills were tried for draining mines; "but though they were powerful machines, they were very irregular, so that in a long tract of calm weather the mines were drowned, and all the workmen thrown idle. From this cause, the contingent expenses of these machines were very great; besides, they were only applicable in open and elevated situations."

No possible concentration of windmills, again, would supply the force required in large factories or iron works. An ordinary windmill has the power of about thirty-four men, [3] or at most, seven horses. Many ordinary factories would therefore require ten windmills to drive them; and the great Dowlais Ironworks, employing a total engine power of 7,308 horses, [4] would require no less than 1,000 large windmills!

In navigation the power of the wind is more applicable, as it is seldom wanting in the open sea, and in long voyages the chances are that the favourable will compensate the unfavourable winds. But in shorter voyages the uncertainty and delay of sailing vessels used to be intolerable. It is not more than forty years since passengers for Ireland or for the Continent had sometimes to wait for weeks until a contrary wind had blown itself out. Such uncertain delays dislocate business, and prevent it from proceeding in the rapid

70

and machine-like manner which is necessary for economy. Hence the gradual substitution of steam for sailing vessels. In the steam boiler, indeed, we have the veritable bag of Æolus; and thus, though steam is a most costly power, it is certain, and our sea captains are beginning to look upon wind as a noxious disturbing influence. In a well-established and connected system of communications, there is little or no use, and often a good deal of harm, in reaching a place before the appointed time. Thus there is a tendency to decline the aid of sails even when the wind is favourable and strong, and, unless for the purpose of saving fuel, a point little attended to as yet, it cannot be said that there is any benefit to be derived from sails equivalent to their trouble and cost. *It is certainty that is the highest benefit of steam communication.*

The regularity and rapidity of a steam vessel render it an economical mode of conveyance even for a heavy freight like coal. The first cost of a steam collier is five times as much as for sailing colliers of equal tonnage. But then capital invested in the steam vessel is many times as efficient as in the sailing vessel. A steam collier can receive her cargo of 1,200 tons at Newcastle in four hours, reach London in thirty-two hours, discharge by steam hydraulic machinery in ten hours, and return to Newcastle with water ballast within seventy-six hours for the round voyage. A single collier has been known to make fifty-seven voyages to London in one year, delivering 62,842 tons of coal with a crew of twenty-one persons. To accomplish the same work with sailing colliers would require sixteen vessels, and 144 hands. [5]

The same necessity for regularity may be still more clearly seen in land conveyance. A wind-waggon would undoubtedly be the cheapest kind of conveyance if it would always go the right way. Simon Stevin invented such a carriage, which carried twenty-eight persons, and is said to have gone seven leagues an hour. [6] Sailing coal-waggons were tried by Sir Humphrey Mackworth at Neath about the end of the seventeenth century, and Waller eulogizes these "new sailing waggons, for the cheap carriage of his coal to the waterside, whereby one horse does the work of ten at all times; but when any wind is stirring (which is seldom wanting near the sea), one man and a small sail do the work of twenty." [7]

Nearly a century later Richard Lovell Edge-worth spent forty years' labour in trying to bring wind carriages into use. But no ingenuity could prevent them from being uncertain: and their rapidity with a strong breeze was such, that, as was said of Stevin's carriage, "they seemed to fly, rather than roll along the ground." Such rapidity not under full control must be in the highest degree dangerous.

"Nothing could at first sight have seemed more improbable than the success of the steam locomotive over the atmospheric locomotive. The power of the air, which was absolutely gratuitous, was proved to be capable of impelling railway carriages as effectually as the power of steam, generated by coals which were procured at a great cost, and were brought from a considerable distance. But the conditions under which the force of the atmosphere

71

could be applied were so onerous that the invention ceased to present the character of an aid, and its use has consequently been discontinued." [8]

It is the characteristic of certainty which led Brindley strongly to prefer canals to improved river navigations. Rivers he regarded as only fit to feed canals, and as being themselves subject to floods and droughts, he characterised them "as out of the power of art to remedy." [9] Many of Brindley's finest engineering works on the Bridge-water Canal were directed to warding off the interference of river floods. Yet even his great canal was subject to be frozen up in winter and to be let dry for repairs in summer, and we could not tolerate the inconvenience and loss which a stoppage of traffic would now occasion in our large and nicely-jointed system of trade.

Uncertainty will for ever render aërial conveyance a commercial impossibility. A balloon or aërial machine does not enjoy like a ship the reaction of a second medium. It is subject to the full influence of the wind. Thus, even if an aërial machine could be propelled by some internal power from fifty to a hundred miles an hour, it could not make head against a gale. To say nothing of the facts that balloon travelling must be dangerous, that it is really dependent on the use of fuel, and cannot, as far as we can yet see, ever be rendered practicable or cheap, *it is, beyond all this, subject to natural uncertainty necessarily precluding its general use.*

Atmospheric or terrestrial electricity has, no doubt, suggested itself to some as a source of power. The thunder-cloud, the aurora borealis, and the earth-current of the telegraphic wire, are natural manifestations of electric power, which might possibly be utilized. But such secondary forces are altogether inconsiderable in amount, compared with the forces of heat and wind, from which they doubtless arise. In fact, they are scarcely sensible, except during thunder, auroral or magnetic storms, when they become destructive, and interrupt our telegraphic communications. We should no more think of waiting for a magnetic storm to move our engines, than Brindley would have thought of waiting for a mountain torrent to float his canal boats. The first essential of a motive force is constancy; natural electricity, on the contrary, possesses all the characteristics of uncertainty and extreme irregularity, which are most opposed to utility.

We meet, however, a constant and manageable source of force in water power. The water-wheel, or the turbine, possesses a natural tendency to uniformity of motion, even more perfect than that bestowed on the engine by Watt's "governor." Water power is, in this respect, the best motive power, and is sometimes used on this account, where a very delicate machine requires to be driven at a perfectly constant rate. When an abundant natural fall of water is at hand, nothing can be cheaper or better than water power. But everything depends upon local circumstances. The occasional mountain torrent is simply destructive. Many streams and rivers only contain sufficient water half the year round, and costly reservoirs alone could keep up the summer supply. In flat countries no engineering art could procure any considerable supply of natural water power, and in very few places do we find water power free from occasional failure by drought.

The necessity, again, of carrying the work to the power, not the power to the work, is a disadvantage in water power, and wholly prevents that concentration of works in one neighbourhood which is highly advantageous to the perfection of our mechanical system. Even the cost of conveying materials often overbalances the cheapness of water power. The splendid Katrine Water Mills recently constructed by Mr. Fairbairn are in the best natural circumstances, and give a nominal power of 100 horses at an annual cost of 1,260l. But Mr. Fairbairn calculates that an equivalent force from coals, at 7s. per ton, would only cost 1,400l., and the difference is probably more than balanced by the cost of conveying raw materials and products to and from the mill, with the possibility, too, of an occasional scarcity of water during drought. [10]

It is usually possible, with more or less labour, to procure water power artificially, to store it up, and convey and expend it where we like. Those who are acquainted with Sir W. Armstrong's beautiful apparatus for working cranes, dockgates, and performing other occasional services, will probably allow that the most perfect conceivable system of machine labour might be founded on hydraulic power. Imagine an indefinite number of windmills, tidal-mills, and water-mills employed to pump water into a few immense reservoirs near our factory towns. Water power might thence be distributed and sold, as water is now sold for domestic purposes. Not only all large machines, but every crane, every lathe, every tool might be worked by water from a supply pipe, and in our houses a multitude of domestic operations, such as ventilation, washing, the turning of the spit, might be facilitated by water power.

The first suggestion of a system of storing and distributing power seems to be due to Denis Papin, the French refugee engineer, the same who suggested the use of the steam-engine piston. [11] In the Transactions of the Royal Society for the year 1687 [12] he described a method of *prolonging the action of water-wheels by drawing and forcing air through tubes,* which seems to involve the principle of the boring machines of the Mont Cenis tunnel, the new coal-cutting machine, and pneumatic and hydraulic apparatus generally. And it was Bramah, a second French engineer, domiciled here, who first showed in practice the wonderful capabilities of hydraulic power. And so controllable, safe, clean, and irresistible is hydrostatic pressure, either of air or water, that, now our mechanical skill in construction is sufficiently advanced, it must come more and more into use. We might almost anticipate from its wide adoption a perfect Utopian system of machine labour, in which human labour would be restricted to the simple direction of the hydraulic pressure.

But before indulging in imaginary approximations to perfection, it is well to inquire into the several conditions of possibility. To the capabilities of hydrostatic pressure there is perhaps physically speaking scarcely a limit, but commercially speaking our command of water power, or hydrostatic power, in whatever form, is nearly limited to our command of steam. It is steam that presents us with hydrostatic power in its most abundant and available form. Water power in uniform abundance is to be had, in this country at least, only through steam; and *all experience points to the fact that, instead of water being a possible commercial substitute for steam, it is steam that from its first use has been a substitute for water power.*

A brief consideration of the history of the steam-engine will put this fact in the clearest light. Though water power had been in use since the time of the Romans, a great want was clearly felt in the seventeenth century of some new power, antithetical to water power, so to speak, and capable of overcoming it, so that drowned mines might be pumped dry, and water might be raised to furnish artificial water power, where a natural supply was not to be had. The earliest explicit patent for a new engine was directed to the raising of water, [13] and the "Exact and True Definition" of the Marquis of Worcester's engine clearly expressed a similar purpose.

"There being indeed no place but either wanteth water, or is overburdened therewith...by this engine either defect is remediable." Hence the Marquis calls his invention a "stupendous water commanding engine," and truly regarded it as a new *primum mobile* which was to overcome the force of falling water.

His appreciation of the value of water power is shown by his remarkable motto: [14] —

"Whosoever is master of weight is master of force,
 Whosoever is master of water is master of both."

"And consequently," said he, "to him all forcible actions and achievements are easy, which are in any wise beneficial to, or for, mankind."

Savery had no less correct and exalted notions of what his engine might accomplish by simply overcoming the gravity of water. It generated an universal motive power; for he said, "I have only this to urge, that water in its fall from any determinate height, has simply a force answerable to, and equal to the force that raises it;" [15] and he hints at "what may yet be brought to work by a steady stream and the rotation, or circular motion of a water-wheel," and "what use this engine may be put to in working of mills, especially where coals are cheap."

Now during the greater part of last century the steam-engine did perform the duty alluded to; it did pump up water and furnish artificial water power for turning mills and winding coals from mines. At the Coalbrookdale Iron Works it accomplished an inestimable service by enabling Darby to maintain and increase the blast of his new coal furnaces, an atmospheric engine being used *to return the water from the lower to the higher mill-pond.* [16]

Had not the introduction of the crank, flywheel, and governor by Watt, enabled us to communicate equable circular motion directly from a steam-engine to a machine, the water-wheel supplied with water by an engine would to this day be the source of motive power. As it is, of course steam power used directly is cheaper than steam power used indirectly. Water power is now only used where a natural fall is easily available. Such falls had in general become monopolised property from time immemorial, and naturally became the seats of factory labour, half a century or more ago. But it was the steam-engine which alone could allow the growth of our factory system, as seen in the fact that steam power employed in factories now exceeds water power six-fold. In 5,117 textile factories existing in the United Kingdom in 1856, the power employed consisted of, [17] —

	Horse power.
Steam power...	137,711
Water power...	23,724
Total...	161,435

The water-wheel, moreover, has, by the continued exertions of our great engineers, from Smeaton down to Fairbairn, been carried near its mathematical maximum of efficiency, whereas the engine yet gives us only a fraction of the power it may be made to give. The improvement of the engine has, in fact, caused it to be substituted successively in many mills before worked by water; and could its efficiency be again doubled, as is not impossible, hardly could the best water power in the country withstand the superior economy of steam.

The predominance of steam over water is seen in many other instances. It is a steam-engine that is used to supply water power for Sir W. Armstrong's apparatus, as at the Liverpool and Birkenhead Docks. A handsome and lofty building will be seen near the Birkenhead Great Float, containing a reservoir of artificial water power thus obtained. Again, it is only the engine that can supply water for the manufacturing and domestic uses of our great towns like Manchester and London. Our factories, printworks, sugar refineries, breweries, and other works, find it a matter of immense cost and difficulty to get a plentiful supply of water from wells and pumping engines, or from natural sources. And if we can hardly supply our boilers with water, how can we dream of ever using water, instead of steam, in the cylinder, and as the motive power?

The predominance of steam is further seen in its actual substitution for the windmill, or the tidal mill. Wind-cornmills still go on working until they are burnt down, or out of repair; they are then never rebuilt, but their work is transferred to steam-mills. Yet the grinding of corn is a work most suitable to the variable power of the wind. Again, if there is anything which could be cheaply done by wind, it is the raising of large masses of water where occasional irregularities are of no consequence, the rain and wind mostly coming together. Yet the windmills long employed to drain the Lincolnshire Fens, as practised in Holland, were at last superseded by powerful steam-engines, on the recommendation of Mr. Rennie. [18] Tidal mills are no novelty. One is mentioned in the first page and column of the Domesday Book as existing at Dover. A tidal pump was long moved by the current under Old London Bridge, and supplied the City with water. A tidal corn-mill, too, of very ingenious construction, subsequently existed at Woolwich. [19] Not long ago Sir Robert Kane, in his "Industrial Resources of Ireland," [20] supposed tidal mills to be capable of supplying motive power to Ireland.

The application of the tides to machine labour is rendered difficult on account of their variation from day to day. To gain a constant head of water always available we must either construct elaborate and costly high and low tide basins, or else we must use the variable tidal wheel to pump up water into a great reservoir. The estuary of the Dee is one of the places best adapted to give a vast tidal power, and an anonymous but apparently able engineer has calculated what power might be utilised there. [21] He considers that the equivalent steam power might be had at a capital cost of £4,000,000, a sum wholly insufficient to provide the tidal works. Hence he concludes that the tidal scheme would be at least commercially impracticable, and he doubts whether it would be at all possible mechanically speaking to construct embankments and tidal basins on loose sands.

And whatever schemes of this sort be proposed we should remember that the tendency of tidal docks and reservoirs to silt up is an insuperable objection in cost. Engineers, from the time of Brindley, have constantly found that there is nothing more nearly beyond the remedy of art than the silting up of harbours, docks, and reservoirs. The great new Birkenhead Docks are threatened with this evil, and a tidal mill and reservoir constructed on the opposite side of the Mersey about half a century ago was soon abandoned for a similar reason.

It will, therefore, appear obvious that *if we are to have a water power millennium of machine labour, which is physically possible, it must yet be using steam as the ultimate source of power.*

To go on to other suggestions, we may notice the very prevalent opinion that the electro-magnetic engine will some day supersede the steam-engine. Such an engine, however, must be worked by an electro-positive metallic element as the source of power. Now it is coal or fuel only by which we can smelt ores and obtain the metal required for the engine, and it is demonstrable that we should get far more force by using coal directly under a steam-engine boiler, than by using it to smelt metals for an electro-magnetic engine. After the exposure of the claims of such an engine by Baron Liebig, [22] I need not dwell upon it. The predominance of steam, too, is shown most clearly in the fact that the steam-engine is used conversely to turn Faraday's magneto-electric machines, and supply electricity for telegraph purposes, and for illuminating lighthouses. And while force is found to be the cheapest source of electricity, it is impossible that electricity should be the cheapest source of force. The electro-magnetic engine might be found a convenient device for applying or concentrating force in some particular circumstances, but the force must ultimately be furnished by coal.

Hitherto we have considered mechanical force only, but it is obvious that if coal were used up we should want some source of heat as well as force. A favourite notion is to employ wind, water, or tidal mills to turn magneto-electric machines, and by the stream of electricity produced to decompose water, thus furnishing a continuous supply of artificial gaseous fuel. Such a plan was proposed in the *Times* during the discussion on the French Treaty. But an answer, attributed to Dr. Percy of the School of Mines, soon appeared, showing the amount of fuel derivable to be inconsiderable. The waste of power must be vastly greater in such a process of transmutation than in the system of artificial water power which we have considered. Besides, if uniform experience is to be trusted, a steam-engine would be a much more economical means of turning the magneto-electric machines than either a wind, water, or tidal machine. We should therefore only use coal in a roundabout manner to generate a less valuable fuel. For the hydrogen gas generated, though in some instances valuable, would in general be immensely less convenient than coal. For equal weights, it gives about four times as much heat as coal, but hydrogen is so light that *for equal volumes it gives one five-thousandth part as much heat.* To compress it in a small space would require more force than the combustion of the fuel itself would furnish, and gas companies do not find it convenient to compress their gas. Hydrogen too has so much higher a diffusive power than coal-gas, that it could hardly be retained in gasometers or ordinary pipes. Even the loss of coal-gas by leakage is said to be nearly twenty-five per cent.

Of course it is useless to think of substituting any other kind of fuel for coal. We cannot revert to timber fuel, for "nearly the entire surface of our island would be required to grow timber sufficient for the consumption of the iron manufacture alone." [23] And I have independently calculated, from the known produce of continental forests, [24] and the comparative heat-producing values of timber and coal, [25] that forests of an extent two and a half times exceeding the whole area of the United Kingdom would be required to furnish even a theoretical equivalent to our annual coal produce. Practically, however, there are inconveniences about the use of timber that would altogether prevent it from nourishing a large manufacturing system. Wood fuel is superior to coal in the single case of the iron smelting furnace; but in most other uses, the greater bulk of wood, and the large areas of forest land over which it is spread, necessarily render it a costly and inefficient fuel compared with coal.

Peat, or turf, again, may no doubt be turned into fuel; but, in spite of what has been said in its favour by Sir R. Kane, [26] all experience shows that it is immensely inferior as regards cost and efficiency to coal. It is usually full, too, of phosphorus and sulphur, and thus has not even those advantages of purity which render timber so valuable for the iron blast furnace.

Petroleum has of late years become the matter of a most extensive trade, and has even been proposed by American inventors for use in marine steam-engine boilers. It is undoubtedly superior to coal for many purposes, and is capable of replacing it. But then, *What is Petroleum but the Essence of Coal,* distilled from it by terrestrial or artificial heat? Its natural supply is far more limited and uncertain than that of coal, its price is about 15*l*. per ton already, and an artificial supply can only be had by the distillation of some kind of coal at considerable cost. To extend the use of petroleum, then, is only a new way of pushing the consumption of coal. It is more likely to be an aggravation of the drain than a remedy.

Coal has all those characteristics which entitle it to be considered the best natural source of motive power. It is like a spring, wound up during geological ages for us to let down. Just as in alluvial deposits of gold-dust we enjoy the labour of the natural forces which for ages were breaking down the quartz veins and washing out the gold ready for us, so in our seams we have peculiar stores of force collected from the sunbeams for us. Coal contains light and heat bottled up in the earth, as Stephenson said, for tens of thousands of years, and now again brought forth and made to work for human purposes.

The amount of power contained in coal is almost incredible. In burning a single pound of coal there is force developed equivalent to that of 11,422,000 pounds weight falling one foot, and the actual useful force got from each pound of coal in a good steam-engine is that of 1,000,000 lbs. falling through a foot; that is to say, there is spring enough in coal to raise a million times its own weight a foot high. Or again, suppose a farmer to despatch a horse and cart to bring a ton of coals to work a portable engine, occupying four hours on the way. The power brought in the coal is 2,800 times the power expended in bringing it, and the amount of useful force actually got from it will probably exceed by 100 times or more that of the horse as employed in the cart. In coal we pre-eminently have, as the partner of Watt said, "what all the world wants—POWER." All things considered, it is not reasonable to suppose or expect that the power of coal will ever be superseded by anything better. It is the naturally best source of power, as air and water and gold and iron are, each for its own purposes, the most useful of substances, and such as will never be superseded.

Of course I do not deny that if our coal were gone, or nearly so, and of high price, we might find wind, water, or tidal mills, a profitable substitute for coal. But this would only be on the principle that half a loaf is better than no bread. It would not enable us to keep up our old efficiency, nor to compete with nations enjoying yet undiminished stores of fuel. And there is little doubt, too, that a century hence the steam-engine will be two or three-fold as efficient as at present, turning the balance of economy so far the more in favour of those who then possess coal, and against those who have to resort to water or wind.

This is a point which I must insist upon as finally decisive of the question. The progress of science, and the improvement in the arts, will tend to increase the supremacy of steam and coal. Any mechanist knows that the water-wheel and the windmill have been brought, by the exertion of our engineers, Brindley, Smeaton, Rennie, Telford, and Fairbairn, near to their mathematical limit of efficiency; so that we can do little more than improve the mechanical construction, and gain some small percentage of additional power by reducing the friction of the machinery. The steam-engine, on the other hand, at least equally admits of improvement in mechanical details; but beyond this, in the principles of heat and vapour, we see clearly the possibility of multiplying at least three-fold the efficiency of fuel. If there is anything certain in the progress of the arts and sciences it is that this gain of power will be achieved, and that all competition with the power of coal will then be out of the question. In short, the general course of science and improvement will only lead us the more to regret the limited extent of our coal resources.

But let us further remember that coal is now a pre-eminent gift in our actual possession, whereas if any wholly new source of power be some day discovered, we have no reason to suppose that our island will be as pre-eminently endowed with it as with coal.

Mr. Babbage has applied his rare genius to this question, and what he has once said is incapable of improvement. Passing over the period which this work considers, when coal will be scarce here and plentiful elsewhere, he has thrown his thoughts forward to the time when coal will be scarce everywhere. Heat, he thinks, may then be got from the hot springs of Ischia. "In Iceland," he continues, [27] "the sources of heat are still more plentiful; and their proximity to large masses of ice seems almost to point out the future destiny of that island.... In a future age *power* may become the staple commodity of the Icelanders."

Power is at present our staple commodity, and Mr. Babbage clearly saw, more than thirty years ago, that with our coal *power* must pass from us.

Among the residual possibilities of unforeseen events, it is just possible that some day the sunbeams may be collected, or that some source of force now unknown may be detected. But such a discovery would simply destroy our peculiar industrial supremacy. The study of electricity has already been zealously cultivated on the Continent with this view,—"England," it is said, "is to lose her superiority as a manufacturing country, inasmuch as her vast store of coals will no longer avail her, as an economical source of motive power." [28] And while foreigners clearly see that the peculiar material energy of England depends on coal, we must not dwell in such a fool's paradise as to imagine we can do without coal what we do with it.

[1] Lardner, On the Steam Engine, 7th ed. 1840, p. 8.
[2] See "Economy of Manufactures," § 17, et passim. In this exquisite work

Mr. Babbage anticipates the modern doctrines of the relations of the natural forces.

[3] Life of Telford. Telford's Memorandum Book, p. 671.

[4] Truran on the Iron Manufacture of Great Britain, p. 242.

[5] C. M. Palmer, Report of the British Association, 1863, p. 697.

[6] See a curious account in the British Museum, under the name Stevin, 1652.

[7] Smiles' Engineers, vol. iii. p. 73.

[8] Plutology; or, the Theory of Efforts to satisfy Human Wants. By W. E. Hearn, LL.D. Professor of Political Economy in the University of Melbourne, 1864, p. 199. This work appears to me both in soundness and originality the most advanced treatise on political economy which has appeared, and it should be familiar to every student of the science.

[9] Smiles' Engineers, vol. i. p. 458.

[10] Fairbairn on Mills and Mill-Work, p. 89.

[11] See p. 103.

[12] No. 186, p. 263, Jan. 1687.

[13] See the patent of 1631, in Rymer's Fœdera.

[14] Harleian Miscellany, vol. iv. p. 526.

[15] Miner's Friend, pp. 28, 29.

[16] See chap. xv.

[17] Chadwick, Report of the Brit. Assoc. 1861, p. 210.

[18] Smiles' Engineers, vol. i. p. 67.

[19] Barlow's Cyclopædia.

[20] First edition, p. 105.

[21] See the Journal "Engineering," 30th March, 1866, p. 195.

[22] Letters on Chemistry, No. 12.

[23] Taylor's Archæology of the Coal Trade, p. 176.

[24] Percy's Metallurgy, vol. i. pp. 71, 72.

[25] Watt's Chemical Dictionary, Article Fuel.

[26] Industrial Resources of Ireland, 1st ed. chap. ii.

[27] Economy of Manufactures, 3rd ed. 1833, § 465.

[28] Liebig's Letters on Chemistry, No. 12, p. 154.

Chapter Nine - Of the Natural Law of Social Growth

Before proceeding with this question we must understand clearly what we mean by the progress of a country. We must ascertain how that progress is to be measured, and when it may be called *uniform*.

Suppose it stated that in a certain country during one year the consumption of coal has increased by one million tons. The statement is almost useless. We learn from it, indeed, that the country is progressing rather than going backwards, but this is all. We do not learn the rate at which it is progressing. If the previous consumption were only one million tons in a year, the increase would be enormous, for it would consist in doubling the consumption. With a previous consumption of ten million tons, the increase, being ten per cent., might still be great. But on the present consumption of England, amounting to eighty-six million tons, an increase of one million is not great, being scarcely more than one per cent.

Again, the population of England and Wales increased between 1811 and 1821 by 1,722,574 persons, and between 1851 and 1861 by 2,172,177 persons, but it increased eighteen for every hundred of the existing population in the former period, and only twelve for every hundred in the latter. Though the recent increase was of greater absolute, it was of less relative, amount; it was, *truly speaking, at a less rate*. We ought, in short, in statistical matters to treat all quantities relatively to each other, and we ought to cultivate the habit of so regarding them.

The reason is not far to seek. One generation naturally imitates the earlier one, from which its education is drawn. The son takes after his father—the same in body and mind, in passion and in judgment. Individual variations of character and career are of course innumerable. But on the average it is true that the son is as the father; he marries at the same age, strives at the same success in business, to gain the same fortune, to rear and educate the same family. If all things then go on the same, if no deterioration, no new obstacle presents itself, a family that rears a double progeny of children may expect a fourfold progeny of grandchildren, and an eightfold progeny of great-grandchildren. And though this could not be expected to occur in a single family subject to every accident of life, it may be expected on an average of a great mass of cases.

There are few countries where the population has ever doubled in a single generation, but the same reasoning holds good of any other rate. We are about doubly as numerous as our grandfathers. If we are in other respects like them—equally vigorous and enterprising, and not subject to any new exterior obstacles, we may expect our grandchildren to be doubly as numerous as ourselves.

This is one way of stating the law that men, as well as all living creatures, tend to increase in an uniform geometrical ratio. And an uniform rate of growth means an uniform ratio—an uniform percentage of increase— *uniform multiplication in uniform periods*. The law is true and necessary as a mathematical law. If children do as their fathers, they must increase like them; if they do not, some change must have occurred in character or circumstances.

Such is the principle of population as established by Malthus in his celebrated essay. Of the moral and social consequences he deduced from it I need say nothing at present. They have been accepted for the most part by political economists. But the statement *that living beings of the same nature and in the same circumstances multiply in the same geometrical ratio,* is self-evident when the meaning of the words is understood.

Now what is true of the mere number of the people is true of other elements of their condition. If our parents made a definite social advance, then, unless we are unworthy of our parents, or in different circumstances, we should make a similar advance. If our parents doubled their income, or doubled the use of iron, or the agricultural produce of the country, then so ought we, unless we are either changed in character or circumstances.

But great care is here necessary. We are getting to the gist of the subject. Even if we do not change in inward character, yet our exterior circumstances are usually changing. This is what Malthus argued. He said that though our

81

numbers tend to increase in uniform ratio, we cannot expect the same to take place with the supply of food. We cannot double the produce of the soil, time after time, ad infinitum. When we want more off a field we cannot get it by simply doubling the labourers. Any quantity of capital, and labour, and skill may fail to do it, though discoveries from time to time do allow of a considerable increase. Yet the powers and capabilities of organic and inorganic nature always present this remarkable contrast. The former are always relative to the number of existing beings, and tend unceasingly to increase. But exterior nature presents a certain absolute and inexorable limit.

Now *the whole question turns upon the application of these views to the consumption of coal.* Our subsistence no longer depends upon our produce of corn. The momentous repeal of the Corn Laws throws us from corn upon coal. It marks, at any rate, the epoch when coal was finally recognised as the staple produce of the country;—it marks the ascendency of the manufacturing interest, which is only another name for the development of the use of coal.

The application, however, is a little complicated. The quantity of coal consumed is really a quantity of two dimensions, the number of the people, and the average quantity used by each. Even if each person continued to use an invariable quantity of coal per annum, yet the total produce would increase in the same ratio as the number of the people. But added to this is the fact that we do each of us in general increase our consumption of coal. In round numbers, the population has about doubled since the beginning of the century, but the consumption of coal has increased eightfold, and more. *The consumption per head of the population has therefore increased fourfold.*

Again, the quantity consumed by each individual is a composite quantity, increased either by multiplying the scale of former applications of coal, or finding wholly new applications. We cannot indeed always be doubling the length of our railways, the magnitude of our ships, and bridges, and factories. In every kind of enterprise we shall no doubt meet a natural limit of convenience, or commercial practicability, as we do in the cultivation of the land. I do not mean a fixed and impassable limit, but as it were an elastic obstacle, which we may ever push against a little further, but ever with increasing difficulty.

But the new applications of coal are of an unlimited character. In the command of force, molecular and mechanical, we have the key to all the infinite varieties of change in place or kind of which nature is capable. No chemical or mechanical operation, perhaps, is quite impossible to us, and invention consists in discovering those which are useful and commercially practicable. No *à priori* reason here presents itself why each generation should not use its resources of knowledge and material possessions to make as large a proportional advance as did a preceding generation.

And it cannot escape the attention of any observant person that our inventions and works do multiply in variety and scale of application. Each success assists the development of previous successes, and the achievement of new ones. None of our inventions can successfully stand alone—all are bound together in mutual dependence. The iron manufacture depends on the use of the steam-engine, and the steam-engine on the iron manufacture. Coal and iron are essential either in the supply of light or water, and both these are needed in the development of our factory system. [1] The advance of the mechanical arts gives us vast steam-hammers and mechanical tools, and these again enable us to undertake works of magnitude and difficulty before deemed insuperable. "The tendency of progress," says Sir William Armstrong, [2] "is to quicken progress, because every acquisition in science is so much vantage ground for fresh attainment. We may expect, therefore, to increase our speed as we struggle forward."

For once it would seem as if in fuel, as the source of universal power, we had found an unlimited means of multiplying our command over nature. But alas no! The coal is itself limited in quantity; not absolutely, as regards us, but so that each year we gain our supplies with some increase of difficulty. There are unlimited novelties to make our own, *had we unlimited force to use them.*

Such are the principles of our progress. But I should be as ill-contented as any of my readers to rest an argument upon such theory alone. I shall appeal to experience, and show that some of the main branches of industry depending upon the use of coal have hitherto obeyed the law of uniform geometrical increase. I can show that up to the present we are in an unchecked course of discovery and growth—that old applications of coal are being extended, and yet admit of great extension, while new ones are continually being added. And I shall infer that a continuance of the same may be expected in the absence of any extraordinary influence; that the consumption of coal will increase at a nearly constant rate until some check, some natural but perhaps elastic boundary of our efforts, is encountered.

For the present our cheap supplies of coal, and our skill in its employment, and the freedom of our commerce with other wide lands, render us independent of the limited agricultural area of these islands, and take us out of the scope of Malthus' doctrine. We are growing rich and numerous upon a source of wealth of which the fertility does not yet apparently decrease with our demands upon it. Hence the uniform and extraordinary rate of growth which this country presents. We are like settlers spreading in a rich new country of which the boundaries are yet unknown and unfelt.

But then I must point out the painful fact that such a rate of growth will before long render our consumption of coal comparable with the total supply. In the increasing depth and difficulty of coal mining we shall meet that vague, but inevitable boundary that will stop our progress. We shall begin as it were to see the further shore of our Black Indies. The wave of population will break upon that shore, and roll back upon itself. And as settlers, unable to choose in the far inland new and virgin soil of unexceeded fertility, will fall back upon that which is next best, and will advance their tillage up the mountain side, so we, unable to discover new coal-fields as shallow as before, must deepen our mines with pain and cost.

There is too this most serious difference to be noted. A farm, however far pushed, will under proper cultivation continue to yield for ever a constant crop. But in a mine there is no reproduction, and the produce once pushed to the utmost will soon begin to fail and sink towards zero.

So far then as our wealth and progress depend upon the superior command of coal we must not only stop—we must go back.

[1] See the chapter on Invention in Mr. Hearn's Plutology.
[2] Resources of the three Northern Rivers, quoted in the Quarterly Journal of Science, No. 2, p. 371.

Chapter Ten - Of the Growth and Migrations of Our Population

It is in several ways essential to our inquiry to examine, briefly, the increase and movements of our population, and the extraordinary effects which the growing use of coal has exercised upon it.

Our examination must be restricted to England and Wales, or at most to Great Britain. Ireland, if referred to at all, must be contrasted with England in natural and social condition. *Practically and commercially* Ireland is devoid of coal. In spite of the large area of the Irish coal measures, there are only 73 collieries in Ireland, of which about 46 are in work. The total produce was 125,000 tons in 1864, and is on the decrease. We can only attribute this extraordinary fact to the inferior quality of the coal, and the great cost of mining it. "The coals of Ballycastle in the north are of a quality so inferior, that English coal is in use within a very few miles from the pits; the coals of Arigna are almost equally inferior in quality; whilst the anthracite or stone coal of Kilkenny, from its deficiency of flame, can only be partially used, and from its weight and density of texture, is three times more expensive in excavation than the bituminous coal of the English fields." [1]

Ireland cannot raise a manufacturing system alongside of England when she has to buy from England the chief requisite of manufacturing industry. The manufactures of Ireland have been abolished by the steam-engines of England, [2] and it is a persistent but strange error of authors and statesmen to suppose that Ireland can still find wealth in imitation and rivalry with England. The industrial efforts of the Irish should be exerted in a *contrary* direction to those of England, and agriculture and handicraft employments in which fuel affords no aid will be their best resource. If it be found that such pursuits will not sustain an increasing population, we must learn to conform to the conditions under which we are placed; and when rightly viewed the recent exodus of the Irish people, by which a population of 8,175,124 persons in 1841 was reduced to 5,798,967 in 1861 is a fact confirming, in the negative way, many conclusions to be drawn concerning the progress of our own population.

Scotland will be occasionally referred to. It exhibits the bright and dark features of English progress, intensified in degree. While the general rise of Scotch industry, especially in the cases of the Glasgow iron trade, and the lowland agriculture, surpasses the highest instances of English progress, the poverty and distress of the Highland and sterile parts, and the emigration thence arising, exceed anything we have suffered in the agricultural parts of England. But the want of statistical data concerning Scotland and Ireland would generally oblige us to give our attention to England alone, were this not also desirable for the sake of simplicity.

The following table exhibits the progress of the population of England and Wales for nearly three centuries, according to the most reliable estimates and enumerations:—

POPULATION OF ENGLAND AND WALES.

Year	Population.	Numerical increase for 10 years.	Rate of Increase per cent. for 10 years.
1570	4,160,321 [1]		
1600	4,811,718	217,132	5 increase.
1630	5,600,517	262,933	5 increase.
1670	5,773,646	43,282	1 increase.
1700	6,045,008	90,454	2 increase.
1701	6,121,525 [2]		
1711	6,252,105	130,580	2 increase.
1721	6,252,750	645	0 increase.
1731	6,182,972	-69,778	1 decrease.
1741	6,153,227	-29,745	0 decrease.
1751	6,335,840	182,613	3 increase.
1761	6,720,547	384,707	6 increase.
1771	7,153,494	432,947	6 increase.
1781	7,573,787	420,293	6 increase.
1791	8,255,617	681,830	9 increase.
1801	9,192,810	937,193	11 increase.
1811	10,467,728	1,274,918	14 increase.

POPULATION OF ENGLAND AND WALES.

Year	Population.	Numerical increase for 10 years.	Rate of Increase per cent. for 10 years.
1821	12,190,302	1,722,574	18 increase.
1831	14,070,681	1,880,379	16 increase.
1841	16,050,542	1,979,861	14 increase.
1851	18,109,410	2,058,868	13 increase.
1861	20,281,587	2,172,177	12 increase.

[1] Preface to Census Returns of 1841, pp. 34-37.

[2] 1701-1861 including army, &c. abroad: Census of 1861, General Report, p. 22. See the Diagram fronting the title-page.

The estimates for the 16th, 17th, and 18th centuries, however carefully calculated from the registers of births, deaths, and marriages, and from other data, are not true to a nicety; but they afford at any rate conclusive evidence that in the first half of last century the population was nearly stationary, and occasionally diminishing. About the middle of the century, it began to grow again; and the rate of growth rose until, in the beginning of this century, it reached a height altogether unprecedented in the history of the country. In the period 1811-21, especially we find the increase as high as 18 per cent. or treble the rate which prevailed in the previous half century.

In passing I will draw attention to the fact that the ratios or rates per cent. of increase show some approach to uniformity over considerable periods of time. The simple numerical increase of population presents no such uniformity, and in late times is thoroughly divergent. In fact the *arithmetic increase of the four years,* 1857-1861, was as great as that of the whole century, 1651-1751. [3] It is clear, from the mere inspection of the table, that *the notion of an arithmetic series is wholly inapplicable to matters of population and statistics.* We must look to the ratio or proportional rate of increase, as measuring progress or marking the changes of condition of our population.

Looking now to the rates of increase from 1821 to the present time, we are at once struck by a very distinct and continuous decrease. The rate of 18 per cent. diminishes successively to 16, 14, 13, and 12 per cent. *There is an appearance of convergency—of a new approach to a stationary condition.*

Properly examined, however, this appearance is found to be very deceptive. When necessary allowances are made, *our growth up to the present time is seen to be one of increasing rapidity.*

In the first place, a nation is a very composite whole, of which each part may change at its own rate. Our population especially is divided into the distinct agricultural and manufacturing masses—contrasted as they are in every point of nature, history, and social condition. The one represents Old England in its maturity; the other, New England, already the greater, yet still growing as in youth.

We may compare the condition of these two great portions by means of the rates of progress of some of the most purely agricultural and most purely manufacturing counties:—

AGRICULTURAL COUNTIES.
INCREASE OF POPULATION PER CENT [1]

	1801-11.	1811-21.	1821-31.	1831-41.	1841-51.	1851-61.
Buckingham...	9	14	9	6	5	3
Cambridge...	13	21	18	14	13	-5
Devon...	12	15	13	7	6	3
Dorset...	9	16	10	10	5	2
Norfolk...	7	18	13	6	7	-2
Somerset...	10	17	13	8	2	0
Sussex...	19	23	17	10	15	8
Westmoreland...	12	12	7	3	3	4
Wilts...	4	14	8	8	-1	-2

MANUFACTURING COUNTIES.
INCREASE OF POPULATION PER CENT.

	1810-11.	1811-21.	1821-31.	1831-41.	1841-51.	1851-61.
Durham...	10	17	24	29	27	30
Lancaster...	22	27	27	24	22	20
Monmouth...	35	22	29	36	17	11
Northumberland	19	15	11	12	14	13
Stafford...	21	17	18	24	20	23
Glamorgan...	19	20	24	35	35	37

[1] Census of 1861. Population Tables, vol. i. p. xviii. The negative sign (-) indicates a decrease of population, as in the cases of Cambridge, Norfolk, and Wiltshire.

Comparing the above tables, we see that in the period 1811-21 both the agricultural and manufacturing populations were in a state of rapid increase. To this is due the extraordinary general rate of increase of the population, namely eighteen per cent. during those ten years. But the subsequent rapid decline of the agricultural rate shows how impossible it was for a growing population to find subsistence on the land. And when we remember the prevalence of pauperism during the period 1811-21 we shall be convinced that the increase of agricultural population which did occur, was unsound and not warranted by any corresponding increase in the means of living.

The following numbers express the average sum contributed by each person in England and Wales to the legal support of the poor:—

	s.	d.
1801...	9	1 [1]
1811...	13	1
1821...	10	7
1831...	9	9
1841...	6	0
1851...	5	6½
1860...	5	6
1864...	6	2 [2]

[1] Porter's Progress (1851), p. 91.
[2] Increase due to the cotton distress.

Some allowance ought to be made for the variation in the value of the currency, but the pressure of pauperism half a century ago would still remain about double what it now is. And this pressure was chiefly felt in the agricultural counties. Mr. Porter, in his "Progress of the Nation," [4] gave a table whence it clearly appeared "that the burthen of the poor's rate in proportion to the population is generally greatest in the most agricultural counties. Suffolk, Norfolk, Wiltshire, Oxfordshire, Buckinghamshire, Essex, and Cambridgeshire, all essentially agricultural, are the most heavily burthened with poor; while Lancashire, the West Riding of Yorkshire, Cheshire, Staffordshire, Nottinghamshire, and Derbyshire, which are of an opposite character, enjoy a comparative exemption from that burthen." This clearly marked difference prevents us from attributing the excessive pauperism of the time to the wars, or the high price of corn, which last circumstance ought to favour the agricultural, at the expense of the manufacturing population.

The laxness of the Poor-laws, the impetus communicated by the rise of our manufacturing and trading system, the demand for soldiers, and perhaps other causes, seem to have induced throughout the United Kingdom, in the early part of this century, habits of unrestricted marriage, which in the absence of any extraordinary outlet for the growing population could only lead to poverty. In Ireland the result of an unsound but rapid growth of agricultural population was that extraordinary emigration which is not yet stopped. In the Scotch Highlands the result was hardly less deplorable, or the emigration less remarkable, though on a minor scale. The harshness of nature rather than the harshness of the landlords is the cause of this emigration, which is clearly shown in the following rates of progress and regress:—

SCOTCH HIGHLAND COUNTIES.
INCREASE OR DECREASE OF POPULATION PER CENT [1]

	1801-11.	1811-21.	1821-31.	1831-41.	1841-51.	1851-61.
Argyll...	6	12	4	-4	-9	-12
Ross...	8	13	9	5	5	-1
Inverness...	7	16	5	3	-1	-8
Sutherland...	2	1	7	-3	4	-2

[1] The negative sign (—) indicates a decrease of population.

It is interesting to compare the above with the rates of progress in counties where the coal and iron trades flourish:—

SCOTCH MANUFACTURING COUNTIES.
INCREASE OF POPULATION PER CENT [1]

	1801-11.	1811-21.	1821-31.	1831-41.	1841-51.	1851-61.
Ayr...	23	23	14	13	15	5
Lanark...	29	28	30	34	24	19
Renfrew...	18	20	19	16	3	10

[1] Census of Scotland, Population Tables, p. xlii.

Now in England our agricultural population has received a check similar to that in the Scotch Highlands. No inconsiderable numbers have gone abroad, but in general the surplus country population has been draughted into the towns. Those nourished among sheep pastured hills, or richly tilled fields, in the quiet village, or the lonely hut, are attracted to the crowded squalid alleys, the busy workshop, or the gloomy mine.

Mr. Smiles has explained how the population of a hill-girt district, like Eskdale, is kept stationary from generation to generation. "Oh, they swarm off," said a native to him. "If they remained at home we should all be sunk in poverty, scrambling with each other among these hills for a bare living." [5]

It is indeed true, as remarked by Mr. Rickman, [6] that an increase of population "may be deemed a solid good, or a dreadful evil, according to the circumstances of the country in which it occurs. If a commensurate increase of food and of raiment can be produced by agriculture and by manufacture, an accession of consumers in the home market cannot but be beneficial to all parties; and the increase of population in such case may be deemed equally desirable in itself, and conducive to national strength and national prosperity."

The effects of an unwarranted growth of population are seen in the poverty of our own agricultural counties, and in the wretchedness of Ireland and the Scotch Highlands.

It is our towns which alone afford the growing subsistence which is the warrant of an increment of population. They not only have room for their own native born, but engulf the best blood of the country districts. They afford that unlimited subsistence, which could alone enable our population to approach a constant geometrical rate of increase.

But it must not be supposed that our towns have maintained a constant rate of growth. I have chosen thirty of the most progressive and important English manufacturing towns, and summed up the number of their inhabitants.

MANUFACTURING TOWNS (NOT INCLUDING LONDON).

	Population.	Numerical increase in ten years.	Rate of increase per cent in ten years.
1801	623,000		
1811	763,000	140,000	22
1821	991,000	228,000	30
1831	1,352,000	361,000	36
1841	1,763,000	411,000	30
1851	2,220,000	457,000	26
1861	2,679,000	459,000	21

Such numbers alone give us an adequate notion of our powers of growth. Our manufacturing population has more than quadrupled itself in sixty years; it has multiplied at a rate equivalent to doubling in twenty-eight years. When the new is thus viewed apart from the old, our growth is seen to be that rather of a new colony, than of an ancient settled country whose history runs back 2,000 years. And when it is considered that this country and the busy towns in question have been sending forth the hundreds of thousands of emigrants who populate Africa, Australia, and America, I assert without fear of contradiction, that the annals of the newest and most flourishing settlements afford nothing so truly astonishing as our growth. England enjoys the stable society, the refinements and comforts, the intellectual and historical renown which belong to an ancient, mature, and honourable monarchy. But she joins the good new to the good old in a manner elsewhere unknown. In our spreading towns, in our factories and fleets, not to speak of our arts and sciences, our yet living literature, and our constitution still perhaps changing for the better, we see the great work which is given into our care to carry on in moderation for the good of ourselves, our posterity, and the world.

But, to return, it will be seen that the rate of progress of our town population has dropped from thirty-six per cent. to twenty-one per cent. Is not this an indication that even our town population is overrunning its means of subsistence, and that we are now converging to a stationary condition? This is far from being true as yet; the rates of increase will probably not continue falling. But in any case our industry is divergent; and the more so, the more nearly we regard it in its first spring. It is the unslackened progress of Durham and Glamorgan, that most truly represents the progress of our national industry. The growth of the populations of those counties has been already shown, but the constant progress of our great northern coal trade is still more clearly shown in the following accounts of the united populations of the five great coal towns, Newcastle, Gateshead, Tynemouth, South Shields, and Sunderland.

NORTHERN COAL TOWNS.

Population.		Numerical increase in ten years	Rate of increase per cent in ten years.
1801	90,825		
1811	99,889	9,064	10
1821	125,128	25,239	25
1831	151,487	26,359	21
1841	192,283	40,796	27
1851	238,890	46,607	24
1861	297,752	58,862	25

London, too, a kind of great resultant and measure of the rest of the kingdom, holds a nearly constant rate—

POPULATION OF LONDON.

Population of London.	Numerical increase in ten years.	Rate of increase per cent. in ten years.
1801 958,863		
1811 1,138,815	179,952	18
1821 1,378,947	240,132	21
1831 1,654,994	276,047	20
1841 1,948,417	293,423	17
1851 2,362,236	413,819	21
1861 2,803,989	441,753	19

The appearance of convergency which our population as a whole presents is due to emigration. And this emigration is not a mere adventitious and disturbing circumstance. It is an integral part—the complement of our general development. The more we grow at home upon our mineral resources and manufacturing skill, the greater demands we make for food and raw materials. And it is to a great extent our demand which raises wages in our African, Australian, and American settlements to rates that attract our population abroad. The gold discoveries have added only an accidental and temporary attraction.

Modern Britain does not and could not stand alone. It is united on the one hand to ancient agricultural Britain, and on the other hand to the modern agricultural nations of our stock, which are growing in several continents. Of the same language, manners, and bound together in the same real interests of trade, Britain and her colonial offspring must be regarded for the present as a single whole. Our own agricultural area being essentially limited, the offspring of the agricultural population must find employment either in our towns or abroad. And the growth of our towns requires a corresponding growth of our foreign agricultural settlements.

But it must not be supposed that emigration from England is caused by internal pressure. It arises rather from the external allurements which the colonial settlements offer in high wages, independence, and a certain charm of novelty and adventure not to be overlooked. The Irish emigration of 1847, indeed, was caused by internal pressure, and is to be contrasted to that still going on, and which is due to a positive attraction exercised upon the Irish by American prosperity. So the gold discoveries formed attractions which greatly accelerated English emigration, and aided the development of colonies now so important to our trade.

When once planted in almost boundless areas of rich country, like those of North America, Australia, and South Africa, population multiplies at a new rate, and manifests its geometrical tendency, freed from the checks which Malthus showed to be a usual restraint.

But the important result to us is the secondary effect of foreign British population in trading with the centres of manufacturing industry, and stimulating the growth of our wealth and numbers at home. Food and raw materials are poured upon us from abroad, and our subsistence is gained by returning manufactures and articles of refinement of an equal value. Provided our skill, our capital, but, above all, our motive power, coal, be equal to the continuous drain, there is no pitch of material wealth and greatness to which our towns might not attain, when thus supplied from our foreign agricultural settlements with the other elements of subsistence. For the present, it would seem, that our home resources are unweakened, and equal to any probable demands.

Hence it is that, in our most crowded towns, we have, in the development of our manufacturing and coal-consuming system, means of subsistence which for the present remove Malthusian checks to increase. Whether our children stay at home, or whether they go abroad, there is the same addition of useful labour, in fields of undiminished fertility, and the same inducements to a future continued multiplication.

The proof that this is the true state of affairs—that our emigration is not due to poverty and pressure at home, but rather to attractions abroad—that our increase of population is rather under than above the increasing means of subsistence—is apparent in many gratifying facts concerning our wealth, comfort, and contentment; but it is most strikingly shown in our marriage-registers. Poverty and superfluity of population would tend to restrain marriage, and free emigration would then, at the most, allow the continuance of the usual rate of marriage. Malthus, Ricardo, and other economists of the same period, were too much inclined to regard this as the normal state of society. Population seemed to them always full to the brim, so that each ship-load taken to the colonies would no more tend to empty the country, than a bucketful of water would tend to empty the ever-running fountain from which it is drawn. They could not bring themselves to imagine such a state of things in this country, that one man should not stand in another's way, and that men, rather than subsistence, should be lacking. But that this country does make some approach at present to such a happy condition, is conclusively shown by the late extraordinary spread of marriage.

"Marriages express the hopes and fears of the country. They go on at all seasons, and at all times; but prudence makes them fluctuate, so that the more and the less indicate the feelings with which the great body of the people regard their prospects in the world." [7] Every year of depressed trade and distress leaves its mark upon the returns of the Registrar-General, in the shape of diminished marriage; and every period of prosperity has a contrary effect. The returns, in consequence, are in no slight degree irregular; but, treating the numbers of marriages in periods of ten years, we get the results shown on the following page. The very considerable rise in the marriage rate is a fact of the utmost significance, and is all the more remarkable when compared with the low rate of increase of persons of marriageable age, as shown later this chapter.

MARRIAGES IN ENGLAND AND WALES.

	Number of marriages.	Numerical increase.	Rate of increase per cent
1801-10	832,151		
1811-20	910,434	78,283	10
1821-30	1,052,095	141,661	15
1831-40	1,179,615	127,520	12
1841-50	1,354,988	175,373	15
1851-60	1,600,596	245,608	18

In stating the marriage returns for the quarter ending September, 1865, the Registrar-General says: "The rate was much above the average. Weddings were more rife than they were in the previous summer, or in the summer of any year since registration began. This implies that the great body of the people were prosperous."

The increasing frequency of marriage presents a strong contrast to the failing rate of increase of the total population. It shows conclusively that *there is no such thing as an internal check to population in England,* and that Nature is taking its appropriate means to remedy the drain from outward attractions.

Wonderful confirmatory evidence is derived from a comparison of the returns of the last two censuses concerning the conjugal condition of the people. It is found that the number of married persons increased 16 per cent. between 1851 and 1861, or four per cent. more than the general population; while the unmarried women of the age 20—40 years increased but little, and the unmarried men of the same age scarcely at all. The numbers are as follows:—

	Husbands.	Wives.
1851...	2,958,564	3,015,634
1861...	3,428,443	3,488,952
Increase...	469,879	473,318
Rate of increase 16 per cent...		16 per cent.
	Bachelors.	Spinsters.
1851...	1,198,050	1,168,386
1861...	1,201,576	1,229,051
Increase...	3,526	60,665
Rate of increase 3/10 per cent...		5 per cent.

To complete this chapter, it would be desirable to present such accounts of the number of emigrants from England as would quantitatively prove emigration to be that check to our population which we have considered it; but statistics are here deficient. Accounts of the number of emigrants since 1814 have been published; but unfortunately no record of the nationality of the emigrants has been preserved. The large and fluctuating amounts of Irish and Scotch emigration render the accounts quite inapplicable to England; but from the accounts, such as they are, I form the following table of emigration to the several parts of the world:—

EMIGRATION FROM THE UNITED KINGDOM.

	United States.	North American Colonies.	Australasian Colonies	Elsewhere.	Total.
1815-20	50,359	70,438	—	2,731	123,528
1821-30	99,801	139,269	8,935	1,805	249,810
1831-40	308,247	322,485	67,882	4,536	703,150
1841-50	1,094,556	429,044	127,124	34,168	1,684,892
1851-60	1,495,243	235,285	506,802	49,875	2,287,205
Total.	3,048,206	1,196,521	710,743	93,115	5,048,585

Statistics of the immigration into the United States [8] enable us to gain some notion of the increase of English emigration apart from that of the Irish and

Scotch. In the American accounts, indeed, the nationality of the larger part of the immigrants is not stated; but if we divide the number of the undistinguished immigrants, in periods of ten years, in the proportion of the numbers of those whose birthplace is distinguished, we get the following probable numbers of emigrants to the United States, whose birthplace was in England or Wales:—

	Persons.
1821-30...	25,365
1831-40...	55,676
1841-50...	175,253
1851-55...	203,508

Since the beginning of 1853 the nationality of emigrants has been registered in our Customhouse accounts; and the Census Commissioners estimate, from the returns, that 640,316 persons, born in England or Wales, emigrated in the ten years between the census days of 1851 and 1861. [9]

Emigrants are chiefly young men and women. The following figures give the proportional numbers of immigrants at New York, and the other ports of entry in the United States, for three intervals of age: [10] —

Years of Age.

9-15...	22
15-30...	50
30-45...	28 [1]

[1] Including, in the American authority, "the small number at older ages."

In short, three out of four emigrants are marriageable, or recently married.

The effect upon the ages of our population is strikingly shown in the following numbers, which express the rates of increase per cent. between 1851 and 1861, of the numbers of persons in England and Wales between the ages stated: [11] —

Age.	Rate of increase per cent.
0-20 years...	12.0
20-40 years...	9.5
40-60 years...	16.0
60-80 years...	14.0
80-100 years...	5.8

The low rate of increase for the ages 20-40 years is very remarkable, and these numbers alone prove that our population, but for the emigration going on, would be increasing at the rate of 16 or 18 per cent. instead of 12 per cent.

It is in strict accordance with the known principles of population, that the great gap in the procreative powers of the population, caused by so large a subtraction of marriageable persons, should be filled by an unusual spread of marriage among those who remain; and the extent to which this is happening has already been stated. But are there no serious reflections that should occur to us, when made acquainted with such facts? Should we forget that we are now in the highest state of progress and prosperity that a country can look to enjoy? A multiplying population, with a constant void for it to fill; a growing revenue, with lessened taxation; accumulating capital, with rising profits and interest. *This is a union of happy conditions which hardly any country has before enjoyed, and which no country can long expect to enjoy.*

It is in such a period that a population becomes accustomed to early marriage, the easy acquirement of a livelihood, the habit of looking for a rise in the social scale, and the enjoyment of leisure and luxuries. Nothing can be more desirable than such a state of things as long as it is possible. It is the very happiness of civilization. But nothing is more grievous than the forcible change of such habits, and the disappointment of the hopes they inspire.

Now population, when it grows, moves with a certain uniform impetus, like a body in motion; and uniform progress of population, as I have fully explained before, is multiplication in a uniform ratio. But long-continued progress in such a manner is altogether impossible—it must outstrip all physical conditions and bounds; and the longer it continues, the more severely must the ultimate check be felt. I do not hesitate to say, therefore, that the rapid growth of our great towns, gratifying as it is in the present, is a matter of very serious concern as regards the future. *I do not say that the failure of our coalmines will be the only possible check.* Changes here, or in other parts of the world, may, even before the failure of our mines, reduce us to a stationary condition, and bring upon us at an earlier period the sufferings and dangers incident to our position. But such a grievous change, if it does not come before, must come when our mines have reached a certain depth.

[1] H. Fairbairn, Political Economy of Railroads, 1836, p. 116.
[2] Ibid. p. 108.
[3] General Report upon the Census of 1861. p. 22.
[4] Ed. 1847, p. 96.
[5] Lives of the Engineers, vol. ii. p. 291.
[6] Preliminary Observations to Population Abstracts, 1822, p. xxx.
[7] Quarterly Report of the Registrar-General, 1849.
[8] Bromwell on Immigration, p. 176.
[9] Census of 1861. Population Tables, vol. i. p. xxxii.
[10] Abstract of Seventh Census of the United States, p. 14.
[11] Census, 1861. Appendix to General Report, p. 111.

Chapter Eleven - Of the Change and Progress of Our Industry

Our rapid but one-sided progress may be shown not only in its effects upon the numbers of the population, but also in the kind and extent of our industry.

In the second half of last century our population, previously stationary, began to grow at a growing rate. When we consider that at this period the engine was coming into use, that Arkwright's cotton machinery was invented, that the smelting of iron with coal was immensely increasing the abundance of the valuable metal, we cannot hesitate to connect these events as cause and effect. It was a period of commercial revolution. It was then we began that development of our inventions and our coal resources which is still going on. It was from 1770 to 1780, as Briavoinne thinks, that the commercial revolution took a determined character. [1]

The history of British industry and trade may be divided into two periods, the first reaching backward from about the middle of last century to the earliest times, and the latter reaching forward to the present and the future. These two periods are contrary in character. In the earlier period Britain was a rude, half-cultivated country, abounding in corn, and wool, and meat, and timber, and exporting the rough but valuable materials of manufacture. Our people, though with no small share of poetic and philosophic genius, were unskilful and unhandy; better in the arts of war than those of peace; on the whole learners, rather than teachers.

But as the second period grew upon us many things changed. Instead of learners we became teachers; instead of exporters of raw materials we became importers; instead of importers of manufactured articles we became exporters. What we had exported we began by degrees to import; and what we had imported we began to export.

It is interesting to observe the reversal which then occurred in several of our ancient trades. Wool had been for a long time esteemed the staple produce of the country. We raised the raw material in plenty, but were so unskilful in its manufacture, that all the Acts of Parliament that could be devised, all the arts and watchfulness of the revenue officer, could not prevent it being "run" for the manufacturers of France and Holland. No efforts of the legislature could enable us to compete with foreigners, and mistaken restrictions only contributed to keep the whole country stationary. But when once our manufacturing ingenuity took its natural rise, no more was heard of the "running of wool," and we have since become by far the first and largest woollen manufacturers, consuming not only our own raw wool, but as much as we can buy in Australia, Germany, Spain, and America.

Again, we had during the early part of the last century imported quantities of fine cotton goods from India, and great was the indignation of Gee and other commercial writers at this "finger labour" being allowed to interfere with our home industry. No exclusion of such Indian cottons could have promoted the invention of cotton-spinning machinery, which is rather due to the general advance of our skill in mechanical construction. But it is curious to reflect upon the different state of things now, and the enormous quantities of cotton we not only draw from India, but return in a manufactured state.

Corn had been next to wool the most esteemed produce of the kingdom. When our population was not one-third of its present amount we were able to raise enough for our own use, with a margin over in plentiful years. This margin the Dutch and French merchants readily purchased from us and stored up, often selling it back to us again in periods of dearth. But as corn is not a material of manufacture, its export was regarded very favourably as bringing treasure into the country, and the whole kingdom looked upon the system of bounties and protective duties, established in 1670, as a piece of skilful political economy. But no sooner had our population about 1761 or 1771 begun to increase than our imports of wheat exceeded our exports, and the inward movement of corn was accelerated by the reduction of the protective duties to a nominal amount. Our dependence on foreign corn, however, increased so rapidly, and was so odious to the general feelings of the country, that a restrictive Act was readily passed in 1791. This was the first of the series of Corn Laws which twenty years ago led to so severe a struggle. The effect of restriction is seen in the stationary amount of imports between 1791 and 1830, the increased demands of the population being met by the enclosure of land, and the improvement of tillage. But the necessary result of pushing a very limited country like England to its greatest capabilities is a comparative rise of the price of food, compared with other articles, and compared with the food of other countries. Thus naturally arose the great Corn Law Question. These facts are apparent in the following table of the average exports and imports of wheat and wheat-meal, during periods of ten years, in the last and present centuries.

	Average Annual Exports of Wheat. Quarters.	Average Annual Imports of Wheat. Quarters.
1701-10...	107,116	217
1711-20...	112,020	4
1721-30...	115,779	11,513
1731-40...	290,512	1,307
1741-50...	378,452	110
1751-60...	272,883	16,229
1761-70...	203,365	96,728
1771-80...	101,739	130,423
1781-90...	110,197	174,728
1791-1800...	82,178	568,896

	Average Exports of Wheat. Quarters.	Annual Average Imports of Wheat Quarters.	Annual
1801-10...	37,738	596,087	
1811-20...	40,087	540,111	
1821-30...	79,510	560,314	
1831-40...	157,852	1,077,370	
1841-50...	71,989 [1]	2,892,094	
1851-60...	-	5,031,266	
1861...	-	8,670,797	

[1] Average of 1841-9.

The exports, it is seen, attained their highest amount about the middle of last century, but were never large. Our imports are now increasing beyond all bounds, and even prices below 40s. per quarter do not stop the influx. With the above we may contrast the average annual quantities of wheat sold in the several market towns of England and Wales, in the undermentioned periods:—

	Quarters of Wheat
1815-20...	1,119,959
1821-30...	2,271,858
1831-40...	3,675,134
1841-50...	4,012,652
1842-51...	5,114,176
1852-61...	4,849,130

The returns for the last two periods are given separately because they refer to a larger number of market towns than the previous returns. As the quantities sold do not include by any means the whole of what is grown or used, we cannot draw any accurate conclusions as to the amount of our subsistence; but it clearly appears that our production of wheat has passed its highest point and is declining.

Such an extraordinary change in the source of subsistence of the country cannot but be accompanied by many secondary changes. Human requirements are various, and arranged in a scale of subordination. A plentiful supply of corn, creating population, creates also a demand for animal food, for dairy produce, for vegetables and fruit, the home production of which is naturally protected by the cost of carriage. Few or no farmers or landowners, then, who would promptly submit to the necessary changes of culture, could suffer any loss from the influx of foreign corn. This view was urged, in 1845, previous to the repeal of the Corn Laws, in Mr. T. C. Banfield's very excellent Lectures on the Organization of Labour: "The farmer and the landlord," he said, [2] "are the parties most interested in the rejection of our present Corn Laws, which make wheat a profitable crop at the expense of every other. They ought to be clamorous for their repeal; for no one can deny that cheapness of corn will increase the demand for every other article of agricultural produce." Similar views had been previously stated in a pamphlet by my father on the subject of the Corn Laws. [3] And no anticipations could have been more thoroughly fulfilled.

In spite of the vast importations, and the very low price to which corn has fallen both in 1850-1 and 1862-5, we have few complaints of the farmers' or the landlords' ruin. Agriculturists are either prosperous, or patient to an extent not to be looked for in human nature. But the fact is, that the substitution of new crops and kinds of culture has been going on very extensively, rendering the price of corn no longer the measure of the farmer's profit. An excellent example of the changes which are more or less going on throughout the rural parts of Great Britain, is furnished by certain statistics of the parish of Bellingham, in Northumberland, communicated by the Rev. W. H. Charlton to the British Association, at Newcastle, in 1863. Comparing the condition of the parish in 1838 and in 1863, it is shown that the acres of land under the plough had been nearly halved, being reduced

from 1,582 acres to 800 acres.

The area of wheat, indeed, had been reduced to one-fifth,

from 200 acres to 40 acres;

while that of oats was less decreased,

from 400 acres to 300 acres.

The number of grazing-cattle had, on the other hand, been multiplied thirteenfold,

from 50 head to 660 head;

and the sheep had increased very greatly,

from 5,102 head to 9,910 head.

The milch cows, however, had decreased

from 460 cows to 220 cows;

and the quantity of cheese produced,

from 1,120 cheeses to 60 cheeses.

The horses employed in farm-work had decreased nearly to one-half,

from 119 horses to 66 horses;

but the increase in horses otherwise employed nearly made up the difference, being   from 17 horses to 56 horses.

Of course such changes must be expected to continue with the growth of our population and consumption, until only the richest of our valley lands bear wheat, while the rest of the kingdom is given up to grazing, or to sheep-walks, dairy-farms, and market-gardens. Under our present system of free-trade, the farmer will find his best advantage, not in clinging to old traditions and customs, but in trying to apprehend the tendencies of the time, and select those new kinds of culture which will give the best money return.

One extraordinary result of the current changes in our old industry was disclosed by the census of 1861. *It is a positive decrease of our agricultural population.* [4]

PERSONS EMPLOYED IN AGRICULTURE.

1851.	1861.
2,011,447.	1,924,110.

The decrease is chiefly in the number of indoor farm-servants, which was 287,272 in 1851, and only 204,962 in 1861. On the other hand, agricultural implement proprietors increased fully fourfold in numbers, from 55 in 1851 to 236 in 1861; while agricultural engine and machine workers were for the first time stated in the census of 1861 as 1,205 in number. The decrease of agricultural population is partly due to the less labour required in grazing than in tillage. But the employment of horse, water, or steam power in many field operations, as well as in thrashing, chopping, churning, &c. has greatly contributed to the same result. The economy of labour in agriculture affords in this country little or no compensation to the labourer in the extension of employment, because the area of land is limited and already fully occupied. Labour saved is rendered superfluous. It is this that keeps agricultural wages so low; and as steam-power is more and more used upon a farm, the number of labourers will continue to decrease. The only relief for the consequent poverty of the labourer, beyond a poor-house allowance, is migration into a manufacturing town or a prosperous colony. In either case the emigrant contributes directly or indirectly to develop our new system of industry, and to render more complete the overbalancing of our ancient agricultural system. Such facts, having been disclosed by the census, are patent to all; but we cannot too often have brought to our notice *the profound changes they indicate in our social and industrial condition.*

When we turn from agriculture to our mechanical and newer arts, the contrast is indeed strong, both as regards the numbers employed and the amounts of their products. But the subject is a trite one; every newspaper, book, and parliamentary return is full of it: factories and works, crowded docks and laden waggons are the material proofs of our progress.

I shall, therefore, give my attention to the *rate of our progress,* and show that *our trade and manufactures are being developed without apparent bounds in a geometric, not an arithmetic series - by multiplication, not by mere addition - and by multiplication always in a high and often a continuously rising ratio.*

Next after coal, the production of which we shall consider in the next chapter, iron is the material basis of our power. It is the bone and sinews of our labouring system. Political writers have correctly treated the invention of the coal blast-furnace as that which has most contributed to our material wealth. Without it the engine, the spinning-jenny, the power-loom, the gas and water-pipe, the iron vessel, the bridge, the railway-in fact, each one of our most important works-would be impracticable from the want and cost of material.

The production of iron, the material of all our machinery, is the best measure of our wealth and power; and the following statement shows that, from the time when the charcoal bloomary and forge gave place to the coke blast-furnace, the production of iron in England has advanced at a rate alike extraordinary in rapidity and constancy:—

PRODUCTION OF PIG IRON.

	Pig iron produced. Tons.	Average increase in ten years. Tons.	Average annual rate of increase per cent.	Rate as for ten years.
1740	17,350			
1788	68,300	10,620	3	33
1796	125,079	70,980	8	113
1806	258,206	133,130	7	107
1825	581,000	169,890	4	54
1839	1,248,781	477,000	6	73
1847	1,999,608	938,530	6	80
1854	3,069,838 [1]	1,528,900	6	85
1864	4,767,951 [1]	1,698,113	5	55

[1] Mineral Statistics. The amounts for previous years are estimates collected from several well-known works.

It is evident that an arithmetical law of increase is totally inapplicable to the above numbers, since the yearly addition increases continuously from little more than 1,000 tons to 170,000 tons, the recent yearly addition. The ratio of increase, on the contrary, has only varied from 3 to 8 per cent. per annum. In the last period, indeed, 1854-64, we observe a fall in the rate, probably temporary, and due to the partial loss of the American trade, in consequence of the enactment of the Morrill tariff.

The same temporary check to the iron trade is more apparent in the following account:—

EXPORT OF PIG IRON.

Year.	Tons of pig iron exported.	Increase.	Rate per cent of increase as for ten years.
1801	1,583		
1812	4,066	2,483	136
1821	4,484	418	12
1831	12,444	7,960	177

EXPORT OF PIG IRON.

Year.	Tons of pig iron exported.	Increase.	Rate per cent of increase as for ten years.
1841	85,866	73,422	590
1851	201,264	115,398	134
1861	387,546	186,282	93

Our export iron trade commenced but little previous to the beginning of this century, so that a generation hardly yet passed away saw its rise. Within a period of sixty years the trade, as regards crude iron only, has been multiplied 245-fold. It is in vain to prophesy how much it may yet in future years be further multiplied. Prodigious resources are now being applied to the extension of the iron manufacture, and the present activity of the trade leads us to suppose that any recent dulness will be amply compensated. A single company, that of the Ebbw Vale Iron Works, managed by Mr. Abraham Darby, a descendant of the founder of our iron manufacture, holds 16,306 acres of land, employs more than 15,000 labourers, representing a population of 50,000 persons, produces 130,000 tons of pig iron annually, with a capability of producing 180,000 tons, or ten times as much as the whole produce of the country 120 years ago. But we must almost tremble when we hear that this single company raises 850,000 tons of coal annually, and with a comparatively small outlay are prepared to increase the yield to a million and a half of tons! Expanding as it does, the iron manufacture must soon burn out the vitals of the country, and it is possible that there are those now living who will see the end of the export of crude iron; so rapid is the development of the trade that its rise and decline may perhaps be compassed by two lifetimes.

The consumption of timber, as Mr. Porter remarked, [5] exhibits forcibly the comparative progress of industry. The following table exhibits the quantities of timber, "eight inches square and upwards," of colonial and foreign growth, consumed in the United Kingdom in the years 1801 to 1841, and the total cubic contents of all timber imported in the years 1843, 1851, and 1861:—

Year.	Quantity of Timber. Loads.	Rate of increase per cent. in ten years.
1801...	161,869	
1811...	279,048	72
1821...	416,765	49
1821...	546,078	31
1831...	745,158	36

Year.	Total Imports. Loads.	Rate of Increase per cent. as for ten years.
1843...	1,317,645	
1851...	2,111,777	80
1861...	3,061,138	45

The extraordinary increase between 1843 and 1851 is due to the partial repeal of the timber duties in 1847 and 1848. The more recent rate of forty-five per cent. is but little below the average rate (fifty per cent.) obtaining since the beginning of the century.

The amount of cotton consumed is a measure of one of the largest branches of our manufacturing system. Excluding from view the recent extraordinary disturbance in that trade, the following numbers exhibit its rate of progress:—

IMPORTS OF COTTON.

Year.	Quantity of Cotton imported. Pounds.	Increase in ten years. Pounds.	Rate of increase per cent. as for ten years.
1785	17,992,882		
1790	31,447,605	26,909,446	206
1801	54,203,433	20,687,116	64
1811	90,309,668	36,106,235	67
1821	137,401,549	47,091,881	52
1831	273,249,653	135,848,104	99
1841	437,093,631	163,843,978	60
1851	757,379,749	320,276,118	73
1860	1,390,938,752	633,559,003	96

No single branch of production can give an adequate measure of the general growth, because our manufactures not only expand in the case of each article, but also branch out into new kinds of work ever becoming more diverse and elaborate. Let us consider the attempts that have been made to estimate the general aggregate of our exchanges.

For a century and a half the amounts of our imports and exports were expressed according to a tariff of invariable prices fixed in 1694. The official values thus obtained have no claim whatever to be considered the real values of the commodities imported or exported, and only furnish a convenient criterion of the increase and decrease of the aggregate quantity of goods. The official account of the value of imports from the beginning of last century, is as follows: [6] —

TOTAL VALUE OF IMPORTS.

Year.	Average official value of imports. £	Increase. £	Rate of increase per cent in ten years.
1701-10	4,267,464		
1711-20	5,318,450	1,050,986	25
1721-30	6,621,725	1,303,275	25
1731-40	6,992,010	370,285	6
1741-50	6,784,409	-207,601 [1]	-39
1751-60	7,826,441	1,042,032	15
1761-70	10,025,235	2,198,794	28
1771-80	10,684,426	659,191	7
1781-90	13,543,418	2,858,992	27
1791-1800	20,660,760	7,117,342	53
1801-10	28,809,778 [2]	8,149,018	39
1811-20	30,864,670	2,054,892	7
1821-30	39,661,123	8,796,453	29
1831-40	53,487,465	13,826,342	35
1841-50	79,192,806	25,705,341	48
1851-55	116,931,262	37,738,458	63 [3]

[1] Decrease.
[2] M'Culloch's Account of the British Empire; Darton's Tables, p. 30.
[3] Rate as for ten years.

Low rates of progress varied by retrogression prevailed throughout the greater part of last century. Before its termination occurred a great burst of trade, only brought temporarily to a stand by the great Continental wars. Starting from the Peace we observe *a continuous acceleration in the rate of multiplication of our aggregate imports, the most recent rate being the highest known.*

The accounts of the official values extend only to the year 1855, the system of official values being then abandoned in favour of real values. These values are computed in the Statistical Department of the Board of Trade from the actual prices of the commodities as given in mercantile price lists, or furnished by the principal mercantile firms. But the increase of our imports from 1854 to 1863, as measured by their real ascertained values, is even more surprising.

Year.	Real value of imports. £	Increase. £	Rate per cent. of increase as for ten years.
1854...	152,389,853		
1863...	248,980,942	96,591,089	73

We have accounts of the declared real value of exports from about the commencement of this century.

TOTAL VALUE OF EXPORTS.

Year.	Average annual declared values of exports. £	Increase in ten years. £	Rate of increase per cent. in ten years.
1801-10	40,737,970		
1811-20	41,484,461	746,491	2
1821-30	36,600,536	-4,883,925 [1]	-1212
1831-40	45,144,407	8,543,871	23
1841-50	57,381,293	12,236,886	27
1851-60	106,513,673	49,132,380	86

[1] Decrease.

Since 1860 the amount of our exports has been greatly influenced by the revolution in the Cotton trade, but there has been a great recent expansion as seen below:—

Year.	Total Exports. Millions Sterling.
1860...	£135,800,000
1861...	125,100,000
1862...	123,900,000
1863...	146,600,000
1864...	160,400,000
1865...	165,800,000

The stationary or retrograde condition of our exports as expressed by the real value, in the earlier part of this century, has been attributed to the restrictive influence of the Corn Laws. But the official values and other statements of quantities of commodities examined in previous pages negative this notion. It was due rather to the great fall of prices which was proceeding from about the year 1810 until about 1851. Allowing for the change of prices it may be said, I believe, that the progress of our trade was slow during the great wars, rapid and constant from the Peace to the accomplishment of Free Trade, and greatly accelerated since that event.

The rise of our commerce is strikingly seen in the continuous growth of the port of Liverpool, which soon will be the greatest of all emporiums of trade. The dock accounts extend over a century, giving the number and since 1800 the tonnage of vessels charged with dock-dues.

PORT OF LIVERPOOL.

Year.	Number of ships.	Tonnage of ships.	Rate of increase per cent. in ten years.
1761	1,319		
1771	2,087	...	58 of ships.
1781	2,512	...	20 of ships.
1791	4,045	...	61 of ships.
1801	5,060	459,719	25 of ships.
1811	5,616	611,190	33 of tonnage.
1821	7,810	839,848	37 of tonnage.
1831	12,537	1,592,436	89 of tonnage.
1841	16,108	2,425,461	52 of tonnage.
1851	21,071	3,737,666	54 of tonnage.
1861	21,095	4,977,272	33 of tonnage.

The above numbers are not so regular as those we might get by taking decennial averages, and yet the rate of multiplication of Liverpool as a port has only varied in a century from twenty to eighty-nine per cent.

Accounts of the shipping of the whole kingdom are available from the beginning of the century. From them we get the following extraordinary results:—

TONNAGE OF BRITISH PORTS.

Year.	Average annual tonnage of ships entering and clearing.	Increase.	Rate per cent. of increase in ten years.
	Tons.	Tons.	
1801-10	3,467,157		
1811-20	4,203,613	736,446	21
1821-30	5,059,522	855,919	20
1831-40	7,175,081	2,115,559	42
1841-50	11,704,796	4,529,715	63
1851-60	20,233,049	8,528,253	73

Multiplication at a growing rate! So far is our shipping industry from increasing in an arithmetical series only, that even a geometrical series does not adequately express its rapid expansion. *The very rate of multiplication progresses.*

But it is the expansion of our ocean steam marine which most fitly represents our mechanical resources, our commercial requirements, and our maritime supremacy. The following are the amounts of tonnage of steam vessels belonging to the United Kingdom, beginning with the decennial period following the introduction of steamboats in 1814:—

BRITISH STEAM VESSELS.

Year.	Tonnage.	Increase of tonnage.	Rate of increase per cent. in ten years.
1821	10,534		
1831	37,445	26,911	256
1841	95,687	58,242	156
1851	186,687	91,000	95
1861	506,308	319,621	171

If we pass over the early period when steam-vessels were quite a novelty, we find that their increase, always extraordinary, has been more rapid even proportionally speaking in the last ten years than in twenty previous years. And the extreme success and prosperity of the iron ship-building trade at the present time is the sure indication of the future extension of steam navigation.

When we consider that the system of ocean steam communication is almost wholly in our hands and supported upon our coal, our pride at its possession must be mingled with anxiety at the enormous drain it directly and indirectly creates upon our coal-mines.

[1] M. N. Briavoinne, De l'Industrie en Belgique. Bruxelles, 1839, p. 197.
[2] Page 53.
[3] The Prosperity of the Landholders not dependent on the Corn Laws. By Thomas Jevons, 1840, pp. 7-11.
[4] See the able investigation by Frederick Purdy, Esq. of the Statistical Department of the Poor Law Board, On the Decrease of the Agricultural Population, 1851-61; British Association, 1863, p. 157. Journal of the Statistical Society, September, 1864, p. 388
[5] Progress of the Nation, 1847, p. 587.
[6] First Report of the Commissioners of Customs, 1857, p. 108. See the diagram fronting the title-page, in which the divergent character of our progress is shown to the eye by curves representing the numbers of the population, the official value of our imports, and the vend of coal from Newcastle.

Chapter Twelve - Of Our Consumption of Coal

In the last three chapters I have tried to make apparent, both from principle and fact, that a nation tends to develop itself by multiplication rather than addition—in a geometrical rather than an arithmetical series. And though such continuous multiplication is seldom long possible, owing to the material limits of subsistence, I have given sufficient numbers to prove that up to the present time our growth is unchecked by any such limits, and is proceeding at uniform or rising rates of multiplication.

Now while the iron, cotton, mercantile, and other chief branches of our industry thus progress, it is obvious that our consumption of coal must similarly progress in a geometrical series. This, however, is matter of inference only because until lately the total quantities of coal consumed were quite unknown.

We can trace the progress of the consumption of coal in previous centuries with some accuracy by means of the accounts of the Newcastle and London Coal Trade, which used to be, far more even than it now is, the largest branch of the trade. The total quantities of coal shipped from Newcastle and the neighbouring ports were as follows: [1] —

VEND OF COAL FROM NEWCASTLE.

Year.	Vend from the Newcastle Coal-field.	Increase for years.	Rate of increase as crease fifty per cent. as for fifty years.
	Tons.	Tons.	
1609	251,764		
1660	537,000	279,643	110
1700	650,000	141,250	27
1750	1,193,467	543,467	84
1800	2,520,075	1,326,608	111
1864	18,349,867 *[1]*	12,367,025	372

[1] Including 7,562,963 tons of railway borne coal.

The progressive consumption of London for two centuries, is seen in the following figures:—

COAL IMPORTED INTO LONDON.

Year.	Total quantity of coal imported into London.	Increase in fifty years, or as for fifty years.	Rate per cent. of increase as for fifty years.
	Tons.	Tons.	
1650	216,000		
1700	428,100	212,100	98
1750	688,700	260,600	61
1800	1,099,000	410,300	60
1850	3,638,883	2,539,883	231
1865	5,909,940	7,570,190	404

We see that it is almost impossible to compare this and previous centuries, and that *the rate of multiplication is in recent years many times as great as during preceding centuries, and is rapidly advancing up to the latest returns.* The simple numerical increase is now almost indefinitely greater than it used to be.

As to the total quantity of coal consumed in the whole kingdom the most erroneous notions were entertained even twelve years ago. Writers on Statistics and the Coal Trade made what they called *Estimates,* by adding together the Sea-borne, and a few other known quantities of coal, and then making a liberal allowance ad libitum for the rest.

The variations in the estimates made by different authors may be judged from the following statement: [2] —

	Tons.
R. C. Taylor, Statistics of Coal, 1848...	31,500,000
J. R. MacCulloch, 1854 *[1]* ...	38,400,000
Braithwaite Poole, Statistics of British Commerce, 1852...	34,000,000
T. Y. Hall, "A Treatise on the Extent and probable Duration of the Northern Coal-field, 1854"...	56,550,000
The same, quoting "a particularly careful writer on the subject of the Coal Trade"...	52,000,000
Joseph Dickinson, Inspector of Coal Mines, in his Report, 1853...	54,000,000

[1] Statistical Account, vol. i. p. 599. This later estimate is substituted for the one given in the Mineral Statistics.

In 1854 was begun the system of Mining Records [3] and Statistical Inquiry, recommended by Mr. Sopwith with reference to our present subject, and carried into practice by Mr. Robert Hunt, with the assistance of the Government Inspectors of Coal Mines, and the voluntary co-operation of the Carrying and Mining Companies. The following are the amounts of coal ascertained to have been raised from our coal-mines:—

Year.	Tons.
1854...	64,661,401 [1]
1855...	61,453,079
1856...	66,645,450
1857...	65,394,707
1858...	65,008,649
1859...	71,979,765
1860...	80,042,698
1861...	83,635,214
1862...	81,638,338
1863...	86,292,215
Total	726,751,516

[1] Statistical Abstract for the United Kingdom, 1864, p. 91.

Since the first edition of this work was published it has been found that the returns from South Staffordshire were under-estimated, owing to a misapprehension of the size of the Staffordshire ton and boat-load.

The correct amounts of coal produced during the last four years are as follows:—

Years.	Tons.
1861...	85,635,214
1862...	83,638,338
1863...	88,292,515
1864...	92,787,873

By adopting the new numbers I might slightly strengthen my conclusions, but I do not think it worth while to make the necessary alterations.

The quantity of small coals consumed upon the colliery waste-heaps is not included in the above, and is unknown. Mr. Atkinson, inspector of the coal-mines of Durham, south of the Wear, estimated the waste in his district in 1860 at 2,404,215 tons; but Mr. Dunn, inspector for Cumberland, Northumberland, and the rest of Durham, considered the waste in his district to be only 834,117 tons. [4] The discrepancy of these estimates is so great and obvious that there appeared in the Mineral Statistics for 1862 [5] the following note:— "The amount of coals burnt or wasted at pits has been so differently represented, and appears such an uncertain although very large quantity, that it is for the present omitted." We may conjecture it to be at least five millions of tons in the whole. But the uncertainty does not affect our subject much, because before long this deplorable waste of coal must come to a natural end.

We see that without considering the waste the lowest of the amounts of coal consumed (1854-1863) exceeds, by eight millions of tons, the largest previous estimate of our consumption, that of Mr. T. Y. Hall writing in 1854; while the estimates of Poole, MacCulloch, and R. C. Taylor are hardly more than half the true amount. With such facts before us we cannot place much credit in previous estimates, but I give such as I have met with.

Year.		Tons.
1819.	R. C. Taylor, Statistics of Coal...	13,000,000
1829.	Estimate...	15,580,000
1833.	J. Marshall, Digest of Parl. Accounts, p. 237...	17,000,000
1840.	J. R. MacCulloch, Dictionary of Commerce...	30,000,000
1845.	J. R. MacCulloch, Dictionary of Commerce...	34,600,000

I much prefer to reject all such estimates, and argue only upon the undoubted returns of the Mining Record Office, given earlier this chapter. We of course regard not the average annual arithmetic increase of coal consumption between 1854 and 1863, which is 2,403,424 tons; *but the average ratio or rate per cent. of increase, which is found by logarithmic calculation to be 3.26 per cent*. That is to say, the consumption of each year, one with another, exceeded that of the previous year as 103.26 exceeds 100.

We cannot help perceiving, however, that the consumption of coal is variable, and dependent upon the fluctuating activity of trade. The year 1854 presents a maximum; for the consumption falls off next year from 64½ millions to 61½, and suffers no great increase until 1859. There is then a very rapid rise up to a second maximum in 1861. We are uncertain when the consumption will again reach a maximum, and under these circumstances it is better to compare the consumption of the two years of maxima, 1854 and 1861, assuming that they are years of a certain correspondent activity. The average rate of increase in the interval is 3.7 per cent., and the comparison of the years 1854 and 1864 would give almost exactly the same result; but in our succeeding calculations I will assume that the *average annual rate of growth of our coal consumption is 3½ per cent.—or the ratio of growth is that of* 103.5 to 100.

This is equivalent to a growth in ten years of 41 per cent. or in fifty years of 458 per cent., or 5½ fold.

Such are the critical numbers of our inquiry.

If we assume the consumption of coal to have grown to its present (1863) amount, at the uniform rate of 3½ per cent., and calculate its former probable amounts backwards, we find no accordance with former estimates of the error of which we were already well assured (p. 236).

Year.	Estimated Amount.	Calculated Amount.
1819...	13,000,000	18,993,000
1829...	15,580,000	26,792,000

Year.	Estimated Amount.	Calculated Amount.
1833...	17,000,000	30,744,000
1840...	30,000,000	39,115,000
1845...	34,600,000	46,456,000

But it is worthy of notice that Mr. Hull, when briefly reviewing the consumption of coal, conjectured the true amount probably not to exceed ten million tons at the beginning of the century, and to be about 36 million tons in 1840. [6] Now these estimates agree well with the amounts we should arrive at from our assumed rate of growth.

Year.	Hull's Conjecture.	Calculated Amount
1801...	10,000,000	10,225,000
1840...	36,000,000	39,115,000

The following are the calculated probable amounts of coal used at decennial intervals as far back as it is safe to assume that the present high rate of progress existed; that is, to the time of the introduction of Watt's engine, the pit-coal iron furnace, and the cotton factory:—

Year.	Probable Consumption Tons.
1781...	5,139,000
1791...	7,249,000
1801...	10,225,000
1811...	14,424,000
1821...	20,346,000
1831...	28,700,000
1841...	40,484,000
1851...	57,107,000

If we take the consumption of 1852 and 1853 as the same as that of 1851, and the consumption in each period of ten years as uniformly the same as that of the first year, we easily get the following:—

	Tons of Coal.
Probable consumption, 1781-1853...	1,436,991,000
Actual consumption, 1854-1863...	726,751,516
Total consumption, 1781-1863...	2,163,742,516

We cannot but be struck by the fact that *the consumption of the last ten years is half as great as that of the previous seventy-two years!* But we gain little notion from the above of the total quantity of coal already burnt or wasted in these islands. An incalculable waste of coal has been going on throughout the period reviewed, both as regards the slack burnt at the pit mouth, and the many times greater quantity of small or large coal left behind in the pit by prodigal modes of mining, which coal cannot for the most part be recovered. And then previous to 1781 there had been a very considerable and more stationary consumption of coal, especially in Northumberland, Staffordshire, and at Whitehaven, during four or five centuries.

But let us now approach the main point of our inquiry, and follow the future probable consumption of coal. Assuming the present rate of growth, 3½ per cent. per annum, to hold, it is easy to calculate the amounts of coal to be consumed in the undermentioned years, starting from the actual consumption of 1861: [7] —

In the year	Consumption at the assumed rate of increase.
1861...	83.6 millions of tons.
1871...	117.9 millions of tons.
1881...	166.3 millions of tons.
1891...	234.7 millions of tons.
1901...	331.0 millions of tons.
1911...	466.9 millions of tons.
1921...	658.6 millions of tons.
1931...	929.0 millions of tons.
1941...	1,310.5 millions of tons.
1951...	1,848.6 millions of tons.
1961...	2,607.5 millions of tons.

The total aggregate consumption of the period of 110 years, 1861-1970, would be 102,704,000,000 tons. [8] Or, if it be objected that 1861 was a year of maximum consumption, we may reduce the above sum in the proportion of 83.6 millions to 80 millions, the average consumption of the five years 1859—63. We thus get 98,281,000,000 tons; or, in round numbers, we may say, always hypothetically, — *If our consumption of coal continue to multiply for 110 years at the same rate as hitherto, the total amount of coal consumed in the interval will be one hundred thousand millions of tons.*

We now turn to compare this imaginary consumption of coal with Mr. Hull's estimate of the available coal in Britain, viz. *eighty-three thousand millions of tons within a depth of 4,000 feet.*

Even though Mr. Hull's estimate be greatly under the true amount, we cannot but allow that — *Rather more than a century of our present progress would exhaust our mines to the depth of 4,000 feet, or 1,500 feet deeper than our present deepest mine.*

I have given reasons for believing that if all our coal were brought from an average depth of some 2,000 feet, our manufacturers would have to contend with a doubled price of fuel. If the average depth were increased to 4,000 feet, a further great but unknown rise in the cost of fuel must be the consequence.

But I am far from asserting, from these figures, that our coal-fields will be wrought to a depth of 4,000 feet in little more than a century.

I draw the conclusion that I think any one would draw, that *we cannot long maintain our present rate of increase of consumption; that we can never advance to the higher amounts of consumption supposed. But this only means that the check to our progress must become perceptible within a century from the present time;* that the cost of fuel must rise, perhaps within a lifetime, to a rate injurious to our commercial and manufacturing supremacy; and the conclusion is inevitable, that our present happy progressive condition is a thing of limited duration.

I may here notice that the exact amount of our stock of coal is not the matter of chief moment. The reader who thoroughly apprehends the natural law of growth, or multiplication in social affairs, will see that the absolute quantity of coal rather defines the height of wealth to which we shall rise, than the period during which we shall enjoy either the growth or the climax of prosperity. For, as the multiplication of our numbers and works proceeds at a constant rate, the numerical additions, as we have fully seen in many statistical illustrations, constantly grow. Ultimately the simple addition to our consumption in twenty or thirty years will become of moment compared with our total stores. The addition to our population in four years now is as great as the whole increase of the century 1651—1751, and the increase of coal consumption between 1859 and 1862 is equal to the probable annual consumption at the beginning of this century. It is on this account that I attach less importance than might be thought right to an exact estimate of the coal existing in Great Britain. Were our coal half as abundant again as Mr. Hull states, the effect would only be to defer the climax of our growth perhaps for one generation. And I repeat, *the absolute amount of coal in the country rather affects the height to which we shall rise than the time for which we shall enjoy the happy prosperity of progress.*

Suppose our progress to be checked within half a century, yet by that time our consumption will probably be three or four times what it now is; there is nothing impossible or improbable in this; it is a moderate supposition, considering that our consumption has increased eight-fold in the last sixty years. But how shortened and darkened will the prospects of the country appear, with mines already deep, fuel dear, and yet a high rate of consumption to keep up if we are not to retrograde.

Doubts have been expressed by Mr. Vivian, Mr. Hull, and others, as to whether the number of our mining population and the area of our coal-fields will admit of any further great extension of our yield. It is said that underground hands must be born and bred to the occupation of coal mining; and if we consider that many children of miners may be induced to emigrate, or to avoid their fathers' occupation on account of its hardship and danger, there may be a positive lack of hands. Facts utterly negative such a notion. The Census returns show the number of coal-miners to have been—

| In 1851... | 183,389 |
| And in 1861... | 246,613 |

The increase is at the rate of 34.4 per cent. in ten years, or about 3 per cent. per annum, which accords well with the rate of increase of coal raised, if we remember that the use of machinery, and the increased investment of capital in coal mining, enlists greater resources and involves greater cost than is expressed in the mere number of miners.

The notion, again, that there is anything in the area or condition of our coal-fields to prevent a present extension of the yield, is completely contradicted by accounts of the number of collieries existing in the United Kingdom. [9]

Year.	Number of Collieries.
1854...	2,397
1855...	2,613
1856...	2,829
1857...	2,867
1858...	2,958
1859...	2,949
1860...	3,009
1861...	3,025
1862...	3,088
1863...	3,180
1864...	3,268

The general increase is at the rate of 36 per cent. in ten years, or 3.1 per cent. per annum. Nearly the same average rate of increase is shown in the number of pits in the Northumberland and Durham coal-field, which were 41 in number in 1799 [10] and 289 in 1864.

If we consider that new pits opened are deeper and larger concerns than the old pits laid in, and capable of much larger yields, we must allow that the coal-owners, at least, both expect and are prepared to meet a largely increased demand for a good many years to come. But we should remember that the more rapid and continued our present expansion, the shorter must be its continuance.

[1] T.J. Taylor, Archæology of the Coal Trade, pp. 177 and 204, in Memoirs of the British Archæological Association, 1858. See the diagram fronting the title page.
[2] Mineral Statistics for 1855. Introd. p. vi.
[3] Proposed long ago by Mr. Chapman. See Holmes, Treatise on the Coal Mines of Durham and Northumberland. London, 1816, p. 218.

[4] Mineral Statistics for 1860, p. 99.
[5] P. 68.
[6] The Coal Fields of Great Britain, 2d Ed. pp. 28, 236.
[7] These numbers are represented to the eye in the diagram fronting the title-page.
[8] The sum of the geometrical series, in millions of tons,

$$83{\cdot}6 \left\{ 1 + 1{\cdot}035 + (1{\cdot}035)^2 + \ldots \ldots + (1{\cdot}035)^{109} \right\}$$

or, which is exactly the same, the value of the definite integral

$$\int_{0}^{110} 82{\cdot}17 \, (1{\cdot}035)^t \, dt$$

in which the constant 82.17 has been determined so that

$$\int_{0}^{1} 82{\cdot}17 \, (1{\cdot}035)^t \, dt = 83{\cdot}6.$$

[9] Mineral Statistics, Passim.
[10] P. Cooper, Mining Journal, Jan. 21, 1865.

Chapter Thirteen - Of the Export and Import of Coal

It has been suggested by many random thinkers that when our coal is done here, we may import it as we import so many other raw materials from abroad. "I can conceive," says one writer, "the coal-fields of this country so far exhausted, that the daughter in her maturity shall be able to pay back to the mother more than she herself received. May we not look forward to a time when those 'water-lanes' which both dissever and unite the old and new world, shall be trod by keels laden with the coal produce of America for the ports of Britain? and in such a traffic there will be abundant use for vessels as capacious and swift as the *Great Eastern*."

I am sorry to say that the least acquaintance with the principles of trade, and the particular circumstances of our trade, furnishes a complete negative to all such notions. *While the export of coal is a vast and growing branch of our trade, a reversal of the trade, and a future return current of coal, is a commercial impossibility and absurdity.*

But why, it may be asked, can we now export millions of tons of coal, and distribute them to all the ports of the globe, and yet cannot hope to bring back our lost riches in the improved vessels of the future? We have been able to reverse the woollen, linen, and cotton trades; to import the copper and tin and lead ores, which we used to draw from our own veins; to buy our supplies of food—wheat, dairy produce, butcher's meat, and eggs from abroad; and, even in such a bulky material as timber, to replace our own oak and elm and beech, by the deal and pine, mahogany and teak, of distant forests. If by our manufacturing skill we can thus successively reverse every great trade, buying raw materials with finished goods, instead of finished goods with raw materials, why not also reverse the coal-trade? Is not Free Trade the sheet anchor that will never fails us? Unfortunately not. *There is a false step of analogy in such reasoning*. Mark what accompanies the reversal of each branch of commerce - it is the increased employment of coal, and coal-driven labour at home, in the smelting-furnace or the factory. *The reversal of every other branch of trade is the work of coal, and the coal-trade cannot reverse itself*. And the facts which may be adduced concerning the coal-export trade, so strikingly illustrate the importance of our coal-mines to our maritime and commercial position, that I shall give, at some length, arguments which demonstrate, more than sufficiently, the impossibility of importing coal.

Trade is manifestly reciprocal, and free trade only allows the development of any peculiar excellence, or advantage, and the exchange of the products for those more easily procured else-where. One most peculiar advantage is the force which coal, skilfully used, places at our disposal. It is our last great resource—the one kind of wealth by the sufficient employment of which we might reverse every other trade, draw every other material from abroad until the kingdom was one immense Manchester, or one expanse of "Black Country." But take away that resource, and our expectations from free trade must be of a very minor character. "Easy access to the raw material," said Mr. Gladstone, "and abundant supplies of fuel, lead to the creation of manufactures. Put these two conditions together, and you have the combination which makes South Lancashire a busy manufacturing country, with the great town of Liverpool behind it." But observe that the fuel of South Lancashire is a condition as well as the raw material from abroad.

The truth is that if coal as well as other raw materials were found abroad in Pennsylvania, Prussia, New South Wales, or Brazil, the whole cost of freight would be a premium upon establishing the system of coal-supported industry on the spot. Even the narrow seas of St. George's and the English Channels are impassable by coal-driven industry. Ireland, especially Dublin, has drawn coal from Whitehaven time out of mind, for domestic purposes and local manufactures. But the practical non-existence of coal-mines in Ireland has rendered it impossible for any branch of manufacture consuming much coal to exist there. If a work paid at all in Ireland, there must be a margin of profit in transferring the work to an English coal-field. Similarly, it is explained in a recent very able Report [1] upon the coal-trade of France, that no great branch of coal-consuming industry could ever arise in France upon English coal.

"We cannot expect," says the reporter, M. Rouher, "to make foreign coal the basis of a great branch of industry. Coal is a cumbersome commodity, and its cost is doubled or tripled by lading and unlading, and conveying it 100 or 200 miles. To demand coal from England and compete with the products raised upon English coal-fields in manifestly to place ourselves in an inferiority. About two tons and a half of coal, for instance, are required to produce one ton of cast iron. It is much easier to draw our cast iron direct from Glasgow, than to transport a weight of coal two and a half times greater. It requires two or three tons of coal to convert cast iron into wrought iron; that is to say, five tons at least are needed to make wrought iron from the ore. It is most economical, then, to demand from England the finished article."

No one will properly understand the trade in coal who forgets that coal is the most bulky and weighty of all commodities. In this, as in other respects, it stands wholly by itself. No other commodity at all approaches it in the vast quantity required, and it is even said that the weight of coal carried over English railways is double the weight of all other merchandise put together. [2] The cost of carriage is the main element of price everywhere except in the coal-field, or its close neighbourhood. The best coal is put on board at Newcastle for 9s. per ton. Before it reaches France, it is about trebled; in the Mediterranean ports, Genoa, or Leghorn, it is quadrupled, while in many remote parts of the world coal cannot be purchased for less than 3*l.* or 3*l.* 10*s.* per ton. [3]

To go back to the suggestion with which we started, that our coal supplies will sometime be imported from America, let us consider that about 1,200 colliers of the size of the *Great Eastern* would be required to maintain our present supplies only. And whatever the size of the steam-vessels in which we may suppose the coal carried, their united tonnage would be at least five times the whole of our tonnage now employed in every trade and in every part of the world. The cost of such an unheard-of fleet would be the weight acting against us and in favour of American industry. And as all the colliers, railways, and canals cannot supply London with coal much under twenty shillings per ton, it is extravagant to suppose that coal could reach us from America for less than forty or sixty shillings per ton. Our industry would then have to contend with fuel, its all-important food, *eight or twelve times as dear as it now is in England and America.*

The complete commercial absurdity of the supposition renders any more accurate calculations superfluous.

But it is asked, How is a large export trade of coal possible, if an import trade is commercially impossible? This export trade is far the most weighty and wide-spread trade in the world. Taking the Mineral Statistics for 1862, we notice with some wonder that shipments of coal, in amounts from five tons up to 482,179 tons (Hamburg), are made to the following number of ports in the several countries:—

No. of Ports					
France...	122	Prussia...	17	Turkey...	17
Denmark...	135	Holland...	24	Africa... 22	
Norway...	50	Belgium...	7	Australia...	9
Sweden...	37	Spain... 36		East Indies...	34
Russia...25		Portugal...	8	West Indies...	37
Austria...	7	Italy... 18		North America... 38	
Germany...	54	Mediterranean... 18		South America... 43	
		Greece...	5	Channel Islands... 3	

119

Heligoland... 1	St. Helena... 1	Number of Coal-ports elsewhere... 203
Iceland... 1	Falkland Islands... 1	
Azores... 3	New Zealand... 4	
Canaries... 3	Sandwich Islands...1	**Total number of Coal-Ports... 783**
Madeira... 1	Number of Coal-Ports	
Ascension... 1	in Europe... 580	

In short, excluding some of the extremely distant North Pacific ports, it may be said that British coal is bought and consumed in every considerable port in the world. It competes on equal terms and gives the price to native coal or other fuel, in nearly all maritime parts of the world. This extraordinary fact is partly due to the unrivalled excellence of Newcastle and Welsh steam-coals, and the cheapness with which they can be put on board ship. But *it is mainly due to the fact that coal is carried as ballast, or makeweight, and is subject to the low rates of back-carriage.*

The subject of the variation of freights and their influence on the currents of trade is a very curious one, but has been so overlooked by writers on trade and economy, that I may be pardoned giving a few illustrations of its nature and importance.

Whether the mode of conveyance be by vessel, canal-boat, waggon, carriage, or pack-horse, the vehicle is always required to return back to the place whence it started. The whole gains of a trip must on the average pay all expenses and leave a margin for profit, but it is immaterial whether the necessary fare or freight-charges be paid on the whole, or any part of the journey. Usually, a hackney coach, post-chaise, or canal-boat starts full, upon its outward trip, without calculating upon any return fare. In hackney-coach regulations the return fare is usually fixed at half the chief fare, but in the case of post-chaises, canal-boats, and perhaps some other conveyances, the return fare is usually the perquisite of the drivers. In the old mode of pack-horse conveyance the same was probably the case.

The advantage of gaining something by a return journey is so obvious that journeys are often planned to allow of profitable return freights. For instance, in the days of pack-horse conveyance, Sir Francis Willoughby built Wollaton Hall, in 1580, of stone brought on horseback from Ancaster in Lincolnshire, thirty-five miles away, but it was arranged that the trains of pack-horses should load back with coal, which was taken in exchange for the stone. And when efforts were made at the beginning of this century to bring Staffordshire coal to London in order to destroy the previous monopoly of the northern coal-owners, it was expected that the expense of canal conveyance would be reduced by the back carriage of manure from London thirty or forty miles up the country, and of flints all the way from Harefield to the Potteries. [4]

The railway tolls on goods traffic, again, are not fixed at an uniform rate per ton, or per cubic foot, as might seem most fair and simple, but are adjusted in a complicated tariff so as to encourage as large a traffic as possible and give the best return. And one chief principle of this is to encourage back traffic by low or almost nominal rates. Trucks carrying various materials into towns may be used to carry manures and refuse out. Waggons carrying coals in one direction may carry back ores, slates, bricks, building-stone, flints, limestone, &c.

But it is in over-sea conveyance that we find the most important instances of the arrangement of freights.

In the year 1325 a vessel is recorded to have brought corn from France to Newcastle and to have returned laden with coal. This is one of the earliest notices of the coal-trade, but it furnishes the exact type of what it has ever since been, a simple exchange of cargoes. And King Charles seems to have been intelligently aware of the reciprocal nature of the coal-trade when at Oxford, in November 1643, he wrote to the Marquis of Newcastle to send a vessel full of coals to Holland and get much-needed arms in return. [5]

The following is perhaps the most remarkable example of an exchange of freight:— "In Cornwall there exist mines of copper and of tin, but none of coal. The copper ore, which requires the largest quantity of fuel for its reduction, is conveyed by ships to the coal-fields of Wales, and is smelted at Swansea, whilst the vessels which convey it take back cargoes of coal to supply the steam-engines for draining the mines, and to smelt the tin, which requires a much less quantity of fuel for that purpose." [6] In this way the copper-smelting trade has been carried across an arm of the sea and settled in a place where there is no copper ore, by the joint attraction of cheap fuel and gratuitous carriage. Vessels must have conveyed coals to the Cornish engines whether they brought back ores or not, and to carry coals for copper smelting too would require a second fleet or vessels.

The whole coasting trade of the British coasts is, and always has been, greatly dependent on coal. Coasters going to any point of the coast to bring away slates, stone, lime, agricultural produce, &c. go out from Liverpool, Cardiff, the Clyde, Newcastle, or other large ports, with a cargo of coals, which everywhere meets a ready sale. Double freights are thus ensured.

In many cases a more complicated circle of traffic is established. Vessels bringing iron from Cardiff to Liverpool, on its way to America, often go on with Lancashire coal to Ulverston, and return to Cardiff with the hæmatite ores required for mixture with the Welsh argillaceous ores. Vessels, again, carrying slates or stone to Bristol from the Welsh quarries often take steam-coal to Liverpool and return to the welsh coast with bituminous coal for household use, the difference of quality being sufficient to establish an exchange trade. By such natural arrangements, not only are the great currents of industrial traffic bound together into one profitable whole, but coal is supplied cheaply to all parts of the coast, where it is landed at the nearest convenient place to a village, or group of villages, and retailed from a central coal-yard. The household coal, with smith's small coal, culm for lime-burning, draining-tiles, and a few other articles, form the only common and general coasting cargoes. On the other hand, whenever there is a great preponder-ance of freight in one direction, the shipping must necessarily return empty like the railway coal-waggons from London. The sailing or steam-colliers which supply the London market not only have no outward freight as a usual thing, but they have to purchase ballast in the Thames and discharge it in the Tyne. The ballast-wharves of the Tyne are often mentioned in the very early history of Newcastle, and the heaps of gravel, and stones, and rubbish drawn from the ships have grown from those days to these.

"To carry on the coasting trade in coal to London, 10,000 tons of gravel are weekly supplied in the Thames, and establishments in the North are actually paid for discharging and conveying it to a convenient place of deposit." [7]

At one period of his life, George Stephenson was brakesman to the fixed engine which hauled up the ballast upon the heap, "a monstrous accumula-tion of earth, chalk, and Thames mud, already laid there to form a puzzle for future antiquarians." [8] And Stephenson often earned extra wages in the evening by taking a turn at heaving the ballast out of the collier vessels, while his engine was taken in charge by his friend Fairbairn.

In the foreign trade the influence of freights is far more distinct and im-portant. A ship is often chartered for a specific voyage out and home, freight being provided both ways; but more commonly the homeward freight is the chief object the British shipowner aims at, and he sends the ship out often at a loss upon the outward passage, depending upon the captain or foreign agents to find a profitable home cargo. This important circumstance concern-ing the shipping and trading interests has often been alluded to, in pam-phlets, speeches, or parliamentary reports. Dr. Buckland, for instance, thus explained the curious fact that Netherland coal was exported to America and avoided France, so much in want of it for her manufactures, by attributing it to the want of back carriage. [9] Mr. T. Y. Hall, again, stated clearly:— "The owners of vessels trading between England and France find that coal an-swers the purpose of ballast when other goods cannot be obtained at remu-nerative freights." [10] But the most distinct statement is in a pamphlet called forth by Sir Robert Peel's proposal, in 1842, to revive the export tax on coal. [11]

"The proposed duty would produce also an indirect but injurious effect upon the importation of the raw materials of manufactures into this country at the lowest cost. It is well known that most of these articles are of a bulky nature; it is important to reduce the expense of freight upon them, and this the present facility for exporting coal secures to a considerable degree, being an article that provides an outward freight to a ship. This is peculiarly illus-trated in the Baltic, from whence tallow, hemp, flax, and timber, articles of low value but great bulk, constitute the objects of imports, while our princi-pal articles of export are indigo, cochineal, dyes, drugs, gums, &c., articles of great value but small bulk; so that it is necessary to have some compensating article of low value for our own exportation, to equalize and reduce the rate of freight. The same reasoning applies to our imports from the Mediterranean, and indeed most places of our intercourse from whence we derive our raw materials; while the export of common goods, such as anchors, chains, and other heavy commodities, of which whole cargoes can never be made up, had materially increased at Newcastle and Sunderland since the facility of shipment of coal by exporting ships has been provided."

In British trade, especially under the present free-trade policy, there is a great preponderance of homeward cargoes. Our imports consist of bulky raw materials and food. Nearly the whole of the corn, fruits, live stock, provisions, sugar, coffee, tea, tobacco, spirits, are consumed here. Timber, hemp, guano, hides, bones, with dye and tan materials; such as logwood, indigo, valonia, are either consumed here, or contribute little to the bulk of our exports. Cotton, silk, wool, and flax are either used up in this country, or returned of a smaller bulk. Our exports of cast and wrought iron, hardwares, and general manufactures are rather heavy than bulky, and of a far higher value than the imports proportionally to the bulk. A large part of our shipping would thus have to leave our ports half empty, or in ballast, unless there were some makeweight or natural supply of bulky cargo as back carriage.

Salt to some extent supplies the Liverpool shipowners with outward cargo, and it is remarkable that the tenth Earl of Dundonald, a man as ingenious and energetic as the late Earl, clearly foresaw the value of the salt-trade in this respect, and urged its extension upon the nation in an able pamphlet [12] of the year 1785. Though the Northern nations then drew their salt from Spain, Portugal, or Sardinia, he held that "salt may become a great article of export trade from this country" to Flanders, Holland, part of Germany, Prussia, Norway, Denmark, Sweden, and Russia, because two-thirds of the outward-going vessels to some of these countries sail in ballast, making their freight upon their homeward voyage, and it was not to be doubted that they would rather accept half freights which, however small, are a clear gain, than incur the cost of ballast. Our export of salt exactly fulfils the purpose explained by the Earl, but on a more extensive scale than he could possibly have anticipated. In 1861 about 700,000 tons of salt were exported from England, by far the largest part of which comes down the Weaver from the Cheshire works to Liverpool, and is there shipped. [13]

There is a curious relation too between the earthenware manufacture and the shipping interest of the Western ports. From early times indeed the Staffordshire earthenware trade has presented a remarkable instance of the arrangement of freights. The materials of earthenware, fuel, flintstones, and clay are never found together like the materials of the iron manufacture; the finished earthenware too is of so bulky a nature when packed in crates, that a large part of its cost depends upon the cost of conveyance. Proximity to a coal-field is the first requisite of a pottery; proximity to a market the next requisite. Both these requisites are combined in the Staffordshire potteries. In the days of pack-horse conveyance their central position was of great importance, because the pack-horses, which brought the flints and clay from the nearest ports, could be used to carry and distribute the crockery slung in crates over the horses' backs. The flints were brought from the chalk districts of the south-east of England, by sea to Hull, and thence up the Trent as far as possible; while the clay came from Devonshire and Cornwall, either by the Severn as far as Bewdley, or up the Mersey and Weaver to Winsford. [14]

In later days the early opening of canal communication and the commercial proximity of the potteries to Liverpool have been of the highest importance to both. So much iron and other heavy articles are shipped at Liverpool, that the shipowners need some light, bulky article to fill up the higher parts of the ships' holds. A considerable part of the produce of the Staffordshire potteries, accordingly, goes to Liverpool, the export of crockery being stimulated by the favourable freights offered. And such is the demand for crockery at the port, that several attempts have been made to attract the manufacture itself to Liverpool or Birkenhead. Further, the Clyde shipowners, having a great superfluity of heavy iron cargoes, and experiencing a like want of light freight to complete the loading of their ships, have actually attempted to create a pottery manufacture about Glasgow with that purpose. [15]

At Liverpool indeed the whole products of the Lancashire factories, the earthenware and hardware of Staffordshire, the iron of South Wales, added to the salt of Cheshire, furnish a large mass of outward cargo, and the export of coal has hitherto been of minor importance. But with the progress of trade, that port will receive such immense masses inwards, that outward cargoes of coal will come more into demand. In 1850, Mr. William Laird urged the suitability of Liverpool for the export of coal, and there cannot be a doubt that in the natural progress of our trade, coal-staiths at Liverpool or Runcorn, supplied by direct lines from the South Lancashire field, will ship great amounts of coal ballast.

At other ports coal is, and long has been, an inestimable benefit to the shipowners. It is destructive to their profits to keep a vessel long in port waiting for cargo, and it is worse to send her off in ballast. Where there are coal-staiths, however, she can be loaded and dispatched in a day or two, with a cargo that will at least pay expenses, and find a ready sale in any part of the world. It is on this principle that the Manchester, Sheffield, and Lincolnshire Railway are raising Grimsby into a port. Just in proportion, it is found, as they offer outward cargoes of coal can they induce vessels to resort to the port with their inward cargoes.

It is in the rates of freight that we can best study the relative demand and supply of cargo. A want of outward cargo causes shipowners to bid for what is to be had, and reduce their prices of freight accordingly. Were there no ballast cargo like coal available, the outward rates must become quite nominal, until it would be profitable to send bricks, flagstones, and paving stones on long sea voyages. But the fact that coal may always be shipped establishes a certain minimum rate of freight depending upon the price at which we can compete with foreign coal or other fuel, and force a trade so essential to our shipowners.

In the current rates of freight (May, 1864) we may detect many effects of demand and supply, as well as a general confirmation of the facts stated. Thus the outward freight to Bombay is only 20s. per ton, the homeward freight being 60s. or three times as much, owing to the large shipments thence of cotton, rice, seeds, &c. The outward rate to Aden, however, is 30s. and to Suez 50s., owing chiefly to the considerable demand at those points for coal for the Peninsular and Oriental Mail steamers, with the absence of freights thence.

At the following Eastern ports the large preponderance of the homeward freights of cotton, sugar, tea, jute, and other Eastern produce, causes the inward to exceed the outward coal-freight several times.

	Outward.		Homeward.	
	s.	*d.*	*s.*	*d.*
Calcutta...	17	6	75	0
Singapore...	27	0	75	0
Shanghai...	40	0	72	10
Mauritius...	20	0	50	0

In South America, again, the demand for carriage of hides, bones, nitrate of soda, &c. raises the freight to England in a considerable ratio.

	Outward.		Homeward.	
	s.	*d.*	*s.*	*d.*
Rio de Janeiro...	28	0	45	0
Pernambuco...	19	0	41	0
Rio Grande...	40	0	50	0

Throughout the West Indies the demand for shipment of coffee, sugar, logwood, mahogany, &c. raises home freights to double the outward.

	Outward.		Homeward.	
	s.	*d.*	*s.*	*d.*
Porto Rico...	25	6	52	6
Jamaica...	28	0	43	0
St. Jago de Cuba...	27	0	60	0
Havannah...	27	6	55	0

The homeward freights from New York chiefly depend upon the shipments of corn. Taking the rate at 6s. and 3d. per quarter, we find the following relation by weight:—

	Outward.		Homeward.	
	s.	*d.*	*s.*	*d.*
New York...	22	0	30	0

For Canadian ports there is a greater disproportion, owing to the inward excess for timber freights and the less outward demand.

	Outward.		Homeward.	
	s.	d.	s.	d.
Montreal (wheat)...	—	30	0	
Halifax...	17	0	—	

In the Mediterranean ports there is far less disproportion on the average, and it is curious that the preponderance of freights is opposite at the two ends. At the lower, or Western ports, outward exceed inward freights, as at Marseilles.

	Outward.		Homeward.	
	s.	d.	s.	d.
Marseilles...	20	0	16	0

At the higher or Eastern ports on the contrary, the fruit freights from the Archipelago, or the wheat, tallow, and other freights from the Black Sea, raise the homeward rates as follows:—

	Outward.		Homeward.	
	s.	d.	s.	d.
Smyrna...	23	6	37	6
Odessa...	23	0	45	0

On the West Coast of South America we meet with an immense excess of homeward cargo. Not only are there large quantities of nitrate of soda, copper ore, and wool to ship to Europe, but there is also the guano trade from Callao, a most remarkable instance of the conveyance of bulky material. Now, as our coal has to compete with the native Chilian bituminous coal on most unequal terms, we find the following immense disproportion of outward coal and homeward guano freights.

	Outward.		Homeward.	
	s.	d.	s.	d.
Callao...	24	0	80	0

A curious exchange has recently sprung up of Newcastle coal for Spanish or Esparto grass, a material much required to make paper for *The Times* newspaper, and the vast masses of recent periodical literature. The following are the rates:—

Outward to the Spanish Ports.		Homeward to Tyne.	
s.	d.	s.	d.
23	0	18	0

The demand for coal apparently is so good in Spain that the coal bears almost the same freight as if sent to the West Coast of South America! And thus while we almost make the Peruvians a present of our coal, the Spaniards in a less degree may be said to make us a present of the materials of paper.

With few exceptions, then, homeward freights are in excess of outward freights from one and a half to three or four-fold. And the very exceptions, arising from an extraordinary foreign demand for coal would, if examined, confirm the view of the important part that coal plays in our trade.

That the facilities for getting coal freights from Newcastle and the other Eastern coal-ports appreciably reduce rates of freights to those ports is clearly shown in the following rates from Dantzig to the east coast of England, during 1861 [16] :—

	Timber per Load.		Wheat Per Quarter.
	s.	d.	s. d.
To Coal Ports...	14	0	3 1½
To other ports...	17	3	3 9

Thirty years ago it was stated that there was no considerable amount of back freight for vessels bringing timber from Memel except coal. [17]

One of the most curious effects of the balance of freights is seen in the North American coal trade. In 1862 we shipped coal to the amount of 448,601 tons to thirty-eight ports of the United States, Canada, and the other British Colonies on the Western seaboard of North America. At the same time an export trade in coal is constantly carried on from the Cape Breton mines, along the coast to New York and Philadelphia. Lastly, there is a trade in American coals to the extent, in 1860, of 140,607 tons from the Pennsylvanian field to the West Indian Islands, probably by the return voyage of vessels bringing sugar, coffee, fruits, and other tropical products. Such a circulation of a bulky, cheap commodity like coal, and the fact that coal is actually shipped to Philadelphia, the port of the American coal-fields, is as paradoxical as carrying coals to Newcastle, and is inexplicable except as a consequence of the balance of freights.

It would be difficult to over-estimate the benefits the trade in coal has conferred upon us. Writers for some centuries back have been unanimous in regarding the Newcastle collier fleet as the nursery of our seamen. The "Newcastle voyage is...if not the onely, yet the especiall nursery and schoole of seamen: For, as it is the chiefest, so it is the gentlest, and most open to landmen." [18] And no one could better have expressed than the writer of the above, the way in which an Englishman regards a ship. "As concerning ships, it is that which every one knoweth, and can say, they are our weapons, they are our ornaments, they are our strength, they are our pleasures, they are our defence, they are our profit; the subject by them is made rich, the Kingdome through them strong; the Prince in them is mighty; in a word by them in a manner we live, the kingdome is, the king reigneth." [19]

Another able anonymous writer, in arguing against the old 5s. tax upon seaborne coal, expresses similar views, his chief purpose being "to show how pernicious this tax upon coal is to Trade and Navigation, the safety and glory of England." [20]

"The collier trade is the true parent and support of our navigation."

"The collier fleet," he says again, [21] "is the great body of the shipping of England, and all our other trades are served by detachments from it. Our East country, Norway, and a great part of the West Indian fleet, are but parts of the collier fleet; from which they may depart one or two voyages in the year, as the contingency of the market abroad, or a chance freight at home offers. From which as soon as performed, they return again into the collier trade; that is indeed, the refuge, as well as the nursery of our navigation." But in the following he expresses still more exactly the part that coal now plays in our coasting and foreign shipping. "It's the collier trade alone that affords constant work to the navigation of England. It is there that every idle ship and every idle saylor are sure never to want a voyage or a berth to Newcastle." [22]

"The collier trade is the most huge and bulky trade that possibly can be managed, and therefore in its nature most proper, above all others, to employ not only vast numbers of people upon it, but to afford continual work for them. All our other trades are by fits and starts. Ships and sailors must have constant work." [23]

And the French so clearly perceive the maritime advantages this trade gives, that they attribute to us in the present day the policy of promoting exportation.

"The English Government uses every possible means to stimulate an exportation which contributes powerfully to its maritime preponderance without hurting its industrial preponderance." [24]

And the Newcastle manufacturers are well aware of the advantages they enjoy.

"The ready communication," they say, "which has been obtained with foreign ports, by means of the numerous vessels employed in the exportation of coals, has greatly facilitated the sale of the various articles manufactured by your memorialists, and has consequently increased the value of property employed in manufactures in this district." [25]

Our exports of coal now amount to about nine million tons in a year, the sale of which in foreign ports must return fully four millions sterling to our coalowners, and six millions or more in the shape of freight to our shipowners. To prohibit this trade would therefore be to incur a burden equal to the income tax at its worst. And though the greater part of this burden would be borne by the community in general as the consumers of foreign produce, it would be inflicted through that branch of our industry, our navigation, which is truly the safety and glory of England.

But on the other hand we cannot look upon our growing exports without anxiety. The following numbers show the extraordinary rate of growth since the repeal of the export tax:—

EXPORT OF COAL.

Year.	Amount of Coal exported.	Coal duty per ton.		Rate of increase per cent of exports in ten years.
	Tons.	s	d.	
1821	170,941	7	6	
1831	356,419	4	0	109
1841	1,497,197	0	0	320
1851	3,468,545	0	0	132
1861	7,855,115	0	0	126
1865	9,170,477	0	0	47

Our exports were more than quadrupled in ten years under a repeal of the duty, and have more than doubled themselves in each subsequent ten years. And though there is a slight check in the last few years, from some fluctuation of commerce, no one can doubt that the extension of our commerce and the growth of continental industry will demand a continued increase of exports.

"Independent of the superiority of the article, the freights of vessels from our shores are getting so low, and the distance between Great Britain and the coast of France is so short, that we shall always be able to have the advantage over Belgian and even French coal in the seaport towns."

And the inevitable progress of free trade will ever increase the tendency to export coal. As we subsist more and more upon foreign corn, meat, sugar, rice, coffee, tea, fruit, &c. and work more and more on foreign timber, ores, cotton, silk, wool, dye-woods, oils, seeds, &c. while returning the costly and elaborate products of our steam-driven factories, there must be an ever-growing surplus of inward freights and a corresponding demand for outward ballast freights.

Our foreign coal trade has been, is, and will be an integral and essential part of our system. It is the alpha and omega of our trade. As it was the earliest nursery of our seamen, so it is now their especial support, and it bids fair to hasten us to an early end. It makes our limited fields the common property of the sea-coast inhabitants of all countries. The Newcastle mines are almost as high a benefit to the French, Dutch, Prussian, Danish, Norwegian, Russian, Spanish, and Italian coast-towns, as to our own. And foreigners not unnaturally think we are simple enough in thus lending ourselves to them. "It has often been repeated, for some time past, that there is one simple means of competing with England in her manufactures. It is to buy her coal from her, and England has lent herself to this design by developing and facilitating her exportation of coal in every possible way." [26]

The extraordinary progress of our steam marine was noticed in a previous chapter. Its close connexion with the export trade of coal cannot escape attention. Our lines of steam-vessels create a demand for coal at the most distant and widely extended points of the globe; while low, outward freights enable coal to be sent cheaply to those points. Accordingly, as long as Britain maintains her present commercial and maritime position, not only the continental and other sea-coasts, in most parts of the world, but also the greater part of the steam-vessels plying on every sea, will draw their supplies from those seaboard coal-fields of Newcastle, South Wales, the Clyde, and the Mersey, which, taken as a whole, in the various quality of their fuel, in their facilities of shipment, and their supply of over-sea freight, are wholly unrivalled by any other coal-fields.

The absurdity of the notion of this country importing coals on any large scale, will now be apparent. The fact that we now export large quantities of coal instead of showing the possibility of a return current, shows its commercial impossibility. The coal exported acts as a make-weight, to remedy in some degree the one-sided character of our trade. Coal is to us that one great raw material which balances the whole mass of the other raw materials we import, and which we pay for either by coal in its crude form, or by manufactures which represent a greater or less quantity of coal consumed in the steam-engine, or the smelting furnace. To import coal as well as other raw materials would be against the essentially reciprocal nature of trade. The weight of our inward cargoes would be multiplied many times, and but little weight left for outward carriage; almost every influence which now acts, and for centuries has acted, in favour of our maritime and manufacturing success, would then act against it, and it would be arrogance and folly indeed to suppose that even Britain can carry forward her industry in spite of nature, and in the want of every material condition. In our successes hitherto it is to nature we owe at least as much as to our own energies.

[1] Situation de l'Industrie Houillère en 1859, p. 8.

[2] Situation de l'Industrie Houillère en 1859, p. 53.

[3] Ryder. Treatise on the Economy of Fuel on board Men-of-War Steamers, p. 3.

[4] Second Report on the Coal-Trade, 1800, p. 22.

[5] Brand's History of Newcastle, vol. ii. p. 286.

[6] Babbage in Barlow's Cyclopædia, 1851, p. 55.

[7] Dunn on the Winning and Working of Coal Mines, p. 338.

[8] Smiles' Lives of the Engineers, vol. iii. pp. 38-41.

[9] Report on the Coal-Trade, 1830.

[10] Trans. N. of England Institute of Mining Engineers, vol. vi. p. 106.

[11] Observations on the proposed Duties on the Exportation of Coals. London, 1842, pp. 14, 15.

[12] The Present State of the Manufacture of Salt Explained. By the Earl of Dundonald. London: 1785.

[13] Braithwaite Poole. On the Commerce of Liverpool, 1854, p. 33.

[14] Smiles' Engineers, vol. i. p. 447.

[15] Hearn's Plutology, p. 310, quoting Journal of the Statistical Society, vol. xx. p. 134.

[16] Commercial Reports from Foreign Consuls, 1862, p. 155

[17] Committee on Manufactures, 1833. Queries, 7,420-5, &c.

[18] The Trades' Increase, p. 25.

[19] The Trades' Increase, p. 2.

[20] The Mischief of the Five-Shilling Tax upon Coal. London, 1699, p. 3

[21] Ibid. p. 5.

[22] The Mischief of the Five-Shilling Tax upon Coal. London, 1699, p. 5.

[23] Ibid. p. 6.

[24] Situation de l'Ind. &c. p. 27.

[25] Memorial of the Manufacturers of the Tyne, of iron, lead, glass, rope, alkali, sail-cloth, &c. (1842?)

[26] Situation de l'Industrie Houillère en 1859.

Chapter Fourteen - On the Comparative Coal Resources of Different Countries

It is essential to our inquiry to view the several coal-producing countries comparatively. Thus only can we gain a true notion of our singular position.

The following statement gives the amounts of coal raised about the years 1858-1860, in the chief coal-producing countries:—

	Annual production. Tons.
Great Britain, 1860...	80,042,698
United States...	14,333,922 [1]
British American Possessions...	1,500,000 [2]
New South Wales...	250,000
Prussia, Saxony, &c...	12,000,000
Belgium...	8,900,000
France...	7,900,000
Russian Empire (estimated)...	1,500,000
Austria...	1,162,900
Spain...	300,000
Japan, China, Borneo, &c. (estimated)...	2,000,000

[1] Reports respecting Coal, 1866, p. 147.

[2] Hull, Coal Fields of Great Britain, 2d ed. p. 29; and Situation de l'Ind. &c. p. 111, quoting a report of M. Gonot, Ingénieur en chef des Mines du Hainaut, 1858.

Of a total produce of 130 millions of tons, 96 millions are produced by nations of British origin and language, and 80 millions are produced in Great Britain itself.

Of the chief material agent of modern civilization, three parts out of five, or 60 per cent. are in the use of Great Britain; and nearly three parts out of four, or 75 per cent. are in the use of Anglo-Saxon nations.

The reader must form for himself, if he can, an adequate notion of the stimulus which the possession of such a mighty power gives to our race.

Let us compare the amounts with the comparative stores of coal existing in the several countries which have been explored. The actual quantities of coal, indeed, are almost wholly unknown; we can only compare the supposed areas of the coal-fields. This has been done by Professor Rogers, in the following statements: [1] —

	Area of Coal Lands in square miles.
United States...	196,650
British North American Possessions...	7,530
Great Britain...	5,400
France...	984
Prussia...	960
Belgium...	510
Bohemia...	400
Westphalia...	380
Spain...	200
Russia...	100
Saxony...	30

Such estimates indeed can pretend to no accuracy, and the area of a coal-field is but slight measure of its value. We can only learn from the statement that our English coal-fields are many times as important as those of any European country, but that the North American coal-fields almost indefinitely surpass ours in extent, and, it may be added, in contents.

Coal may also be said to exist more or less in most other parts of the world—in India, China, Japan, Labuan, New Zealand, Australia, Brazil, Chili, and Central Africa. Many details concerning the frequent occurrence of coal may be found in R. C. Taylor's "Statistics of Coal," [2] but they have in reality little bearing upon our inquiry. With the exception of the great North American fields, none are at all capable of competing in quality or extent with our coal-fields. They will prove very useful in furnishing a supply for local industry and steam navigation. Upon and around each coal-field will grow up, we hope, a prosperous community, enjoying those uses of coal which older nations are discovering; but the only way in which those coal-fields could interfere with, and reduce the consumption of our coal would be, either by—

1. Supplying sea-board coal markets which we now supply, or

2. Supporting a system of manufacturing industry capable of competing with ours.

Now, if the comparatively cumbersome and heavy nature of coal be considered, it will be seen that the cost of conveyance is a main element. A small extent of mountainous country, a considerable distance from a port, or a position far from the general current of trade, removes a coal-field from competition. Thus the French Official Report regards the difficulty and cost of conveyance as the great obstacle in the way of the French coal-mines. Otherwise, without being comparable with English fields, they are rich enough for home consumption. [3] "In France the deposits of combustible mineral are numerous, but there is only a small number which are susceptible, either from their extension or the quality of their products, of development upon a great scale. Most of these basins, too, are situated in mountainous countries, difficult of access, where lines of communication have penetrated but slowly and at great cost. This circumstance explains why at present the price of coal at market exceeds, in a very high proportion, the wholesale price at the pit mouth."

An English report expresses a similar opinion.

"At St. Etienne, the heart of the French mining district, coal can be extracted as low as in Wales, and the expense of it throughout France is imputed to the absence of easy lines of carriage and communication, which enable English coal to be sold on the French coast at a profit." [4]

On the other hand, the favourable natural conditions of our mines are thus described by the writers of the French report: [5] —

"England is the most favoured country of Europe in the extent and richness of its coal-fields. Its superiority is confirmed by the varied and generally excellent quality of its coal, and by a regularity of the strata very favourable to the working of coal-mines.

"Lastly, as if nature had striven to unite in these coal-fields all the circumstances most conducive to mining and trading in coal, the two richest basins, those of Wales and Newcastle, are intersected by the sea. The coal-owners can load and ship their products in the most economical manner, and thus consign them to any point of the home or continental coasts.

"Over-sea conveyance, too, is the more cheap, because in English commerce the outward voyage may be considered as a voyage in ballast, and the return freight covers the chief part of the expenses.

"A like union of favourable conditions does not present itself at any other point of the globe, and constitutes a natural privilege with which no other country can entertain the notion of contending as regards industry founded upon the working and trading in coal. Any attempt at competition of the kind would necessarily be followed by defeat."

Foreign coal-fields then are almost wholly excluded from competition with ours as regards sea-borne coal, because even if there were any coal-fields comparable with ours, in intrinsic natural advantages, there would still be wanting the extrinsic advantages of the vast trading system and the mercantile marine of England capable of conveying and distributing the coal. In a great many parts of the world, at Sydney, Cape Breton, at Newcastle in Australia, Labuan, Chili, Asturias in Spain, and on the coast of the Black Sea, there are seams of coal almost abutting on the sea, but the set of trade and navigation in the wrong direction enables, or rather obliges, us to carry our coals out to these local Newcastles. And if coal situated actually on the sea-board cannot drive our coal away, the high cost of land conveyance completely removes all inland coal-fields from direct competition with our mines in the general sea-board coal markets of the world.

That French and continental mines generally cannot possibly compete with our coal mines is further shown in the remarks of Mr. R. C. Taylor: [6] —

"It is due to the unrivalled accessibility by sea to the best coal basins of England, Scotland, and Wales—where coals of many varieties and admirable qualities can be shipped at the very sites where they are mined—that Great Britain has hitherto been able to furnish such enormous and cheap supplies, not only to the home consumers, but nearly to every maritime country in Europe. In this respect she is far more favourably circumstanced than her rival continental producers, France, Belgium, Prussia, and Austria, whose coal-fields lie remote from the sea-shore.

"From Dunkirk to Bayonne, an extent of 300 leagues of coast, there are but two coal-fields, and those are at some distance from the sea. In regard also to the quality of the coal, France is less fortunate than England; for with the exception of the basins of Anzin, St. Etienne, and a few others, the collieries of the interior yield but an inferior species of fuel. Both these circumstances combine to render France, to a certain extent, dependent upon Great Britain for the better sorts of coal; and hence the French Government annually make large and increasing contracts for the delivery of English coal at their depôts, for the use of their steam marine on service. The incapability of Belgium, with her increasing domestic consumption, and in view of her diminished powers of production, and the remoteness of her coal-fields from the sea-ports, to supply the steam navy of France with any material portion of its regular fuel, is perfectly well understood....

"The manner in which the coal-tracts of Great Britain are distributed, is fortunately such that every coal-field in England and Wales can meet the next adjoining coal-field nearly on a radius of thirty miles, thus forming such a range of deposits, from Scotland to South Wales and Somersetshire, that the whole interior of the country can be supplied with coals, through the railroad system, from several central points."

So long then as the currents of trade and navigation continue in their present general course, there are no coal-fields capable of competing with and reducing the demand for our coal in regard to the over-sea coal-trade. The only other way in which a foreign coal-field could affect the prosperity of our coal-consuming industry would be by nourishing abroad great systems of manufacturing industry capable of withdrawing from us a part of the custom of the world which we now enjoy as regards coal-made articles almost to the extent of a monopoly.

It there were plenty of good coal in France, such a system of iron and coal industry might rise upon it as at any rate to deprive us of the custom of French consumers. Strange to say, this result has taken place to some extent. The good order and enlightened commercial policy of the Imperial Government has had such an extraordinary effect upon French industry, that the produce of coal from the interior French mines has advanced at the rate of 6.7 per cent. per annum—at nearly double the rate of increase of our consumption of coal. The French iron manufacture has advanced in a manner equally surprising, so that instances are not uncommon now of English orders for iron goods being executed in France! And it is no doubt owing to this advance of French industry in a manner parallel to our own, that the French treaty of commerce has had much less remarkable results than was expected. Even the imports of coal into France have remained stationary, as seen in the following accounts:—

	Coal raised in France.	Coal imported.	Coal consumed in France.
	Tons.	Tons.	Tons.
1860...	7,900,000	5,900,000	13,800,000 [1]
1862...	9,400,000	5,900,000	15,300,000 [2]

[1] Situation de l'Industrie Houillère, p. 7.
[2] Journal of Science, No. 2, pp. 337, 338.

The natural riches and skill of the French are, however, so comparatively higher in many other branches of industry, that it cannot be supposed the competition of their coal industry can proceed far, or prove permanent and formidable.

The extraction of coal in Belgium, again, has been increasing at the rate of 2.7 per cent. per annum, as seen in the following accounts of the extraction:—

	Tons.
1854...	7,950,000
1859...	9,160,702
1862...	9,935,645
1863...	10,345,000

But the Belgian coal-proprietors are afraid that the produce of their mines has nearly reached its maximum. The fact is that the Belgian mines have been worked longer than our Newcastle mines, and have reached still greater depths. They are further advanced towards exhaustion than our own; and as their produce is not one-eighth part of our coal-produce, it would be absurd to suppose that they can support any industry capable of seriously competing with ours.

Prussia, by its somewhat inland position, as well as for other reasons, is also incapable of taking any considerable share of the trade of the world, and no other European country has coal mines worth consideration here.

It is only when we turn to North America that we meet a country capable of comparing in coal resources with our own, and the future of England greatly depends therefore upon the future of America. The areas of American and British coal-fields have already been compared, and the current statement is sufficiently true, that the American fields exceed ours as 37 to 1.

Canada, indeed, is devoid of any trace of the coal-measures, and presents a remarkable contrast to the regions by which it is surrounded. The British American Provinces of Newfoundland, New Brunswick, and Nova Scotia contain the North-easterly extensions of the great American fields. But so far as yet known the coal-measures are here more interesting to the geologist than to the economist. Their area is very considerable, and the seams are numerous, but are spread through masses of strata many thousand feet in thickness. Thus the Cumberland coal-field in Nova Scotia, according to Prof. Rogers, has an area of 6,889 square miles, exceeding the whole area of British coal-fields. But the greater portion consists of the lower and upper carboniferous strata, destitute of valuable coal-seams. The thickness of the whole series of rocks is not less than 14,570 feet. [7] The Sydney coal-field with an area of 250 square miles, and a thickness of about 10,000 feet of strata, is of more present importance, since four seams of workable coal crop out at Sydney Harbour, and are easily available for an export trade so far as shipping can be had.

It is, however, the basin of the Mississippi which contains the main mass of productive coal-measures. There is reason to suppose that the carboniferous formation was originally spread in one continuous sheet over the whole of Central America, from the flanks of the Rocky Mountains to the shores of the North Atlantic, and from the Gulf of Mexico to Newfoundland. Large portions must have been removed by denudation, but enough remains in five distinct fields of which the areas are thus stated by Prof. Rogers:

Basin	Length Miles	Breadth Miles	Area Miles
Appalachian...	875	180	55,500
Illinois, Indiana, and Kentucky...	370	200	51,100
Missouri and Arkansas...	550	200	73,913
Michigan...	160	125	13,350
Texas...	160		3,000

Total area, 196,863 square miles.

The Appalachian field is of the highest economic importance. On the east-ward it has been crumpled up into the series of ranges forming the Alleghany Mountains. At the same time the bituminous portion of the coal has been more or less distilled off, producing the anthracite coal of Mauch Chunk and the other Eastern Pennsylvanian mines. The seams of coal, however, retain their bituminous character and their horizontal position on the west of the Alleghany Mountains. "In that less elevated country, the coal-measures are intersected by three great navigable rivers, and are capable of supplying for ages, to the inhabitants of a densely-peopled region, an inexhaustible supply of fuel. These rivers are the Monongahela, the Alleghany, and the Ohio, all of which lay open on their banks the level seams of coal. Looking down the first of these at Brownsville, we have a fine view of the main seam of bituminous coal ten feet thick, commonly called the Pittsburg seam, breaking out in the steep cliff at the water's edge.... Horizontal galleries may be driven every-where at very slight expense, and so worked as to drain themselves; while the cars, laden with coal and attached to each other, glide down on a railway, so as to deliver their burden into barges moored to the river's bank. The same seam is seen at a distance, on the right bank, and may be followed the whole way to Pittsburg, fifty miles distant. As it is nearly horizontal while the river descends, it crops out at a continually increasing, but never at an incon-venient, height above the Monongahela. Below the great bed of coal at Brownsville is a fire-clay eighteen inches thick; and below this, several beds of limestone, below which again are other coal seams. I have also shown in my sketch another layer of workable coal, which breaks out on the slope of the hills at a greater height. Here almost every proprietor can open a coal-pit on his own land, and the stratification being very regular, he may calculate with precision the depth at which coal may be won." [8]

The Appalachian coal-field, of which these strata form a part, is remarkable for its vast area. According to Professor H. D. Rogers, it stretches continuous-ly from N.E. to S.W. for a distance of 720 miles, its greatest width being about 180 miles. On a moderate estimate its superficial area amounts to 63,000 square miles.

We have no extensive seams of coal now which can compare in ease of working with those above described. The "thick coal" of Staffordshire almost within the memory of those now living might be comparable, and four or five centuries ago it is supposed there were seams on the bank of the Tyne, and at Whitehaven, which could be worked by natural drainage, and with the great-est ease. But shallow coal has necessarily almost disappeared in England. The consequence is that we cannot now produce coal, even with the aid of the best engineering skill, and of abundant trained labour, nearly so cheap as it can be had on the banks of the Ohio. At Pittsburg the best bituminous coal may be had at one-half, or one-third the general price at European mines, as shown in the following comparative table of prices at the pit: [9] —

		s	d		s	d.
France...		6	0	to	14	0
Germany...		7	0	to	10	0
England...		6	0	to	10	0
Pennsylvania (anthracite)...		8	0	to	9	0
Pittsburg (bituminous)...		2	0	to	4	0

In short, on the Western coal-fields coal can be obtained at the expense of digging it; that is, at a cost of a cent or a cent and a quarter per bushel. [10]

Beyond the reach of doubt there is no portion of the earth's surface so naturally fitted for becoming the seat of great industries "What is the value, it may be asked," in the words of an American writer, [11] "of 63,000 square miles of country, which yields coal, iron, oil, and salt, beneath its fertile soil? Here are the elements of strength, heat, light, food, and the giant steam, opened at once to the science, skill, and untiring energy of an enterprising people."

It can excite no surprise that a people of British extraction, endowed with the absolute possession of lands so rich, so extensive, and so easily accessible as those of the United States, should spread and multiply. It is nature in its kindest and most liberal mood that has chiefly contributed to the growth of the United States. And a certain remarkable talent for the application and invention of all practical devices for saving labour and overcoming obstacles is the next chief attribute of the American nation that concerns us here. The moral and political characteristics of that people, and the influence they may exert for good or for evil upon the world, are not here in question.

But why does not such wonderful wealth in coal affect our prosperity already, if so much depends upon the price of coal? It is because America has not and cannot for a long period reach that state of industrial development in which a great system of manufactures naturally grows up. Great as is the wealth of coal, the wealth of land is comparatively to European countries, greater still; and agriculture has, and should have the natural preference over manufactures. Nor has America long emerged from that earlier stage of the iron manufacture in which timber is the best fuel. Coal-smelting furnaces in the United States have not existed more than thirty years. And the future relation of American coal to English industry cannot be better expressed than in the words of the very able Report of the South Shields Committee on Coal Mines, in the year 1843.

"It is not the want of coal, but of capital and of labour that allows the more cheaply wrought British mineral to seal up the American mines. It is within the range of possibility to reverse it.

"When the expense of working British coal mines leaves no remuneration to the capital and labour employed, when brought into competition with the mines of other countries, then will they be as effectually lost to Britain for purposes of ascendancy, and their produce as exports, as if no longer in physical existence; and her superiority in the mechanical arts and manufactures, cæteris paribus, it may well be feared, will be superseded."

[1] Edinburgh Review, vol. cxi. p. 88
[2] 1st ed. 1848; 2d ed. revised by S. O. Haldeman
[3] Situation de l'Industrie Houillère en 1859, p. 9.
[4] Report of the South Shields Committee, 1843.
[5] Situation de l'Industrie Houillère en 1859, p. 15.
[6] Statistics of Coal, 1st ed. p. 275, quoted by the Edinburgh Review, vol. xc. p. 534.
[7] Coal-Fields of Great Britain, 2d ed. p. 208.
[8] Lyell, Manual of Elementary Geology, 1852, p. 333.
[9] Overman, On the Manufacture of Iron. p. 102.
[10] Overman, On the Manufacture of Iron, p. 462.
[11] Gesner, Practical Treatise on Coal, Petroleum, &c. New York 1861, p. 30.

Chapter Fifteen - Of the Iron Trade

Solon said well to Crœsus, when in ostentation he showed him his gold, "Sir, if any other come that hath better iron than you, he will be master of all this gold." [1] And it will hardly be denied that the retention of our supremacy in the production and working of iron is a critical point of our future history. Most of those works and inventions in which we are pre-eminent, depend upon the use of iron in novel modes and magnitudes. Roads, bridges, engines, vessels, are more and more formed of this invaluable metal. And it was well remarked by Wilberforce in opposing an intended tax upon iron, that "the possession of iron was one of the great grounds of distinction between civilized and barbarous society; and in the same proportion that this country had improved in manufactures and civilization, the manufacture of iron had been extended and improved, and found its way by numerous meandering streams into every department of civil life." [2]

As our iron-furnaces are a chief source of our power in the present, their voracious consumption of coal is most threatening as regards the future. Though iron is only one of the many products of coal, the making and working of iron demands at present between one-fourth and one-third of our whole yield of coal, and the iron trade certainly offers the widest field for a future increase of consumption. We have seen that for a century our produce of iron has grown at a constant rate, [3] and the pre-eminent usefulness of iron places it beside coal and corn as a material of which there cannot be too much—which itself excites and supports population, offering it the means of constant multiplication.

But it is essentially a suicidal trade in a national point of view. Once already, in an earlier period of iron metallurgy, the iron trade exhausted our resources, and quitted our shores. Its absence contributed to produce that dull and unprogressive period in the early part of last century which is so strongly marked upon our annals.

The former vicissitudes of the iron trade are of a very instructive character. There are two natural periods in the history of the iron manufacture—the charcoal period and the coal period. We require antiquarian writers like Mr. Nichols, Mr. Lower, or Mr. Smiles, to remind us of the very existence of a considerable manufacture of charcoal iron in England in former centuries. It is now so utterly a thing of the past, that only two or three furnaces are kept in work at any one time. [4]

Until the middle of last century, however, iron was always made with charcoal, and a woody country was necessarily its seat. Coal or cole was then the common name for charcoal, pit-coal being distinguished as sea-coal. The *collier* or *collyer* was the labourer who cut the timber, stacked it in heaps, *charked* it, and conveyed the coal on pack-horses to the *iron bloomary* and forge, situated in some neighbouring valley, where a stream of water gave motion to the bellows and the tilt-hammer.

The ore or *mine* was also brought by pack-horse from some neighbouring mine or deposit—for there are few geological formations or districts of this country which do not yield iron ore. Often the mine used was derived from heaps of old slag or offal, the refuse of still earlier iron works. For in a previous age, even the use of water-power was unknown, and the furnace was blown by the foot-blast, double bellows alternately pressed by a man as he stepped from one to the other. The low heat thus obtained was not capable of half withdrawing the metal from its matrix. The thousands of tons of cinder and slag— "old man," as it is locally called—left by the Romans, for the most part, as the included coins and antiquities prove, on the Forest of Dean, the Weald of Sussex, or the Cleveland Hills, were long a source of wonder and profit to the manufacturers of a later period.

Here we see a curious instance of the reaction and mutual dependence of the arts. The use of water-power, by giving a blast and heat of greater intensity, raised the iron manufacture to a new efficiency, but it could not enable us to use coal in smelting iron. It was the advance of the art of iron-working and its special application in the steam-engine that gave us the blowing-engine, and coal-blast furnace, which contributed in a main degree to our commercial resuscitation and our present strong position.

It was in the 17th century that the charcoal iron manufacture most flourished in England, and its chief seat was Sussex. "I have heard," says Norden in his Surveyor's Dialogue, "that there are, or recently were in Sussex neere 140 hammers and furnaces for iron." And Camden says of Sussex, [5] "Full of iron-mines it is in sundry places, where, for the making and founding thereof, there be furnaces on every side, and a huge deal of wood is yearly burnt; to which purpose divers brooks in many places are brought to run into one channel, and sundry meadows turned into pools and waters, that they may be of power sufficient to drive hammer-mills, which beating upon the iron, resound all over the places adjoining."

The increase of the trade threatened to denude England of the forests which were considered an ornament to the country, as well as essential to its security, as providing the oak timber for our navy. Poets and statesmen agreed in condemning the encroachments of the ironmasters.

"These iron times breed none that mind posterity"—

says Drayton. And George Withers in 1634 [6] speaks of—

"The havoc and the spoyle,
Which, even within the measure of my days,
Is made through every quarter of this Isle—
In woods and grooves which were this Kingdom's praise."

Stowe at the same period clearly describes the growing scarcity of wood-fuel, the falsification of previous anticipations, and the necessity felt for resorting more and more to coal.

"Such hath bene the plenty of wood in England for all uses that *within man's memory it was held impossible to have any want of wood in England, but contrary to former imaginations* such hath bene the great expense of timber for navigation; with infinite increase of building of houses, with the great expense of wood to make household furniture, casks, and other vessels not to be numbered, and of carts, waggons, and coaches; besides the extreme waste of wood in making iron, burning of bricks and tiles," &c.

"At this present, through the great consuming of wood as aforesaid, there is so great a scarcity of wood throughout the whole kingdom, that not only the city of London, all haven towns, and in very many parts within the land, the inhabitants in general are constrained to make their fires of sea-coal, or pit-coal, even in the chambers of honourable personages; and through necessity, which is the mother of all arts, they have of very late years devised the making of iron, the making of all sorts of glass, burning of bricks, with sea-coal or pit-coal. Within thirty years last, the nice dames of London would not come into any house, or room, where sea-coals were burned, nor willingly eat of the meat that was either sod or roasted with sea-coal fire." [7]

Norden says, "He that well observes it and hath knowne the welds of Sussex, Surrey, and Kent, the grand nursery of those kind of trees, especially oke and beech, shall find an alteration within lesse than thirty years, as may well strike a feare, lest few yeares more, as pestilent as the former, will leave few goode trees standing in these welds. Such a heat issueth out of the many forges, and furnaces, for the making of yron, and out of the glasse kilnes, as hath devoured many famous woods within the welds." [8]

Evelyn in his Diary, deploring the fall of a fine oak, expresses "a deep execration of iron mills, and I had almost sayd ironmasters too."

141

It was against those "voracious iron-works" that statutes of the 1st and 27th years of Elizabeth were directed, to prevent the destruction of timber trees which were necessary to maintain the wooden walls and maritime power of England. But in spite of statutes the waste went on. Postlethwayt writing in 1766, says, [9] "The waste and destruction that has been of the woods in Warwick, Stafford, Worcester, Hereford, Monmouth, Gloucester, Glamorgan, Pembroke, Shropshire, and Sussex, by the iron-works, is not to be imagined. The scarcity of wood is thereby already grown so great, that where cord wood has been sold at five or six shillings per cord, within these few years it is now risen to upwards of twelve or fourteen shillings, and in some places is all consumed. And if some care is not taken to preserve our timber from these consuming furnaces, we shall certainly soon stand in need of oak to supply the royal navy, and also shipping for the use of the merchants, to the great discouragement of shipbuilding and navigation, upon which the safety and figure of these kingdoms, as a maritime power, depend."

Now, I particularly beg attention to the curious fact that about the end of the 17th century, the iron manufacture to some extent migrated to Ireland. The woods of that country were full of timber when those of England were nearly exhausted. *The trade at once followed the fuel in spite of a want of ore in Ireland.* As appears in tables of Irish exports, and in Sir F. Brewster's New Essays on Trade, [10] of the year 1702, Ireland became an iron exporting country. Sir William Temple says, [11] "Iron seems to me the manufacture that of all others ought the least to be encouraged in *Ireland;* or if it be, which requires the most restriction to certain places and rules. For I do not remember to have heard that there is any ore in Ireland, at least I am sure that the greatest part is fetched from England; so that all this country affords of its own growth towards this manufacture, is but the wood, which has met but with too great consumptions already in most parts of this kingdom, and needs not this to destroy what is left. So that Iron-works ought to be confined to certain places, where either the woods continue vast, and make the country savage; or where they are not at all fit for timber, or likely to grow to it; or where there is no conveyance for timber to places of vent, so as to quit the cost of the carriage."

Postlethwayt alludes to the migration of the manufacture and the necessary result. "It is generally allowed that within about these seventy years, Ireland was better stored with oak-timber than England; but several gentlemen from hence, as well as those residing there, set up iron-works, which in a few years swept away the wood to that degree, that they have had even a scarcity of small stuff to produce bark for their tanning, nor scarce timber for their common and necessary uses."

When Ireland was in a condition to compete with England in a given manufacture, no artificial encouragement was needed. Frequent attempts on the other hand were made to gain a supply of iron from our American plantations. "Certainly," as Evelyn remarked, "the goodly rivers and forests of the other world would much better become our iron and saw-mills, than these exhausted countries, and we prove gainers by the timely removal." But perhaps from the want of labour American iron could not compete with continental iron.

England had for a length of time made and used much iron. "The Forest of Deane," says Yarranton, "is, as to the iron, to be compared to the sheep's back as to the woolen; nothing being of more advantage to England than these two are." And the Commanders of the Spanish Armada are said to have had especial orders to destroy the Forest of Dean, as being a main source of England's strength. And though coal could not yet be used in the smelting-furnace, it had long been chiefly used in the finery, the chafery, and the blacksmith's hearth. A great portion of the coal and culm that had for centuries been exported to France, and the coasts of the Northern Sea, was used in the smithy. And it was undoubtedly the abundance of coal that reared from early times the iron-working arts at Sheffield, Dudley, and Birmingham.

When our home production of iron was rapidly failing, there was a considerable demand for foreign iron in England. Hewitt, in his Statistics of the Iron Trade, [12] after expressing his surprise that in 1740 the total produce of England was only 17,350 tons, made in 59 furnaces, adds his conviction that the total production of Europe at the time did not exceed 100,000 tons, of which 60,000 were made in the forest countries of Sweden, Norway, and Russia. One half of this was imported into England. The consumption of iron in England, he thinks, was 15 lbs. per head of the population; while in Europe, on the average, it did not exceed 2 lbs. Of the iron we used, four-fifths were considered to be imported from one country or another. Joshua Gee speaks of our market as "the most considerable in Europe for the vast consumption of iron," and represents the Swedes, Danes, and Russians as striving to gain our market. [13] Our production of iron by the middle of the century was believed to have declined to one-tenth part of its former amount, and the high cost of foreign iron formed the main check upon the progress of those arts which were to be so great. By this time the substitution of coal for charcoal had become a necessity. Postlethwayt, in a pamphlet possessed by the Statistical Society, [14] describes the condition of the iron-trade in 1747, remarking that "England not being so woody a country as either Sweden or Russia, we do not abound, nor ever shall, with a sufficiency of wood-coal;" and that as cordwood was doubled, or trebled in price, *six* or *eight* times dearer than pit-coal, and very dear compared with its price in foreign iron-making countries, it was no wonder home-made iron decreased. This scarcity of wood was really due of course to the superior profits to be derived from using the land as pasture. Norden allowed this a century before: "The cleansing of many of these welde grounds hath redounded rather to the benefite than to the hurte of the countrey: for where woods did growe in superfluous abundance there was lacke of pasture for kine, and of arable land for corne."

And Houghton had acutely anticipated the subsequent course of things by suggesting that it would be profitable to cut down all wood near navigable waters where coal could be had, of which he remarked *we had enough*. [15]

To make iron with pit-coal was the great problem, the practical solution of which was all-important to the nation.

It was no new notion. From the early part of the seventeenth century it had been the object of eager experiments, and the cause of ruin to many of the experimenters. The history of the establishment of our great iron trade has been described in the works of Mr. Smiles, Dr. Percy, and others, but it possesses points of interest which we cannot pass over.

Simon Sturtevant, a German metallurgist, about 1612, was the first to take out a patent for making iron with pit-coal. His specification of the invention, entitled "A Treatise of Metallica," is an eccentric but clever production. In the practical part of his work he seems to have had less success than in the literary; and others who followed up his notions—mostly Dutchmen and Germans, such as Rovenson, Jorden, Franche, and Sir Phillibert Vernalt—had no more success.

The following verses of the year 1633 quaintly allude to such attempts:—

"The yron mills are excellent for that;
 I have a patent draune to that effect;
 If they goe up, downe goe the goodly trees.
 I'll make them search the earth to find new fire." [16]

It was Dud Dudley, a natural son of Lord Dudley, of Dudley Castle, manager of his father's iron forges in the neighbourhood, who, in 1621, first succeeded in smelting iron with coal. According to his own account in his "Metallum Martis," he made considerable quantities of pit-coal iron at Cradley, Pensnet, Himley, and Sedgley. But various disasters and troubles, the jealousy of other iron-masters, and the civil strife of the time, frustrated all his undertakings, and left him a ruined man. His history may be read in his own work, or in Mr. Smiles' "Industrial Biography."

Dudley's invention, it would seem probable, depended upon *charking* or coking the coal, in a manner analogous to the making of wood charcoal. The coke thus prepared was comparatively free from sulphur, and more readily gave a strong heat. Dudley was thus able, according to his own account, to make five or seven tons of iron a week; selling his pig-iron at 4*l.* per ton, and his bar-iron at 12*l.*, while charcoal iron cost in pigs 6*l.* or 7*l.*, and in bars 15*l.* or 18*l.* He relied for commercial success upon the cheapness of his iron compared with its fair quality, and he expresses clearly the true inducing cause and purpose of his invention, "knowing that if there could be any use made of the small-coales that are of little use, then would they be drawn out of the Pits, which coles produceth oftentimes great prejudice unto the owners of the works and the work itself, and also unto the colliers." [17]

The almost gratuitous use of fuel thus alluded to obviously led to Dudley's remarkable efforts towards our great manufacture. After Dudley's misfortunes his invention was not followed up. The want of wood was not yet severely felt, and the owners of woodland country and iron forges, of course, considered their interest in the charcoal iron manufacture as one to be protected. When Dr. Plot wrote his curious "Natural History of Staffordshire," the making of pit-coal iron was a matter of unfortunate history, and he speaks of a certain German, Dr. Blewstone, as making "the last effort in that country to smelt iron ore with pit-coal." [18]

Thus the matter rested for half a century. The iron trade, which Andrew Yarranton, about this time, truly designated the keystone of England's industrial prosperity, was checked by the high and rising price of the metal; and the efforts made to get iron from Ireland, or the Transatlantic Plantations, had but a slight or temporary success.

It was Abraham Darby who revived the forgotten method of smelting with pit-coal. The earliest adventurers in the process, we have seen, were Germans, and it is curious that the success of the Darby family was founded upon foreign experience. The eldest Abraham Darby went over to Holland in 1706, and learnt the method of casting hollow iron pots, or Hilton ware, as it was then called. Bringing over skilled Dutch workmen, he took out a patent to protect his newly-acquired process, and then, in 1709, started the celebrated Coalbrookdale Works in Shropshire. At first the oak and hazel woods furnished fuel, but the supply presently proving insufficient for the growing trade, it became customary to mix coke and brays, or small coke with the charge of fuel. Eventually, when an increased blast was obtained, coke took the place of charcoal entirely.

There is much uncertainty and discrepancy concerning the history of the Coalbrookdale Works. Scrivenor, in his "History of the Iron Trade," represents pit-coal as used in 1713. Dr. Percy, on the other hand, describes the younger Abraham Darby as first employing raw coal in the smelting furnace between the years 1730 and 1735.

In his first successful experiment he is said to have watched the filling of his furnace for six days and nights uninterruptedly, falling into a deep sleep when he saw the molten iron running forth. The success of the work was probably secured by the erection of a water-wheel of twenty-four feet diameter, capable of giving a powerful blast. But water was scarce, and a fire-engine, or old atmospheric steam-engine, was set up to pump back the water from the lower to the upper mill-pond. Here is one of those significant instances which teach us the power of coal and the interdependence of the arts. Employed in this engine as a source of motive power, it enabled coal to be also used in the smelting-furnace. And this is typical of the iron trade, as it is of other trades to the present day; for our iron industry in all its developments is as dependent on coal for motive power as for fuel in the furnace.

In December, 1756, we find the works "at the top pinnacle of prosperity, twenty or twenty-two tons per week, and sold off as fast as made, at profit enough." And from this time and from this success arose England's material power. To this invention, says M'Culloch, "this country owes more perhaps than to any one else." [19]

The subsequent history of the iron trade is best to be read in the growth of its produce. Already in 1788 the produce had risen to 68,300 tons, and the increase has since proceeded, as we have seen, in a nearly, constant rate of multiplication. [20]

The chief difficulty experienced in the extension of the trade was the want of motive power. Thus Mr. J. Cookson introduced the coal iron manufacture into the Newcastle district, the blast being worked by a water-wheel on Chester Burn. But "frequent interruption for want of water to drive their wheel, led at length to the furnace being 'gobbed,' and ultimately abandoned, about the close of the last century." [21]

Roebuck originated the great iron trade of Scotland, and his success was due to the command of a good blast.

"Dr. Roebuck was one of the first to employ coal in iron-smelting on a large scale, and for that purpose he required the aid of the most powerful blowing apparatus that could be procured. Mr. Smeaton succeeded in contriving and fixing for him, about the years 1768, a highly effective machine of this kind, driven by a water-wheel." [22] This contrivance is said to have been the blowing cylinder now used. [23]

Wilkinson was another great promoter of the iron manufacture, and his success arose from applying the steam-engine directly to work the blast-engine of his furnace near Bilston in Staffordshire. [24]

Cort's improvements in the puddling, faggoting, and rolling of iron blooms followed. The extensive use of such improvements depends upon the use of coal as the only fuel sufficiently abundant for the puddling, or reheating furnaces, and to supply the enormous power required in rolling iron bars of large size.

The discovery of the hot-blast process by Mr. Neilson is the next great step, and one of the most surprising instances of economy in the history of the Arts. Ironmasters had previously adhered to the mistaken notion that a very cool blast was essential to making good iron, and some even tried the use of ice in cooling the air of the blast. But when a blast of air, hot enough to melt lead, was used instead, the consumption of coal per ton of cast iron made, was reduced *from seven tons to two, or two and a half tons*. But was this enormous saving equivalent to a decrease of consumption? The produce of pig iron in Scotland has increased as follows:—

Year.	Tons.
1820...	20,000
1830...	37,500

Year.	Tons.
1839...	200,000
1851...	775,000
1863...	1,160,000

Now, if we compare the consumption of coal in 1830 and 1863, we find—

$$37,500 \times 7 \text{ tons} = 262,500 \text{ tons of coal.}$$
$$1,160,000 \times 2 \text{ tons} = 2,320,000 \text{ tons of coal.}$$

Or the consumption of coal was increased tenfold, not to speak of the consumption of coal in puddling or working the iron, or in the machine industry which cheap iron promotes.

A subsequent step of economy has been the utilization of the waste gases of the blast-furnace in heating the blast, or the boilers of the steam engines which drive the blast-engine. This improvement, however, was adopted extensively on the Continent, and in the United States, before it was introduced here in 1845. Now it is applied in South Wales, Scotland, and Derbyshire with perfect success. [25]

The most recent, and one of the most ingenious improvements of the iron manufacture, that of Mr. Bessemer, needs only a brief notice. At present, indeed, the process is but half completed because the stream of air forced through the molten cast-iron is found to remove only the carbon and the silicon, leaving the injurious elements, sulphur and phosphorus, nearly untouched. [26] It is, therefore, necessary to use, in the making of Bessemer steel, ores which are free from impurities, and the price of the steel must remain high. But if Mr. Bessemer could remove the phosphorous also, and make all our poor iron into good steel, the invention would be one of those modes of economy which, in reducing the cost of a most valuable material, lead to an indefinite demand. It would, indeed, be one of the greatest advances in the arts ever achieved. Such are the wonderful qualities of steel, that if it were cheap enough, its uses would be infinite. Our engines, machines, vessels, rail roads, conveyances, furniture would all be made of it, with an immense improvement in strength, durability, and lightness. Our whole industry would be thrown into a new state of progress. It would be like a repetition of that substitution of iron for wood, in mill work, which Brindley, and Smeaton, and Rennie brought about. And by still further multiplying the value of our coal and iron resources, it would accelerate alike our present growth and the future exhaustion of our resources.

When we reflect upon the conditions of our great production of iron, we shall see them to consist, apart from the ingenuity and perseverance which gave us the inventions, in the following:—

1. Cheapness and excellence of fuel.
2. Proximity of fuel, ores, and fluxes.

Of the first little need here be said. It will be remembered that the first success of Dudley was obtained in the neighbourhood of the "Thick coal," where up to the end of last century coal was a "drug;" and almost the same may be said of Coalbrookdale, where the final success was attained. And now, whether in South Wales, Scotland, Yorkshire, Staffordshire, or Northumberland, the iron manufacture most flourishes where suitable coal is to be had at the lowest rate.

As regards the second condition, it has been the constant reflection of English writers that the co-existence of the materials of the iron-manufacture was not undesigned. "The occurrence of this most useful of metals, in immediate connexion with the fuel requisite for its reduction, and the limestone which facilitates that reduction, is an instance of arrangement so happily suited to the purposes of human industry, that it can hardly be considered as recurring unnecessarily to final causes, if we conceive that this distribution of the rude materials of the earth was determined with a view to the convenience of its inhabitants." In South Wales, Staffordshire, and elsewhere, there are often found in conjunction the coal, ironstone, limestone flux, as well as the refractory clay and gritstone necessary for the construction of the furnaces. The fact, however, is, that this is rapidly becoming an imaginary condition of our trade. The exhaustion of the ironstone seams in some places, the cost of working them in others, the increased facilities of transport by rail, new discoveries of superior ore, are rendering our iron-works more and more dependent on distant supplies of ore. Scrivenor says, "The great superiority of our iron manufacture has generally been considered (independently of the excellent quality of the coal) to consist in having all the materials necessary to the manufacture found on, or immediately in the neighbourhood of the very spot where the furnaces are erected. South Staffordshire, as it was, will serve to illustrate this point—abundance of good coal—amongst other seams that of the tenyard—excellent ironstone and limestone; this last from Dudley; celebrated for its beautiful fossil slabs; but now limestone is brought from the vale of Llangollen, and the ironmasters are looking to Northamptonshire and other places to assist them with the required supply of ironstone. Is not this, as regards South Staffordshire, the beginning of an end?

"This scarcity of materials is certainly most beneficial to districts where, from the want of coal, it was never contemplated having any share in the manufacture of iron; but it alters the general character of the circumstances under which we have been accustomed to view our superiority, and casts the first shadow upon the iron trade." [27]

Blackwell, in his lecture on the Iron Resources of Britain, although asserting that "in no other countries does this proximity of ore and fuel exist to the same extent as in England," [28] describes how the facilities of transport are developing a new system. The iron trade, he says, fosters itself by its own creation, the railroad. It is by this that the new-discovered or rather the re-discovered ores in the oolitic formation, stretching obliquely across England, are made available, saving the North of England and the South Staffordshire iron-works from stoppage under the competition of the Scotch black-band works. Of South Staffordshire he says: "Hitherto the second most important iron district in the kingdom, it could no longer have maintained its ground against other localities had it not been for this discovery. South Wales had its cheap and good coals, its blackbands, and its supplies of sea-borne hæmatites, as well as its own argillaceous ironstones; Scotland its beds of blackbands; and the North of England its oolitic ores; but up to the present time South Staffordshire had only its argillaceous ironstones, always the most expensive to raise, with such admixture of hæmatite and North Staffordshire stone as the great cost of carriage would permit." [29]

It is even possible that recourse will some day be had to the Wealden ores, used in the old charcoal iron-works of Sussex, and which are both rich and plentiful, though too distant from coal for present use.

It is an all-important fact of this subject, that the ore is carried to the fuel, not the fuel to the ore. This was the case when the pack-horse conveyed ore to the forges situated among the wood lands which supplied the charcoal. When timber-fuel was abundant in Ireland, ore was sent thither from England. In the still earlier times of the foot-blast the smelting hearth was shifted about the hills to the parts most abounding in timber, as may be inferred from heaps of scoria scattered here and there up to the very summit of the hills. And it is the case now with all our superior means of transport and diminished consumption of fuel. The same fact is found elsewhere.

"Prussia is rich in iron ores, but they seldom occur along with the coal. In former times, the blast-furnaces were built where wood abounded and water power was available; but in later times, as the use of coal and coke became more and more general, it was found that the coal-basins were the fittest localities for the erection of works, as it was more easy and economical to take the ore to the fuel than the fuel to the ore." [30]

Let us now consider the present position and prospects of the English iron manufacture comparatively to those of other countries. The following are the amounts of pig iron produced by the three chief iron making nations in 1862:—

	Tons.
Great Britain...	3,943,469
France...	1,053,000
United States...	884,474

If the produce of all other countries were added, it would still be found, no doubt, that *our produce exceeds that of the rest of the world,* in spite of the recent rapid progress of the manufacture in France and America. Not long ago *our exports of iron were scarcely inferior to the gross produce of the rest of the world.* [31] This is not due to the quality of our iron. On the contrary, our cheap iron is some of the worst made anywhere. If we compare European iron-producing countries as to the quality and quantity of produce, the following are the orders, the higher place denoting the higher quality or quanti-ty:— [32]

Quality of Iron.	Quantity of Iron.
Sweden.	England.
Belgium.	France.
Prussia.	Austria.
Austria.	Prussia.
France.	Sweden.
England.	Belgium.

The inferiority of our iron is due to the sulphur, phosphorous, or other im-purities of our fuel and ore. It is on this account that steel, even in Mr. Bes-semer's process, has to be made from Swedish iron or other choice metal. And the exceptionally fine and high-priced English iron made by the Low Moor and Bowling Companies is chiefly due to the quality of the coal used.

The vast extension of our manufacture is due to *cheapness,* and this is the point of all importance in the great mass of cases,—in bridges, rails, ships, heavy framework, pipes, fences, &c. *The use of iron is altogether boundless, provided it can be had cheap enough.* As Dr. Percy remarks, in spite of the marvellous advancement of the iron trade, "yet it may be safely affirmed that the uses of iron will be vastly more extended than at present, and that there is no just ground for apprehension lest there should be over-produce of this precious metal. Even the railway system is in a state of rapid growth, and the time will come, when every habitable part of the earth's surface will be retic-ulated with iron or steel roads."

Of the greatly increased supplies of iron required in the future general progress of nations, we shall continue for many years to supply a large part, and to enjoy the wealth and influence which it gives us. But this cheapness depends upon raising coal from our mines and running it into our furnaces at a very low price. Now low prices cannot hold very long with a consumption of coal growing as it has been shown to grow. Were there no other demands upon the South Wales and Scotch coal-fields than that of the iron trade, yet this is of so unlimited an extent that sooner or later the voracious iron fur-naces will exhaust our seams as they exhausted our woods. And the result must be a new migration of our great trade.

It is impossible there should be two opinions as to the future seat of the iron trade. The abundance and purity of both fuel and ore in the United States, with the commercial enterprise of American manufacturers, put the question beyond doubt.

"In the North," says Dr. Percy, "the indefinite expansion of the anthracite iron manufacture is equally certain, whatever may be the policy of the gov-ernment, or the result of the present civil war. The wonderful iron-ore wealth of New Jersey has hardly yet been explored; and another anthracite iron region about Morristown would already have been added to the rest, had there been any direct facilities for bringing the coal to the ore. Now that the Carbondale or Wyoming coal basin, and the Mohanoy or middle coal basin, have both been opened up to the Hudson river market, the vast magnetic ore beds of Lake Champlain will have many more high stacks erected near them than those which already stand upon the shore. Some of these are noble works, mounted on iron pillars. But the principal manufacture must always cling to the Lehigh and Schuykill and Lower Susquehanna valleys in Pennsylvania, where the ore is abundant, the coal near at hand, and the flux on the spot; where the whole land is a garden, and therefore food cheap and labour plentiful, and the great seaports not far off." [33]

The American iron manufacture has been retarded by two chief causes:—

1. The fact that the coal, ore, and flux are not in such close conjunction as in England.

2. The high rate of wages in the United States.

The first obstacle will disappear. The Americans, of all people in the world, are the most forward in driving canals, river navigations, and railways where profit can be made. And while the materials of the iron manufacture are being wedded together in the States, our iron-masters, as we have seen, are seeking their materials at greater distances. The very railway system, which is said to have saved the North of England and the South Staffordshire iron works from a scarcity of materials, will enable the Americans to overcome their great obstacle, and thus one advantage of the English manufacturer becomes illusory.

The high rate of wages in a new country like the States is a true and natural obstacle to the progress of a manufacture, but as we shall see in the next chapter it is one which time will overcome.

If the Americans have obstacles to overcome, they have advantages in cheap and good mineral fuel, which cannot be over-estimated. The anthracite of Mauch Chunk, or the bituminous coal of Ohio, is got almost for the mere price of quarrying, as coal used to be got in Staffordshire, and it is laying the foundation there, as it did here, of a great iron-working industry. Pittsburg is the American Sheffield and Wolverhampton. The steel as well as the iron manufacture has made a secure lodgment there, [34] and its development is a question only of time.

[1] Bacon.

[2] Hansard's Debates, vol. vii. p. 79

[3] See Chapter Eleven.

[4] Newland and Backbarrow in Lancashire, Duddon in Cumberland, and Loon in Scotland, are the only charcoal furnaces in the United Kingdom. Mineral Statistics, 1863, p. 70.

[5] Quoted by M. A. Lower. Contributions to Literature, 1854, p. 120.

[6] Quoted by Smiles. Lives of the Engineers, vol. i. p. 292.

[7] Stowe's Annals, 1632, p. 1025.

[8] Surveyor's Dialogue, p. 175.

[9] Commercial Dictionary, Art. coal.

[10] Pp. 94, &c.

[11] Essay upon the Advancement of Trade in Ireland, Works, 1720, vol. i. p. 119.

[12] Statistics and Geography of the Production of Iron: New York, 1856, p. 7.

[13] Trade and Navigation of Great Britain, 1738, p. 104.

[14] Considerations on the making of Bar Iron with Pit or Sea Coal Fire, 1747.

[15] Houghton's Collection of Letters for the Improvement of Husbandry and Trade, 1727-1728, vol. iv. p. 259.

[16] The Costlie Whore, quoted by Percy, Metallurgy of Iron and Steel, p. 144.

[17] Metallum Martis, London, 1665, p. 8.

[18] Smiles' Industrial Biography, p. 77.

[19] Literature of Political Economy, p. 238.

[20] Chapter Eleven.

[21] Report of the British Association, 1863, p. 738

[22] Smiles' Engineers, vol. ii. p. 61

[23] Percy's Metallurgy, Iron, p. 889.

[24] History of Wednesbury, p. 116.

[25] H. Blackwell, Iron-making Resources of the United Kingdom, 1852, p. 174

[26] Percy's Metallurgy of Iron and Steel, p. 187.

[27] Scrivenor on the Iron Trade, p. 301.

[28] Page 150.

[29] Blackwell, p. 165.

[30] Percy's Metallurgy of Iron, p. 564.

[31] Truran on the Iron Manufacture of Great Britain, pp. iii. iv.

[32] Canada at the Universal Exhibition of 1855, p. 296.

[33] Percy's Metallurgy, Iron and Steel, p. 382. The last remarks are mistaken in their present application, as will be explained in the following chapter.

[34] Percy's Metallurgy of Iron, p. 381.

Chapter Sixteen - The Problem of the Trading Bodies

The position of this country in future years will not be rightly appreciated if we confine our attention near home. Without foreign commerce, but with our coal, it is possible we might have done much that we have done, but we could never have supported such masses of busy population, enjoyed such a variety of foreign products, or reared such a great system of industry. We should have been a happy ingenious self-dependent people, but not numerous nor rich, and neither endowed with our present world-wide influence, nor subjected to its dangers and responsibilities.

But as we are, unfettered commerce, vindicated by our political economists, and founded on the material basis of our coal resources, has made the several quarters of the globe our willing tributaries. "Though England," it has been truly said, "were one vast rock, where not an acre of corn had never waved, still those four hundred millions of men, whose labour is represented by the machinery of the country, would extort an abundance of corn from all the surrounding states." [1] The plains of North America and Russia are our corn-fields; Chicago and Odessa our granaries; Canada and the Baltic are our timber-forests; Australasia contains our sheep-farms, and in South America are our herds of oxen; Peru sends her silver, and the gold of California and Australia flows to London; the Chinese grow tea for us, and our coffee, sugar, and spice plantations are in all the Indies. Spain and France are our vineyards, and the Mediterranean our fruit-garden; and our cotton-grounds, which formerly occupied the Southern United States, are now everywhere in the warm regions of the earth.

But great as is our own system, it is not the whole. Commerce is undoubtedly making its way by its own subtle force, and is uniting the parts of the globe into a web of interchanges, in which the peculiar riches of each are made useful to all. The sum of human happiness is thus being surely increased, but we should be hasty in assuming that the growth of general commerce ensures for this island everlasting riches and industrial supremacy.

We ought not to forget that the enjoyments of a commercial country are not without probable drawbacks. We are no longer independent. The rise and decadence of other trading nations is no longer a matter of indifference to us. Our profits depend upon comparative not absolute riches, and as an individual nation we may find harm in foreign wealth.

And our anxiety must be indefinitely increased in reflecting that *while other countries mostly subsist upon the annual and ceaseless income of the harvest, we are drawing more and more upon a capital which yields no annual interest, but once turned to light and heat and force, is gone for ever into space.*

So far indeed as trade is dependent on legislation and social and political conditions, its future must be almost wholly uncertain and beyond the reach of reasoning. The development of history cannot be predicted, for in the "still and mental parts" of a single unborn individual may reside the forces which are to move the world. But industry and riches must have a material basis, and it is in this respect their future course comes somewhat within the grasp of science. The principles of economy have been so far investigated by our own writers, that with given material conditions the tendency of trade may often be certainly inferred. And if we may assume that the spirit of commercial freedom will spread and suffer no serious relapse, it is quite possible to foresee the necessary course of trade.

Taking commerce as the free growth of the instincts of gain, we find it resolved into a case of complex attractions and perturbations, as between several gravitating bodies. Trade between two bodies is a case of simple attraction, each naturally attracting and buying the articles which are made *with greater comparative facility and cheapness* by the other, paying with its own *comparatively cheaper products.* There is or should be no competition between them; each state should develop the kinds of industry and sources of wealth opposite to those of the other state. Free interchange of products then raises the economy of labour to its highest pitch.

In proportion, too, as the circumstances or industries of two states are more diverse, will trade between them be more to the advantage of each. Two countries whose circumstances are exactly alike can have no motive to trade with each other. Prices will bear the same proportions in each, and thus will leave no margin of profit on exchange, even to pay the freight. And this result will hold too even if one country were naturally richer in every way than another, provided it were in every particular equally richer. Thus if a man with a given amount of labour could raise both twice as much corn and twice as much wool in Australia as in England, we could have no trade with Australia in these articles. But if the same labour could raise twice as much wool but only just as much corn there as here, profit will evidently be gained on the exchange of wool and corn. To the writings of Ricardo, and especially of John Stuart Mill, [2] we are indebted for the discovery and distinct explanation of these principles.

When three states trade with each other, the problem is one of some complexity. A state possessing any peculiar kind of riches may profit and confer profit by trade with each of the other two, and the highest advantage will arise when each devotes its labour exclusively to kinds of industry in which it has comparatively the greatest facilities, or natural riches. If two of the states, however, are of similar circumstances, they cannot trade with each other, but only each of them with the third. And the total trade will have to be shared between the two similar states in some proportion to their absolute capacities of production. For if one had a larger share than this, its powers would be harder pushed and prices somewhat raised, which would at once cause trade to flow more towards the other similar state. If one of these similar states were to grow in absolute powers of production, it must take a greater share of the trade with the third state and positively abstract a portion of the trade between the other two, to the injury not of the third, but of the second similar state.

The question is now sufficiently complex to illustrate our actual position. In reality the countries with whom we trade present a problem of almost infinite complexity, but for simplicity we may form a few great groups according to similarities of condition. Five groups may be made to comprehend all countries with which we have relations of importance to our present subject.

1. Great Britain, capable for the present of indefinitely producing all products depending on the use of coal.

2. Continental Europe, capable of an indefinite production of artistic, luxurious, or semitropical products, but debarred by comparative want of coal from competition with us.

3. Tropical, Eastern, and other regions, capable of supplying food and raw materials, but of climate and other natural conditions wholly different from those of Great Britain.

4. Australasian, African, and American colonies, capable of an immense production of raw materials, but endowed with no considerable coal resources.

5. United States of North America, capable of an immense production of corn and raw materials, but also possessing coal deposits thirty-seven times as great as our own.

At present Great Britain carries on a growing trade with all the other four bodies. The older nations of Europe, indeed, check the trade by restrictions upon the repeal of which we cannot certainly count. Our trade with Western Europe, too, is of a different character from that we enjoy elsewhere, because as the ancient seat of the arts, and endowed with considerable mineral riches, we find there our own superiors in many finer kinds of manufacture. With respect to France and Western Europe, then, we are mainly producers or traders in raw materials. Towards the Tropical, Eastern, Colonial, and American bodies, in fact to the world generally, we are manufacturers, seeking materials to operate, or food to live upon, and giving in exchange the products of our machine labour.

Suppose trade to spread according to that spirit of progress which seems almost the established order of things. For many years to come our relations will remain of the same kind as at present. Europe will receive more and more crude iron, coal, metals, and other materials, returning food, or elegant articles, while other parts of the world will take more finished products and return their appropriate raw materials. Wherever we trade it will be upon coal, or its more or less refined products. There is no saying that we may not thus progress for the greater part of a century, allowing our manufacturing population to quadruple itself, and our industry to multiply itself many times.

Let us now consider the changes that are going on within the several trading bodies. In Great Britain the agricultural population is about stationary, and its offspring has to find employment in the towns, or else to migrate. So familiar too is emigration becoming to us, so great are the facilities and foreign attractions to it, and so congenial is it to the British character to seek independence and adventure across the seas, that a continuous exodus of our population is already a necessity. Our emigrants either reside as agents and merchants in foreign ports and countries where they powerfully stimulate trade with England, or they settle in the colonies and States of which they increase the productive powers. And we must not forget that the kindred nations of Germany are suffering an exodus almost comparable to our own, and are similarly contributing to the growth of our colonies and the United States.

Supposing protective and restrictive tendencies not to gain ground, we shall continue to grow on the one side as a great manufacturing body, while the colonies and most foreign states will find a source of wealth and advantage in supplying us with raw materials and developing the kinds of industry for which their facilities are almost boundless as compared with ours.

But the growth of production cannot go on *ad infinitum;* natural limits will ultimately be reached on the side both of the agricultural and of the manufacturing country, even if no political events intervene to check the trade. Suppose some event to occur and prevent our growing population from meeting a corresponding increase of subsistence. From established habits of prosperity and early marriage we shall continue to grow with a certain inertia, but the rising generation will not find the comfort and early independence they were brought up to expect. They will turn to emigration as a congenial resource, and apply their labour to stimulate trade and the production of raw materials in many parts of the world. The corresponding demand for our manufactures will then tend to support or revive the progress of industry at home, and maintain the long existing rate of multiplication.

It is by a process of this sort that the recent emigration, incited to a great extent by the gold discoveries, has contributed to the late extraordinary increase of wealth. It has encouraged our population to adopt new habits of early marriage. And in America, Australia, Africa, Asia, and the Pacific Archipelago there are open lands and undeveloped natural resources which still admit of a vast extension and continuance of the same process.

Not to speak of the maritime nations, especially the Spanish and the Dutch, who preceded us in extensive colonization, the custom of planting out colonies with us dates back three centuries, to the time of Queen Elizabeth. As early as 1681 an English writer [3] clearly explained that *plantations* were not an exhausting drain upon the mother country, but rather "a wheel to set most of our other trades agoing."

"The plantations," he said, "do not depopulate, but rather increase, or improve our people," and they "have increast the profitable employments, not only by building of ships, carrying out our manufactures and products thither, but also by returning theirs hither to supply ourselves, and also a great part of the rest of the world."

When we look either to the trade the colonies carry on with us, to the internal happiness they enjoy, or the benefits which they promise to the world in the future, it is impossible to overvalue the Anglo-Saxon spirit of colonization [4] But when we follow out a policy of free colonization to its necessary ultimate result, the prospect is more pleasing to a citizen of the world than to a citizen of this small kingdom. For free and voluntary emigration enables and induces our home population to go on multiplying at high rates, otherwise impossible. Not only then have we a growing population, but a growing margin also, who, even in times of the highest prosperity, must seek abroad the subsistence not to be had at home. The longer our prosperity continues unslackened the more necessary a free outlet will become. But the moment to be apprehended is when the first general check to our prosperity and growth at home is encountered. Then the larger part of the rising generation will find themselves superfluous, and must either leave the country in a vast body, or remain here to create painful pressure and poverty. A less active people than the English might endure the latter alternative, and sink by degrees into the stationary condition which characterised some continental nations, and England herself in the early part of the last century. But we may well refuse to look forward to such a change here, so painful must be the disappointment of the best hopes which must accompany it. Nor could we feel sure that our popular institutions could pass unharmed through a period of general pressure and want of employment among a vast artisan population.

The alternative, I say, is wholesale emigration. "The only immediate remedy," says Mr. Senior, [5] "for an actual excess in one class of the population, is the ancient and approved one, *coloniam deducere*.... It is a remedy preparatory to the adoption and necessary to the safety of every other." We have seen in the chapter on Population how our agricultural districts in 1811—31 passed through a period of pauperism and excess of population due to an unwarranted growth of population. The gravest fears for our social soundness were excited, and the evil was only overcome by extensive migration into our towns and colonies. The Scotch Highlands and more lately Ireland have presented still more striking instances of the choice between pressure at home and migration abroad. It is only a question of time when our whole population, including that of our present most progressive towns, will be placed in the same dilemma, and the result must be a vast and continuous exodus.

But now comes the most serious point of all. *After a certain period emigration will begin to have a very different effect upon the destinies of this country from that it now exercises.* Instead of extending across the seas an agricultural system in harmonious union, with our own manufacturing system, it will develop, or rather complete abroad, systems of iron and coal industry in direct competition with ours. The process will be of a two-sided nature.

It is well known that in spreading over a new country, settlers are naturally apt to exhaust the virgin soil they get so cheap, regardless of manures and agricultural arts by which its fertility might be maintained. Upon a process of this kind the able argument of Prof. Cairnes in his "Slave Power" is founded, but exhaustive agriculture and migration are the necessary results in any country or social system of a boundless supply of rich lands. It must pay better to take the cream off the land when the farmer can freely select new farms of untouched richness. A gradual inland migration is the result, and so rapidly has this gone on in the United States towards the West, that already the settlers in Minnesota, Washington, and Nebraska territories are on the verge of deserts that never can be cultivated. And we cannot but acquiesce in the apparently extravagant estimates of American writers concerning the future constant growth of their population. So long as there is security for life and property left, people will multiply over lands so rich that, as an American orator said, "if you tickle them with a hoe, they will laugh with a harvest."

To appreciate the growth of the American people we need only look upon the results of the American census.

POPULATION OF THE UNITED STATES.

Year.	Population.	Numerical Increase.	Rate per cent. of increase.
1790	3,922,827		
1800	5,305,937	1,383,110	35
1810	7,239,814	1,933,877	36
1820	9,638,191	2,398,377	33
1830	12,866,020	3,227,829	33
1840	17,069,453	4,203,433	33
1850	23,191,876	6,122,423	36
1860	31,445,080	8,253,204	36

If we compare the above with the corresponding results for our population, [6] it will be seen that we have scarcely anything here to equal the rate of American increase in constancy or amount. The general rate of growth in America is double our highest rate (18 per cent.) for the country as a whole, and is just equal to the rate of progress of Glamorgan at present, or of our manufacturing towns at their period of most rapid increase.

The very emigration which checks the rapidity of our growth contributes to maintain that of America, and nothing is more probable in political matters than that their population will grow both by internal multiplication and by vast and ceaseless increments from Europe. It is not an extravagant estimate of the Superintendent of the American Census, that the population of the States will number 100 millions of persons before the year 1900. [7]

With such a growth of population agriculture must soon be carried to its first limits. Within a century the choicest lands will have been taken up, and the second and third rate must be settled, or the old exhausted lands revived by more diligent culture. Agriculture will begin to lose its extremely easy and profitable character in the States.

On the other hand, coal, yet to be had at the mere cost of quarrying, will offer more and more tempting employment comparatively to agriculture. In other words, labour no longer drawn away by the superior attractions of agriculture will become abundant in manufacture, and at last a sound system of metallurgical industry will grow up on the banks of the Ohio, capable of almost indefinite extension.

It is this decadence of agriculture joined to the rise of a manufacturing system which most distinctly threatens our commercial position. Corn will be growing dearer in the States, while coal and iron are growing dearer here. The industrial conditions of England and the States will thus approximate to equilibrium, and the advantages of trade will diminish. We shall neither buy corn from them, nor sell iron articles to them. And at the same time America will tend to supplant us in the European market for iron and other crude materials, and in all parts of the world in the market for textile and useful manufactured articles in general.

Then, if not before, the continuous multiplication of our home population and industry will receive a check, and a definitive choice of wholesale emigration or a change of habits will be presented to us. And it must be further observed that by the time in question our consumption of coal will certainly be several times as great as at present. Our total available stores of coal divided by the annual consumption will give a proportionately shorter period of even stationary duration. And while our colonial states will be growing in the vigour of youth, receiving our whole offspring, and establishing new currents of trade far from our shores, our strength will tend to fail continuously.

Of course at the worst we shall not be devoid of many resources. Our position, "anchored by the side of Europe," and close to the terrestrial centre of the globe, gives us a claim to the carrying and trading business of the world, which previously belonged to our close neighbours the Dutch. And our manufactures, though they must diminish in size and importance, may improve in finish and artistic merit. Our work will be that of the trinket and the watch rather than that of the Herculean engine—handiwork rather than machine work. We shall probably approximate to the manufacturing condition of Western Europe, and the extreme elegance of our earthenware, glass, and many small manufactures raises the hope that we may attain a high rank in artistic manufactures.

But excellence in such smaller matters can ill compensate the loss of our supremacy in the elements of engineering and maritime success. When navigation and the construction of a fleet is a pure question of coal mining and iron metallurgy, it is hard to see how we can insure that invincibility on the seas which is essential to the safety of an insular nation dependent on commerce for its very bread.

The rate of our progress and exhaustion must depend greatly upon the legislation of colonies and foreign states. Should France revert to a less enlightened commercial policy; should Europe maintain or extend a prohibitory system; should the Northern States succeed in erecting a permanent Morrill tariff for the benefit of Pennsylvanian manufacturers; and should the tendency of all our colonies towards Protection increase, the progress of trade may indeed be vastly retarded. Under these circumstances the present rapid rate of our growth may soon be somewhat checked. The introduction of railways, the repeal of the Corn Laws, the sudden settlement of our Australian colonies, may prove exceptional events. Then, after a period of somewhat painful depression, we may fall into a lower rate of progress, that can be maintained for a lengthened period, passing out of sight.

But on the whole Free Trade is likely to extend itself on the Continent. Our colonies after a brief experience may see through their mistaken and highly prejudicial views; and the Americans will hardly succeed in their apparent object of rendering their continent a self-contained Chinese-like Empire, unknown to European trade and intercourse. And in other parts of the world—Africa, Asia, and South America—there is sure to be a general and perhaps a very great opening for future trade.

It may reasonably be questioned whether a great and continuous increase of our industry is desirable in a national point of view. But for those colonies and countries which trade with us it is an unalloyed benefit. Corn would be a drug in North America, animal products in South America, and wool in Australia, but for the market we offer; and were not political economy a rather rare and difficult study, the inhabitants of the States, and of our colonies generally, would be aware that the development of the pastoral and agricultural powers of a new country is the first and most appropriate source of riches. It is the very profits thus gained that render wages high, and labour, as it is said, too scarce for manufactures to exist. To receive the products of a mature system of labour, like that of England, in return for the raw products of the soil, is the true mode of creating a rich and populous colony. When the soil is fully occupied it will be time to think of imitating and competing with older countries.

But manufacturers are always the first, as Adam Smith and Sir Robert Peel remarked, to desire artificial restrictions. Colonial manufacturers constantly aver that the overflowing pauper population of the old world enables it to undersell the productions of a colony. And they seize upon a paragraph in Mr. Mill's Political Economy, [8] in which that eminent writer cautiously recommends Protection as a convenient mode of giving a first impulse to a branch of manufacture. Mr. Mill can hardly know the evil which his words are working, misapplied and distorted in meaning as they are for interested purposes.

It is indeed a reproach constantly hurled upon England, even by her own offspring, that she only removed her restrictions—her navigation laws, her prohibition of the export of machinery, and of the import of continental manufactures—when they were no longer necessary. It is, however, quite doubtful whether we derived any real benefit from the navigation laws; there is no doubt that the other restrictions were a great injury to our progress, and in no way assisted the rise of our arts. The attempted strict exclusion of continental manufactures greatly conduced to our stationary condition in the first half of last century, and I am wholly unable to see how it the least forwarded those great inventions in metallurgy and mechanism which did cause our rise. Yet we continually meet in foreign authors such remarks as these: "The requisite skill and development of the mineral resources have been obtained by a century of experience, when *foreign competition was religiously excluded by prohibitory duties,* until England could make iron cheaper than all the world, and since then domestic competition has cheapened the processes, and reduced the cost to the lowest practicable limit."

The falsity of the statement as regards the point in view is apparent. From the very same writer I have already quoted the statement that *about the*

middle of last century England imported fourth-fifths of the iron she consumed.
[9] The high price of iron had long *retarded, not forwarded*, the progress of the engine, the railway, and the mechanical works generally by which alone our manufacturing system could be adequately developed.

Our growth has been nourished by freedom, not by restrictions; and if kindred colonies and nations and foreign states wish to raise the world into the earliest and highest state of wealth, they will push trade to its utmost without jealousy of the immediate wealth it confers upon us, in virtue of our coal resources and our well-developed skill.

Any attempt on the part of foreign nations to cripple the development of our trade injures them far more than us. The Morrill tariff almost wholly recoils upon the nation which submits to it. The effect upon us is seen in a temporary and inconsiderable check to one or two of our branches of industry. Its effect upon America is to cut it off from intercourse with the rest of the civilized world, to destroy its maritime influence, and to arrest, as far as human interference can arrest, the development of a great state. No doubt it enables a manufacturing interest to grow half a century or more before its time; but just so much as one interest is forcibly promoted so much are other interests forcibly held back. And no system of industry thus requiring the unnatural stimulus of government protection can compete with foreign systems stimulated by natural circumstances. When manufacture is naturally more profitable in America than in Britain we shall be supplanted, and not before then. The advent of that period can be hastened only by freedom of industry and trade, not by legislative devices.

[1] H. Fairbairn, Political Economy of Railroads, p. 113.
[2] Principles of Political Economy, book iii. chap. xvii; or, Essays on some unsettled Questions of Political Economy. Essay No 1.
The subject "Of the Competition of different Countries in the same Market" is treated by J. S. Mill. Principles, book iii. chap. xxv.
[3] John Houghton. Collection of Letters for the Improvement of Husbandry and Trade. London, 1681, pp. 35, 36.
[4] See the admirable lecture of Prof. J. E. Cairnes to the Dublin Young Men's Christian Association, "On Colonization and Colonial Government," Oct. 26th, 1864.
[5] Three Lectures on Wages. Preface, p. v.
[6] Chapter Ten.
[7] See American Finances and Resources. Letter No. V. of R. J. Walker, M.A. London, 1864, p. 13.
[8] Principles, &c. Book v. chap. x., Third edition, vol. ii. pp. 507, 508.
[9] Chapter Fifteen.

Chapter Seventeen - Of Taxes and the National Debt

A few pages may be given to considering the policy of imposing duties and restrictions with a view to limit the consumption of our fuel.

The prohibition of the export of coal is the first step which naturally suggests itself, and it has often been advocated. Dr. Buckland, when asked, before the Committee on the Coal Trade of 1830, his opinion of the policy of allowing exportation, answered: "It is permitting foreigners to consume the vitals of our own prosperity. I consider coals the stamina upon which the manufacturing prosperity of the country primarily depends; and I think it our duty not to spare one ounce of coals to any person but ourselves."

The imposition of a more or less heavy duty on the export of coal is certainly the way we should commence a prohibitory system. Such a duty might be imposed for any of the following purposes:—

1st. To raise revenue.

2d. To cripple the competing manufactures of other nations.

3d. To discourage exportation, and thus spare our stores of coal.

It is plain that the first purpose is more or less inconsistent with the other two.

I can see no general reasons against levying revenue by an export duty. Sir R. Peel adopted as a principle of English finance, "that with respect to exports there shall be no duty leviable. I am unwilling to make any exception to this principle." [1] And to the present day the rule has, I believe, been upheld without exception. Yet there are no principles of economic science, so far as I know, bearing against export duties that do not equally bear against import duties. There are only the general arguments against any restrictions on commercial intercourse. In fact, Sir R. Peel had himself previously said, when proposing the coal-tax of 1842: "I must say I cannot conceive any more legitimate object of duty than coal exported to foreign countries. I speak of a reasonable and just duty, and I say that a tax levied on an article produced in this country—an element of manufactures—necessary to manufactures—contributing by its export to increase the competition with our own manufactures—I think that a tax on such an article is a perfectly legitimate source of revenue." [2]

Lord Overstone, too, asserted in his speech on the Commercial Treaty with France—a speech distinguished by his usual clearness and soundness of thought—that an export duty on a commodity of peculiar value and limited supply, like coal, may be an advantageous and legitimate source of revenue.

Instances of export duties of a similar kind are not wanting, but they are rather unfortunate instances. The Spaniards taxed Peruvian gold; the Sicilian Government, sulphur; Russia, its products of tallow, hemp, and flax. In India we raise a large revenue of the kind on opium, and the Slave States propose an impost on cotton. Too high a duty, indeed, is apt to draw out foreign competition, and ruin at once the trade and revenue, as the sulphur trade of Italy was for a time ruined. But we do not fear competition with Newcastle coal; we rather desire to avoid the foreign competition to buy it, and there seems accordingly to be no abstract objections to a duty on coal exported.

But I think that Lord Overstone in advocating such a duty, as a source of revenue, must have overlooked that peculiar relation of coal to our shipping interest which I have endeavoured to explain in chapter xiii. The fact is, that such a tax would be paid by ourselves as entirely as the tax on dogs or men-servants, with the further disadvantage that *we should pay it through and to the discouragement of our navigation. It would be equivalent to a duty on out-ward tonnage.*

For as our coals, in nearly every part of the world, meet and compete with inferior native coals or other fuel, the freight and price have to be lowered until the competition is successful. Witness the rate to Callao, which is no more than that to Spain. If a 4s. coal duty were imposed, our shipowners would receive about 4s. less freight to most places, which consumers would ultimately pay in the shape of increased inward freights and prices of foreign articles. At the same time it must be allowed that the reduction of outward freights would stimulate the exportation of any other heavy commodities like bricks, cement, earthenware, slates, flag-stones, paving-stones, salt, pig-iron, &c, which could be found profitably to take the place of coal as ballast. On the whole it may be said that there are even more reasons against a tax on coal as a source of revenue than might be urged concerning most taxes. It would be paid out of our pockets as much as the income-tax, and would act besides as a restriction on commerce and a burden on navigation.

To impose a duty on coals to injure continental manufactures on the sea-board towns, is a purpose that no English statesman in the present day would avow. It was on the contrary argued by Mr. Gladstone and others, in carrying the Commercial Treaty through the House of Commons, that a large manufacturing interest on the French coasts dependent on English coal, would be an excellent guarantee for the peace and extended intercourse we so ardently desire with that country.

There only remains the question of a partially or completely prohibitory duty on the simple and legitimate ground of self-defence, to save our posteri-ty, if possible, from the misery and danger that a failure of our coal mines would bring upon them. If, indeed, we are again to resort to restrictions on trade, it is not apparent why we repealed the Corn Laws, which might have been far more efficient in preventing the exhaustion of our coal mines than any measures we are now likely to adopt. Nor is it quite apparent why we should stop the export of coal and not that of pig-iron, every ton of which represents the consumption of two or three tons of coal. The question of a prohibitory tax is but a part of the general question whether we do wisely in allowing a suicidal development of trade, and this question will be again re-ferred to in my concluding remarks.

It is hardly necessary to discuss a duty on all coal raised from the pit's mouth. Such a duty of 2s. per ton was proposed by Pitt in 1784, at the beginning of his great financial career. But it was on the express ground that sea-borne coal was already burdened with duties of long standing, and that equalization of burdens was desirable. He intended, too, to exempt manufacturers from the impost as far as possible. But only a week after proposing the tax Mr. Pitt said, with the candour that distinguished his greatness, "From the information he had been able to collect upon the subject, he found men's minds so adverse to the tax, and that it would be necessary to make such a variety of exceptions and regulations in order to prevent it from having an injurious effect on one or other of our manufactures, that he thought it more expedient to abandon the tax." [3]

The character of a general tax on coal was truly stated by Robert Bald. "It would unnerve the very sinews of our trade, and be a death-blow to our flourishing manufactories. Were our determined enemy set in council, to deliberate upon a plan to wound us in a vital point as a nation, the advising the imposing of this tax would be the most successful he could possibly suggest." And again he says truly, "A small tax on the ton of coal would be a heavy tax on the ton of iron. The whole of our mining concerns depend as to their prosperity upon the abundance and cheapness of fuel, and if the price be increased by means of taxes, the utility of the steam-engine will be greatly abridged." [4]

Lord Kames, Sir J. Sinclair, and Adam Smith were the most distinguished of the many writers who deplored the mischief wrought by the old taxes on sea-borne coal, in retarding the progress of towns and country places, where cheap coal might otherwise have been enjoyed. But it is impossible to describe adequately the all-pervading bane that a general tax on coal would be. A rise in price of coal, whether from taxation or scarcity, must levy open and insidious contributions upon us in a manner with which no other tax whatever can compare. Sydney Smith described how a man in former days was taxed at every step from the cradle to the coffin. But through coals we shall be taxed in everything and at every moment. Our food will be taxed as it crosses the ocean, as it is landed by steam upon the wharf, as it is drawn away by the locomotive, as the corn is ground and the bread mixed and kneaded and baked by steam, and the meat is boiled and roasted by the kitchen fire. The bricks and mortar, the iron joists, the timber that is carried and sawn and planed by steam, will be taxed. The water that is pumped into our houses, and the sewage that is pumped away, and the gas that lights us in and out, will be taxed. Not an article of furniture or ornament, not a thread of our clothes, not a carriage we drive in, nor a pair of shoes we walk in, but is partly made by coal and will be taxed with it.

And most things will be taxed over and over again at each stage of manufacture. Materials will be burthened in the cost of steam-carriage, and the want of outward coal-freight—in their steam conveyance here—in the machinery that is to manufacture them—the engine to drive the machinery. At every step some tool, some substance, some operation will suffer in cost from the use of taxed coal.

A general coal-tax, too, would be subject to practical difficulties. Coals differ so much in kind and quality and size, that a uniform tax would be prohibitory of the use of small or inferior coals, and great quantities would be lost and burnt upon the waste heaps. An ad valorem duty, or one graduated to the size of the coal, would entail endless trouble and fraud.

On coals for domestic use a tax would in theory be very desirable; but it would entail a change of national habits among a people who look upon a cheerful fireside as one of the most pleasant things in life. It was really a tax on domestic consumption that Pitt proposed, for he intended to exempt all factories largely consuming coal. But to discriminate the coal used for different purposes would be a difficult or impossible task for the Inland Revenue department.

A tax on coal-gas in domestic consumption might be most readily collected from the inspection of the Gas Companies' books, and would be a beneficial tax in some ways.

Little need be said of other possible modes of legislating with a view to saving coal. To oblige manufacturers to discard old wasteful engines and furnaces would be a wholly unjustifiable interference. It would destroy much property that is now profitable, and render necessary the investment of other capital now profitably engaged elsewhere. And in the building of new engines and furnaces individuals can alone judge properly what forms are most suitable for their purposes, and they are sure not to forget the profit to be derived from a reduced consumption of fuel.

We could hardly prohibit the burning of duff and slack coal on the colliery heaps, seeing that if not lighted they will take fire by spontaneous combustion of the pyrites. To prohibit the screening of coal, again, would deprive many manufacturers of the cheap small coal which is essential to their business. And to attempt to enforce economical modes of mining and working coal, would be to interfere by legislation in the most uncertain of enterprises, where no rules can be laid down, but the individual circumstances of each pit determine its mode of working.

Nothing is more easy than to suggest that the Legislature should interfere to check the waste of coal so much wanted by posterity. But when we examine the several possible modes of interference it will be found that they all break the principles of industrial freedom, to the recognition of which, since the time of Adam Smith, we attribute so much of our success. Equal objections can be urged against interference with internal industry, or external commerce. To tax home industry would strike more at the root of our wealth; a coal export duty would be less burdensome, but it would lay us open to the imputation of perfidy. The greater part of the world would regard any approach to a new restrictive system as the appropriate sequel to that cunning and successful course of commercial manœuvre, which they consider we have pursued since the time of Cromwell. It would seem that we have placed ourselves in a painful dilemma; we must either retract the professions we have made to the world and the principles we have so recently adopted, or else we must submit to see our material resources exhausted in a shorter period than could have been thought possible.

The only suggestion I can make towards compensating posterity for our present lavish use of cheap coal is one that it requires some boldness to make. I mean the reduction or paying off of the National Debt. It has long indeed become a fashion to talk of this as a chimerical notion. And on various pretexts, but really from "the ignorant impatience of taxation," we go on enduring this vast gap in the capital of the country.

An annual appropriation towards the reduction of the debt would serve the three purposes of adding to the productive capital of the country, of slightly checking our present too rapid progress, and of lessening the future difficulties of the country.

If commenced without delay, and continued with perseverance, the vast debt, now nearly eight hundred millions sterling, might be easily reduced to inconsiderable dimensions within that period now before us, which we must believe to comprise England's climax of prosperity.

A most suitable and unobjectionable mode of effecting the payment presents itself. It is well known that the legacy and succession duties are of a very improvident nature, because they yearly convert a portion of the property of the country into income, and expend it, instead of expending the annual interest only. [5] The country, to the extent of about one-twentieth of its revenue, acts the part of a spendthrift in spending what it ought to invest, and trade upon, and transmit to its descendants for their similar use.

Now this investment would be duly made by transferring the whole proceeds of the duty to the Commissioners for the Reduction of the National Debt, not allowing it to enter into the annual balance sheet of the Chancellor of the Exchequer. Of course it would be useless to do this unless the remaining revenue were maintained at least equal to the expenditure. It would be absurd to pay debts on one hand and contract them on the other, in the manner of the old sinking fund. But such is the growing condition of our revenue, that the appropriation could easily be made, had we the patience to refrain for a very few years from *those constant demands for the remission of taxes which are now become an unreasonable habit.* After a very brief period remission of taxes might again go on, gradually accelerated by the reduction of the annual charge of the debt.

At the present time we enjoy the rising tide of prosperity due to the unprecedented commercial reforms of the last twenty years. Are we wise in pushing our present enjoyment to the extreme by remitting every penny of taxes we can possibly spare? And would not the present appropriation of the legacy duty to a special purpose ensure us future remissions at a time when they will be grateful and useful in contributing to uphold for a little longer a rate of progress which is now, if anything, too rapid?

It cannot be doubted that before long, if at all, an effort must be made to relieve the country of this burden. Writers of the last century entertained most gloomy anticipations concerning the growing debt, and they were only wrong in undervaluing the industrial revolution which was then proceeding. But now we run the risk of being too confident, and losing the grand opportunities we enjoy. It is growing wealth that makes a happy and prosperous country, and, no matter what be the absolute wealth of the country at a future time, it is idle to suppose that a popular government with a stationary revenue would ever impose new taxes to pay off an old debt. It is when a surplus revenue grows of its own accord, as at present, that we can alone expect a successful effort to be made.

As a common pretext against any attempt to repay the National Debt it is said that we had better remit taxes instead, and "leave the money to fructify in the hands of the people." But this is wholly erroneous. Taxes are, partly at least, paid out of income which would otherwise be unproductively expended; part only is subtracted from the fund of productive capital. But in investing the proceeds of a tax in Consols towards the reduction of the great debt, almost the whole money will be added to the productive capital of the country, and will be placed most certainly in the hands which will make it fructify in trade and industrial enterprises. [6]

The present Chancellor of the Exchequer has already devoted a good many millions of surplus revenue to the reduction of the debt, and has converted several millions more into terminable annuities. What is still better, he has often spoken of the debt in a manner which shows he would like to do more. Could a minister be found strong and bold enough to carry out a permanent and large measure towards the same end, he would have an almost unprecedented claim to gratitude and fame. And were the work once taken in hand, the notions that the payment of the debt is impossible, or Utopian, or undesirable, would quickly be dispersed. They are mere fallacies of habit.

In regard to our present subject we find, in the above proposed measure, a legitimate and practicable mode of giving some compensation to our posterity, who will undoubtedly suffer from an increased price of coal, the worst of taxes.

[1] Hansard's Debates, third series, vol. lxxvii. p. 478.
[2] Hansard's Debates, third series, vol. lxi. p. 448.
[3] Hansard's Parliamentary History, vol. xxiv. p. 1215.
[4] On the Scotch Coal Trade, p. 197.
[5] J. S. Mill, Principles of Political Economy, 3d Ed. vol. ii. p. 455.
[6] J. S. Mill, Principles of Political Economy, Book v. chap. vii. § 3.

Chapter Eighteen - Concluding Reflections

My work is completed in pointing out the necessary results of our present rapid multiplication when brought into comparison with a fixed amount of material resources. The social and political consequences to ourselves and to the world of a partial exhaustion of our mines are of an infinitely higher degree of uncertainty than the event itself, and cannot be made the subject of argument. But feeling as we must do that they will be of an untoward character, it is impossible to close without a few further remarks upon the truly solemn question—Are we wise in allowing the commerce of this country to rise beyond the point at which we can long maintain it?

To say the simple truth, will it not appear evident, soon after the final adoption of Free Trade principles, that our own resources are just those to which such principles ought to be applied last and most cautiously ? To part in trade with the surplus yearly interest of the soil may be unalloyed gain, but to disperse so lavishly the cream of our mineral wealth is to be spendthrifts of our capital—to part with that which will never come back.

And after all commerce is but a means to an end, the diffusion of civilization and wealth. To allow commerce to proceed until the source of civilization is weakened and overturned is like killing the goose to get the golden egg. Is the immediate creation of material wealth to be our only object? Have we not hereditary possessions in our just laws, our free and nobly developed constitution, our rich literature and philosophy, incomparably above material wealth, and which we are beyond all things bound to maintain, improve, and hand down in safety? And do we accomplish this duty in encouraging a growth of industry which must prove unstable, and perhaps involve all things in its fall?

But the more there is said on the one side of this perplexing question, the more there is to say on the other side. We can hardly separate the attributes and performances of a kingdom, and have some without the others. The resplendent genius of our Elizabethan age might never have been manifested but in a period equally conspicuous for good order, industrial progress, and general enterprise. The early Hanoverian period, on the other hand, was as devoid of nobility as it was stationary in wealth and population. A clear and vigorous mind is to be looked for in a wholesome state of the body. So in our Victorian age we may owe indirectly to the lavish expenditure of our material energy far more than we can readily conceive. No part, no function of a nation is independent of the rest, and in fearlessly following our instincts of rapid growth we may rear a fabric of varied civilization, we may develop talents and virtues, and propagate influences which could not have resulted from slow restricted growth however prolonged.

The wish surely could never rise into the mind of any Englishman that Britain should be stationary and lasting as she was, rather than of growing and world-wide influence as she is. To secure a safe smallness we should have to go back, and strangle in their birth those thoughts and inventions which redeemed us from dullness and degeneration a century ago. Could we desire that Savery and Newcomen had abandoned their tiresome engines, that Darby had slept before the iron ran forth, that the Duke had broken before Brindley completed his canal, that Watt had kept to his compasses and rules, or Adam Smith burnt his manuscript in despair? Such experiments could not have succeeded, and such writings been published, among a free and active people in our circumstances, without leading to the changes that have been. Thence necessarily came the growth of manufactures and of people; thence the inexplicable power with which we fought and saved the Continent; thence the initiation of a Free-trade policy by Pitt, the growth of a middle class, and the rise of a series of statesmen—Canning, Huskisson, Peel, Cobden, and Gladstone—to represent their views and powers.

Our new industry and civilization had an obscure and unregarded commencement; it is great already, and will be far greater yet before it is less. It is questionable whether a country in any sense free can suffer such a grand movement to begin without suffering it to proceed its own length. One invention, one art, one development of commerce, one amelioration of society follows another almost as effect follows cause. And it is well that our beneficial influence is not bounded by our narrow wisdom or our selfish desires. Let us stretch our knowledge and our foresight to the furthest, yet we act by powers and towards ends of which we are scarcely conscious.

In our contributions to the arts, for instance, we have unintentionally done a work that will endure for ever. In whatever part of the world fuel exists, whether wood, or peat, or coal, we have rendered it the possible basis of a new civilization. In the ancient mythology, fire was a stolen gift from heaven, but it is our countrymen who have shown the powers of fire, and conferred a second Promethean gift upon the world. Without undue self-gratulation, may we not say in the words of Bacon?—"The introduction of new inventions seemeth to be the very chief of all human actions. The benefits of new inventions may extend to all mankind universally, but the good of political achievements can respect but some particular cantons of men; these latter do not endure above a few ages, the former for ever. Inventions make all men happy without either injury or damage to any one single person. Furthermore, new inventions are, as it were, new erections and imitations of God's own works."

When our great spring is here run down, our fires half burnt out, may we not look for an increasing flame of civilization elsewhere? Ours are not the only stores of fuel. Britain may contract to her former littleness, and her people be again distinguished for homely and hardy virtues, for a clear intellect and a regard for law, rather than for brilliancy and power. But our name and race, our language, history, and literature, our love of freedom and our instincts of self-government, will live in a world-wide sphere. We have already planted the stocks of multiplying nations in most parts of the earth, and, in spite of discouraging tendencies, it is hardly for us to doubt that they will prove a noble offspring.

The alternatives before us are simple. Our empire and race already comprise one-fifth of the world's population; and by our plantation of new states, by our guardianship of the seas, by our penetrating commerce, by the example of our just laws and firm constitution, and above all by the dissemination of our new arts, we stimulate the progress of mankind in a degree not to be measured. If we lavishly and boldly push forward in the creation and distribution of our riches, it is hard to over-estimate the pitch of beneficial influence to which we may attain in the present. *But the maintenance of such a position is physically impossible. We have to make the momentous choice between brief greatness and longer continued mediocrity.*

www.ingramcontent.com/pod-product-compliance
Lightning Source LLC
Chambersburg PA
CBHW032000190326
41520CB00007B/307